McGraw Hill

4 **HESI A2**
Practice
Tests

McGraw Hill

4 HESI A2 Practice Tests

Fourth Edition

Kathy A. Zahler

New York Chicago San Francisco Athens London Madrid Mexico City
Milan New Delhi Singapore Sydney Toronto

1 2 3 4 5 6 7 8 9   LHS   28 27 26 25 24 23

ISBN   978-1-265-53539-1
MHID   1-265-53539-6

e-ISBN   978-1-265-53590-2
e-MHID   1-265-53590-6

Evolve Reach Admission Assessment Exam is a registered trademark of Elsevier, Inc., which was not involved in the production of, and does not endorse, this product.

Interior design by THINK Book Works

McGraw Hill books are available at special quantity discounts to use as premiums and sales promotions or for use in corporate training programs. To contact a representative, please visit the Contact Us pages at www.mhprofessional.com.

McGraw Hill is committed to making our products accessible to all learners. To learn more about the available support and accommodations we offer, please contact us at accessibility@mheducation.com. We also participate in the Access Text Network (www.accesstext.org), and ATN members may submit requests through ATN.

*Dedicated to the extraordinary nurses
at Memorial Sloan-Kettering.*

Contents

McGraw Hill

4 HESI A2 Practice Tests

CHAPTER 1

Introduction
to the A2

This book contains four practice tests for the HESI A2 (Admission Assessment Exam). They follow the format used in the A2 online exam. Taking these practice tests will give you a good idea of what you'll encounter when you take the real exam. As you complete the tests, you'll become familiar with the directions, structure, and content that you're likely to see at the testing site.

A2 VERSUS OTHER NURSING SCHOOL EXAMS

Who Takes the A2 Exam?

The A2 Exam is used for admission to certain nursing schools. It is a product of Evolve Learning Systems, a division of Elsevier Publishing. Different nursing programs require different exams; for example, some schools expect applicants to take the Nursing Entrance Test (NET) or the Test of Essential Academic Skills (TEAS). Other schools give you a variety of entrance exams from which to choose. Still others require the A2 exclusively.

How Do I Know Whether I Should Take the A2 Exam?

To know whether the school or schools of your choice require the A2, visit their websites or call their admissions offices. They may call this particular test the HESI A2 test, the Evolve Reach A2 test, or the Admission Assessment Exam. Before you begin to study, make sure that you are studying for the correct test. You may need to use McGraw Hill's *5 TEAS Practice Tests* or *Nursing School Entrance Exams* instead.

PLANNING TO TAKE THE A2

When Is the A2 Given, and How Do I Register for It?

The exam is given at a variety of sites, often at nursing schools or community colleges. The dates of the exam may depend on the application dates for the nursing school where you take the test. Some schools offer the test every few weeks throughout the year. You may also take the exam at one of more than 350 Prometric™ testing sites around the country.

To register for an exam, first set up an Evolve account at evolve .clsevier.com/cs. Once you successfully create an account, you should see the HESI Assessment-Student Access link under "My Content." Choose a test date and pay your fee.

To take the exam at the nursing school or community college of your choice, log on to that school's website to learn how to sign up for the next available test.

To take the exam at a Prometric site, start by setting up an account on the Evolve Elsevier site listed above. Submit a registration to take a distance exam. Use the confirmation information you receive to log on to http://www.prometric.com/Elsevier. Clicking on "Admission Assessment," typing your zip code, and listing a range of dates lets you locate the testing site and date that best suit your needs. From there, you may follow the directions to schedule the test at a time convenient for you.

You will pay for the test online when you set up your test date. You will need your credit or debit card and your school's ID number. Use your school-related email address if you have one.

When Should I Take the A2?

Check with your chosen nursing programs to find out when they need score transcripts. Then work backward from that date to determine when you should take the test.

If you take the test at the nursing school that you hope to attend, the date of the test will be designed to mesh with that school's application dates.

Which Modules of the A2 Must I Take?

The A2 contains several modules in the areas of English language, mathematics, and science. Not all nursing programs require every module. If you take the test at a nursing school or community college, the school will probably only test you on the modules that its nursing program requires. For example, some programs do not require any of the science modules. Some require Reading Comprehension and Grammar, but not Vocabulary and General Knowledge. If you wish to send transcripts to several schools, visit their websites to learn which modules they require. Then make sure that the site where you are taking the test offers all of those modules.

What Do I Need on the Day of the Test?

The A2 is only available online. You must present one form of government-issued identification. Passports, driver's licenses, or green cards are fine; credit cards or student IDs are not.

You may need your payment or a copy of your payment receipt. You will definitely need the username and password assigned to you by Elsevier when you registered for the test.

You may not use any resources such as calculators or reference books. A basic calculator is included in the software. You may not carry in a cell phone, tablet, or other electronic device. You may not bring food or beverages into the testing site.

SCORING THE A2

How Is the A2 Scored?

The A2 consists of eight academic modules. Your scores may be reported in three ways—as a percentage score for each module administered; as a subject-area composite score (for all science modules, for example); and as a composite score (the average score for all the modules you complete).

When Will I Receive My Score?

As soon as you complete your online test, you will receive a printed score report from the proctor.

How Do I Submit My Score to Nursing Programs?

Your testing fee automatically includes the submission of scores to the school where you took the test. If you took the test at a Prometric center, or if you want your transcript sent to additional schools, order transcripts from Elsevier via its website or by calling 1-800-950-2728. Elsevier will charge a processing fee for each transcript sent.

Is My Score Good Enough?

Whether your score is acceptable depends on the program to which you are applying. Some nursing programs have specific cutoff points for each module. Others require a certain composite score.

Some nursing programs allow you to take the A2 two or three times if your first scores are unacceptable. They may require you to wait several weeks or months between exams. Again, the rules vary from program to program.

PARTS OF THE TEST

The A2 is divided into eight academic modules within three broad content areas: English language, mathematics, and science. In addition, the A2 may include a section on critical thinking, which may be graded or ungraded, plus one or two ungraded tests under the heading "Learner Profile." This chart shows the number of items (which may vary year to year) and time suggested for each section. Notice that ungraded pilot items are included in most modules. These are used to build tests in future years. Because the test is given online, the times given are only suggestions that will allow you to complete the entire test within a reasonable time.

Content Area and Module	Number of Items	Time Suggested
ENGLISH LANGUAGE		
Reading Comprehension	50 (+ 5 pilot items)	60 minutes
Vocabulary and General Knowledge	50 (+ 5 pilot items)	50 minutes
Grammar	50 (+ 5 pilot items)	50 minutes
MATHEMATICS		
Basic Math Skills	50 (+ 5 pilot items)	50 minutes
SCIENCE		
Biology	25 (+ 5 pilot items)	25 minutes
Chemistry	25 (+ 5 pilot items)	25 minutes
Anatomy and Physiology	25 (+ 5 pilot items)	25 minutes
Physics	25 (+ 5 pilot items)	50 minutes
LEARNER PROFILE		
Critical Thinking	30	30 minutes
Learning Style	14	15 minutes
Personality Profile	15	15 minutes

FORMAT TIP
Rarely will anyone be administered every module on the A2. Check with your preferred nursing program to see which modules it requires. Depending on the modules required, the typical test may run from three to four hours.

Reading Comprehension

Reading items test your comprehension of informational reading passages. You will be asked to read a short, multiparagraph passage and answer a variety of questions about it. Some of the most common skills tested involve the following:

- Main idea
- Supporting details
- Meanings of words in context
- Author's purpose
- Fact and opinion
- Drawing conclusions and making inferences
- Summarizing
- Author's tone

The passages used for A2 all have a science or health theme and may be typical of the type of reading you will do in your professional life.

> **FORMAT TIP**
> With the exception of some math questions, all questions on the A2 are multiple choice and give you four possible choices from which to pick.

Here is an example of an A2 reading comprehension question. On the test itself, most reading passages will be longer than this one.

Counterfeit medicine may be contaminated, or it may contain the wrong or no active ingredient. Counterfeit medicine is illegal and may be dangerous. The quality, safety, and efficacy of counterfeit medicines are not known. Counterfeit medicine is often sold illegally over the Internet or by illegal operators posing as licensed pharmacies.

1. What is the author's primary purpose in writing this passage?

   A. To inform
   B. To persuade
   C. To entertain
   D. To analyze

Explanatory Answer: This question tests your understanding of the author's purpose or intent. This author defines *counterfeit medicine* and presents some facts about it, which indicates that the purpose is to inform (choice A). The author makes no judgments or calls to action, as might take place in a persuasive essay (choice B), and there is no analysis or in-depth investigation of the topic (choice D).

Vocabulary and General Knowledge

This section of the test includes vocabulary terms that appear regularly in health care contexts as well as in general and academic use. You may be asked to select a word or phrase that defines an underlined word in a sentence or to identify a synonym for a given word.

Here are two examples of A2 vocabulary questions.

1. Select the correct definition of the underlined word.

   The patient received a <u>potent</u> dose of sleeping medication.

   A. Average
   B. Invasive
   C. Powerful
   D. Initial

   Explanatory Answer: *Potent* means "strong," so a potent dose is a strong, or powerful, dose (choice C).

2. A person who is compliant is _____.

   A. flexible
   B. obedient
   C. whiny
   D. appreciative

   Explanatory Answer: To comply is to act in accordance with a rule or request, so someone who is compliant is obedient (choice B).

Grammar

The grammar section requires you to locate sentences that are grammatically correct, words or phrases that are not used correctly, and words that best complete a sentence to make it grammatically correct. Questions might focus on any of the following topics, among others:

- Subject-verb agreement
- Pronoun-antecedent agreement
- Misplaced modifiers
- Pronoun case
- Serial commas

- Sentence fragments
- Run-on sentences
- Troublesome word pairs (*between/among*, *good/well*, *fewer/less*, *its/it's*, *lie/lay*, etc.)

Here are two examples of A2 grammar questions.

1. Select the word or phrase that makes this sentence grammatically correct.

    Could you please hand _____ the tongue depressors?

    A. myself
    B. me
    C. I
    D. ourselves

    Explanatory Answer: The pronoun required is an object pronoun (it receives the action of the verb), so only *me* (choice B) completes the sentence correctly.

2. Select the correct order of words to fit the sentence structure.

    The students placed _____ finished essays over _____; _____ glad to be done.

    A. there, their, they're
    B. they're, there, their
    C. their, there, they're
    D. their, they're, there

    Explanatory Answer: The essays belong to the students and thus are *their* essays. They placed them in that spot, *there*. They are (*they're*) glad to be done. The correct answer is choice C.

> **FORMAT TIP**
> For questions with multiple answers like the preceding one, all answers must be correct. There is no partial credit.

Basic Math Skills

The mathematics section of the A2 focuses on the sort of math you may need to use on the job. For that reason, there is an unusual emphasis on measurements and fractions. Here are some of the subskills that you might see on the test:

- Computation (addition, subtraction, multiplication, division) with whole numbers
- Computation with decimals
- Computation with fractions
- Fractions, decimals, and percentages
- Ratios and proportions
- Money
- Military time
- Roman numerals
- Measurement conversions

FORMAT TIP
A few items in the math section may be short answer—you must compute the answer rather than choosing from four possible responses.

Here are two examples of A2 basic math questions.

1. Multiply: (4.3)(3.4) =
   A. 146.2
   B. 14.62
   C. 12.12
   D. 7.7

   Explanatory Answer: Many questions of this sort may be easily answered by estimating. 4.3×3.4 will be somewhere midway between 4×3 and 4×4, so choices A and D are clearly incorrect. The answer is choice B.

2. How many fluid ounces are in a pint? (Enter numeric value only.)
   _____

   Explanatory Answer: There are 8 ounces in a cup and 2 cups in a pint, so the answer is 16.

TIPS FROM TEST TAKERS
Know your conversions, especially liquid measurements. Study a chart of metric-to-standard conversions, too! No conversion chart appears with the test, so you must have these memorized.

Biology

The biology tested on the A2 is basic, which does not mean that it is easy. Expect to see questions on any of these topics:

- Scientific method
- Taxonomy
- Molecules
- Cells
- Photosynthesis
- Cellular reproduction
- Genetics

Here are two examples of A2 biology questions.

1. What is the result of meiosis II?

   A. Two secondary sex cells
   B. Four haploid daughter cells
   C. Two primary sex cells
   D. Duplication of primary sex cells

   Explanatory Answer: Mitosis results in two primary sex cells (choice C), and meiosis I leads to two secondary sex cells (choice A). In meiosis II, the resulting four cells have half the chromosomes of the parent cell. The answer is choice B.

2. Which organelle in animal cells is most similar in function to the chloroplast in plant cells?

   A. Cell membrane
   B. Vacuole
   C. Ribosome
   D. Mitochondrion

   Explanatory Answer: Chloroplasts are the site of photosynthesis, or energy conversion, in plants. Mitochondria are the site of respiration, or energy conversion, in animals. The answer is choice D.

Chemistry

Organic and inorganic chemistry are tested on the A2. All health professionals should have a basic understanding of chemistry. You may find questions on any of these topics:

- States of matter
- Atomic structure

- Chemical equations
- Chemical reactions
- Acids and bases
- Radioactivity
- Chemical bonds
- Molarity
- Stoichiometry
- Reaction rates
- Redox reactions
- Electron configurations

TIPS FROM TEST TAKERS
Review the periodic table of elements, and know the basics!
Unlike some tests, the A2 doesn't show you the table.

Here are two examples of A2 chemistry questions.

1. What is the expected pH of orange juice?

   A. Between 3.0 and 4.0
   B. Between 6.0 and 7.0
   C. Between 8.0 and 9.0
   D. Between 11.0 and 12.0

   Explanatory Answer: Orange juice is fairly acidic, meaning that it would fall toward the lower end of the pH scale. The answer is A.

2. Sodium's ground state electron configuration may be represented as $1s^2 2s^2 2p^6 3s$. How many energy levels does sodium have?

   A. 1
   B. 2
   C. 3
   D. 6

   Explanatory Answer: The first energy level of any atom contains just an s subshell. The second may include an s and a p subshell. Looking at sodium in table form may make this easier to solve:

   $1s^2$
   $2s^2 2p^6$
   $3s$

Sodium, in other words, has electrons in three energy levels, so the answer is C. In the first level, it has two electrons in subshell s. In the second level, it has two electrons in subshell s and six electrons in subshell p. In the third level, it has one electron in subshell s. Adding up the electrons, 2 + 2 + 6 + 1, gives you the total number of electrons in sodium, or sodium's atomic number, 11.

Anatomy and Physiology

This is the part of biological sciences that applies specifically to nursing—the human body and its systems, organs, and processes. You may see any of these topics on the A2:

- Cells and tissues
- Body planes and directions
- Skeletal system
- Muscular system
- Nervous system
- Endocrine system
- Circulatory system
- Respiratory system
- Digestive system
- Urinary system
- Reproductive system

TIPS FROM TEST TAKERS
Review basic anatomical directions (proximal, distal, and so on) and know your organs and functions!

Here are two examples of A2 anatomy and physiology questions.

1. Which arm bone is most proximal to the shoulder?
   A. Radius
   B. Ulna
   C. Humerus
   D. Carpal

Explanatory Answer: To be proximal is to be close to the point of attachment. The radius (choice A) and ulna (choice B) are forearm bones, and the carpal (choice D) is in the wrist. Of the four bones listed, the humerus (choice C) is the arm bone that is closest to the shoulder.

2. Somatotropin is secreted by the _____.

   A. pituitary gland
   B. adrenal glands
   C. hypothalamus
   D. thyroid

   Explanatory Answer: Somatotropin is also known as growth hormone. It is secreted by the pituitary, which regulates growth. The answer is choice A.

Physics

This section of the test focuses specifically on those skills a radiologist or other imaging scientist might need. Most of the physics section is set up as problems. Tested topics may include:

- Speed and acceleration
- Momentum
- Linear and rotational motion
- Newton's laws
- Kinetic and potential energy
- Gravitation
- Wave classification and theory
- Optics
- Static electricity
- Coulomb's law
- Electric fields and charges
- Currents, voltage, and resistance
- Ohm's law

Here are two examples of A2 physics questions.

1. A go-kart is set into motion with an initial speed of 5 m/sec. It moves for 20 seconds. At the end of that time, its speed is 25 m/sec. What is the magnitude of the go-kart's acceleration?

   A. 1.0 m/sec^2
   B. 2.5 m/sec^2
   C. 15 m/sec^2
   D. 20 m/sec^2

Explanatory Answer: Find acceleration by dividing the change in velocity by the length of time the object is in motion:

$$\frac{25 \text{ m/sec} - 5 \text{ m/sec}}{20 \text{ sec}} = \frac{25 \text{ m/sec}}{20 \text{ sec}} = 1.0 \text{ m/sec}^2$$

The answer is A.

2. In one minute, 15 waves break onto the shore. What is the frequency of the waves?

  A. 0.15 Hz
  B. 0.2 Hz
  C. 0.25 Hz
  D. 0.4 Hz

Explanatory Answer: To find frequency, first find period, the time in seconds between one crest and the next. In this case,

$$T = \frac{60 \text{ seconds}}{15} = 4 \text{ seconds}$$

Frequency is the reciprocal of period, expressed in seconds $^{-1}$, or Hertz.

$$f = \frac{1}{4} = 0.25 \text{ Hz}$$

The answer is choice C.

TIPS FROM TEST TAKERS
Review all your basic formulas—especially those for motion, force and work, power, gravitation, and electricity. Most physics questions will be problems that require those equations.

Critical Thinking

You have not yet worked as a nurse, but your program administrators may want to know how well you are able to apply common sense and critical thinking to specific nursing situations. This section may set up scenarios and ask you to choose among four strategies to triage patients or to deal with a specific medical or ethical situation. It looks at your ability to solve problems, to prioritize, to dissect arguments, to interpret data, and to overcome biases.

Some nursing programs use the Critical Thinking section as pre- and posttests to see how well students improve over the course of training. Others require a particular score for entry. There is no way to study for this section, although some students recommend reading through a practical nursing guide if you know that your chosen nursing program requires a high score on this section.

Learning Style

This part of the test, which is not graded, assesses your preferred learning style and provides you with study tips based on your responses. Because you cannot study for this part of the test, which is purely subjective, we will not cover it in this book.

Personality Profile

This ungraded part of the A2 determines your level of introversion or extroversion and classifies your personality type. It is primarily to be used by your teachers in your chosen nursing program. We will not discuss this part of the test in this book.

CHAPTER 2

Tips and Strategies for Test Takers

HOW TO USE THIS BOOK

Preparing for the A2 ahead of time is worth the effort. This book will help you do the following:

- Familiarize yourself with the test format
- Recognize the skills tested on the A2
- Practice your test-taking skills using sample A2 exams

Here is a practical study program that will help you make the best use of this book. The amount of study and review you do between tests will depend on what weaknesses you discover as you assess your responses and compare them to the explanatory answers that follow each test.

Step 1: Think About Your Weaknesses

If it has been a long time since you took biology or thought about parts of speech or algebraic equations, you might want to brush up on those long-lost skills. Chapter 1 of this book lists the major skills that are covered on the A2. If your preferred nursing program requires some of the science sections of the A2, you may need to review formulas, anatomy, the periodic table, and so on—even before you take your first practice test.

Build some review time into your test-prep schedule. Pull out your old textbooks, go to the library, or do some online review. McGraw Hill offers a study guide specifically focused on A2 skills and concepts: McGraw Hill *HESI A2 Review*.

Step 2: Take the Practice Tests

There are four practice tests, and each contains eight modules, just as the real A2 does. If you know which modules are required by your chosen school or schools, focus on those and ignore the others. As you take each test, try to simulate actual test conditions. Sit in a quiet room, time yourself, and work through as much of the test as time allows. If you wish, take a break after each section of the test. When you are done, check your answers against the explanatory answers that follow the test you took. Use the explanatory answers to figure out where you went wrong on any questions you did not answer correctly.

The practice tests in this book are parallel. This means that in most cases, similarly numbered questions on tests 1, 2, and 3 will measure the same sort of skill. This fact will help you determine where your problem areas are. For example, if you consistently miss question number 3 in the Basic Math Skills section of practice tests 1, 2, and 3, you will know that you need to study up on the concept of ratios.

Keep in mind that you will be taking the real test online. That may affect the speed with which you read questions or respond.

Step 3: Review and Improve

Each time you take a practice test, review the explanatory answers. Give yourself a break of a few days. Then take the next practice test and see whether you do better. Look for patterns. Did you miss the same kinds of questions on practice tests 1 and 2? Make a list of skills to review, and do some serious studying before you take practice test 3. If you have kept track of your weaknesses and studied those skills in depth, you should see a noticeable improvement in your score.

TIPS FROM TEST TAKERS
No review book or sample test will provide you with all the material you need to study, especially when it comes to the Anatomy and Physiology (A&P) section of the test. Pull out your old anatomy books and spend some time reviewing before you take a practice test.

STRATEGIES FOR TOP SCORES

As with any test, you can use certain strategies to improve your A2 score. You already know whether you are better at math or at science, or whether you understand grammar well enough to score high on that part of the test.

STUDY STRATEGIES

- **Get to know the format of the exam.** The practice tests in this book are designed to be similar to what you will see on the A2.

- **Get to know the test directions.** The A2 is not different from other multiple-choice tests you have taken over the years. There are always four choices, and most questions are stand-alone or refer to a given passage or problem. Only in the math section are there occasional short-answer questions where choices are not given.

- **Get to know what topics are covered.** Chapter 1 lists the major skills that are covered on the A2.

- **Test and review.** If possible, give yourself time to take each of the practice tests in this book. These are long tests, so you will need to map out big chunks of time with breaks in between. Do not plan to take more than one test in a day. Study the answers, look for patterns, and review those skills that consistently cause problems for you.

TEST-TAKING STRATEGIES

- **Answer all the questions!** Your time is limited across the entire test, but depending on where you take the exam, you may be able to spend more time on chemistry and less on reading comprehension if you prefer. Unfortunately, the A2 is given in a format that does not allow you to go back and review questions you may have had trouble on, so do your best with each question as it is presented.

- **Use the process of elimination.** Even if you feel completely stumped, you will probably be able to eliminate one or more choices simply by using common sense. That improves your odds of getting the right answer.

- **When in doubt, guess.** On the A2, every question has the same value, and no points are taken off for guessing. Use the process of elimination, but if you're baffled, go ahead and guess. On multiple-choice questions with four possible responses, you have a 25 percent chance of getting the answer right by guessing. If you leave the answer blank, your chance drops to zero.

- **Beware of answer choices that look reasonable but are not correct.** Because most questions on the A2 are multiple choice, the test makers have many chances to mislead you with tricky distracters (wrong answers). Focus, use scratch paper to solve problems if it is allowed, and use the process of elimination to help narrow your choices.

TIPS FOR TEST DAY

- **Get a good night's sleep.** You need energy to face a test that is more than three hours long, and you won't have energy if you're exhausted from worry or from excessive last-minute review. If you have taken all three practice tests, reviewed those skills that troubled you, and improved your scores on your final test, you have done what you need to do to succeed. Arriving at the test site well rested and alert will improve your chances dramatically.

- **Be careful as you indicate your answers.** The computer-based A2 does not allow you to go back and fix questions. Make sure that you answer questions as they are presented. If you use the calculator provided in the software, double-check your answers.

TIPS FROM TEST TAKERS

Buttons on the online calculator can occasionally "stick," so be sure to estimate your answers and not rely entirely on the calculator.

- **Watch the time.** Wear a watch and check yourself from time to time. If you have timed yourself on the practice tests, you should be pretty good at estimating the time you have left as you progress through the A2. Individual sections may not be timed, but you may have an overall time deadline; you will be told this as you begin the exam.

A2 TRAINING SCHEDULE

Are you ready to get started? Use this sample schedule to plan your attack.

My A2 Test-Prep Schedule

TEST CENTER: _____ **DATE:** _____ **TIME:** _____

4 Weeks Before	Register for the test via www.evolve.elsevier.com. Check your preferred nursing program's website to see which modules are required—or call to confirm.	
3 Weeks Before	Take Practice Test 1 (required modules only). Review using McGraw Hill *HESI A2 Review* and other resources.	Number of correct answers divided by _____ questions: Problem Areas
2 Weeks Before	Take Practice Tests 2 and 3 on two separate days (required modules only). Review using McGraw Hill *HESI A2 Review* and other resources.	Number of correct answers divided by _____ questions: Problem Areas: Number of correct answers divided by _____ questions: Problem Areas: Tests 2 and 3 compared to Test 1:
1 Week Before	Take Practice Test 4 (required modules only). Review using McGraw Hill *HESI A2 Review* and other resources.	Number of correct answers divided by _____ questions: Problem Areas: Test 4 compared to Tests 2 and 3:

CHAPTER 3

A2 Practice Test 1

READING COMPREHENSION

| 50 items | Suggested time: 55 minutes |

High Fructose Corn Syrup

Lately, there has been a lot of discussion—within the medical community as well as across the kitchen table—about the supposed harmful effects that high fructose corn syrup (HFCS) has on the human body. Many people wonder if its use as a sweetener is contributing to the population's overall rate of obesity.

In the late 1970s, many of the largest food manufacturers in the United States shifted away from using refined table sugar to using the much cheaper HFCS. Soon HFCS was used to sweeten many products, including cereal, steak sauce, soft drinks, bread, baked beans, and yogurt.

Table sugar and HFCS share a similar biochemical structure: both contain the simple sugars glucose and fructose, though HFCS is produced from corn and undergoes additional processing to increase the amount of fructose.

The American Medical Association does not take the view that one sweetener is better or worse than another. However, researchers at Princeton University have recently released a study showing that rats who consumed HFCS gained more weight, especially in the abdominal area, than rats who consumed table sugar.

| GO ON TO THE NEXT PAGE |

Other medical professionals say that more research is needed before conclusive results can be drawn. Meanwhile, nearly everyone can agree that both table sugar and HFCS are high in calories—nearly 50 per tablespoon—and that neither form of sweetener provides any measurable nutritional value.

1. What is the main idea of the passage?

    A. The American Medical Association has identified preferred sweeteners.
    B. High fructose corn syrup may be contributing to obesity in America.
    C. Refined table sugar is a natural product, whereas corn syrup is manufactured.
    D. Rats show a decided preference for high fructose corn syrup over other sweeteners.

2. Which of the following is *not* listed as a detail in the passage?

    A. HFCS and sugar share a biological structure.
    B. HFCS is cheaper to use than sugar is.
    C. HFCS is now used to sweeten a variety of products.
    D. HFCS contains more calories than aspartame does.

3. What is the author's primary purpose in writing this essay?

    A. To inform
    B. To persuade
    C. To entertain
    D. To analyze

4. Choose the best summary of the passage.

    A. After extensive studies of HFCS and its effect on humans, scientists recommend its removal from grocery products.
    B. A recent study on rats seems to confirm doctors' suspicions that HFCS is contributing to people's unhealthful weight gains.
    C. Until more research is done on HFCS, people are better off using it than replacing it with refined sugar.
    D. The AMA suggests that avoiding HFCS can have immediate, healthful results on overweight patients.

GO ON TO THE NEXT PAGE

Hypertension

The term *hypertension* is used to describe the condition of chronically high blood pressure. People who are obese, experience a lot of stress, smoke tobacco products, have a diet with too much salt in it, or have diabetes are often at a higher risk for hypertension. As well, African Americans are more likely to have hypertension than other population groups.

Hypertension often develops over many years. Older people are most often diagnosed with hypertension. One reason for this is that blood vessels lose elasticity and stiffen as a person ages. This creates more resistance to the blood flowing through the body and elevates blood pressure.

Symptoms of hypertension can include blurred vision, headaches, a buzzing in the ears, fatigue, an irregular heartbeat, and nosebleeds. Hypertension that goes untreated over a period of time can lead to serious complications such as kidney disease, heart disease, loss of vision, heart attack, brain damage, and even early death. Fortunately, treating hypertension reduces blood pressure and can lower the risk of complications. For many people, losing weight can result in a significant decrease in blood pressure. For others, physicians may prescribe one or more medications to help bring blood pressure down into a safe range.

One thing is certain: physicians believe that people over the age of 20 should monitor their blood pressure by having it checked at least once a year. Those with a history of hypertension in the immediate family should have it checked more frequently.

5. What does the term *elasticity* mean, as used in the second paragraph?

   A. Firmness
   B. Compactness
   C. Flexibility
   D. Rigidity

6. Which is the best title for this passage?

   A. "How to Manage Hypertension Successfully"
   B. "Doctors Discover the Hidden Dangers of Hypertension"
   C. "Doctors Work to Understand the Causes of Hypertension"
   D. "Causes, Symptoms, Complications, and Management of Hypertension"

GO ON TO THE NEXT PAGE

7. Which of the following statements is an opinion?

A. Obese people are at risk for hypertension.
B. Losing weight can decrease blood pressure.
C. Older people must pay attention to their blood pressure.
D. Blurred vision or dizziness may be a sign of hypertension.

8. Which statement would *not* be inferred by the reader?

A. Maintaining a healthy weight may help prevent hypertension.
B. There is presently no reliable treatment for hypertension.
C. Your ethnicity may contribute to your risk for hypertension.
D. A 60-year-old is more likely to have hypertension than a teenager is.

Concussion

A concussion is a traumatic injury to the brain that can interfere with the way the brain processes information and functions. A concussion often results in severe headaches, diminished alertness, and even unconsciousness.

While more than one million people in the United States suffer concussions every year, many believe that, like people, no two concussions are identical. Recently two professional baseball players suffered concussions. The first player was injured early in the season and tried twice to return to regular play, but was not medically cleared to play until the following year. Even after eight months, this player reported a recurring condition of "fogginess" that seemed to linger. The second player had brief symptoms of sleepiness and involuntary movement, or "shakiness." A few days later, and after several tests, the second player reported that the effects of the concussion had subsided, and he was cleared to play.

No matter the duration of a person's recovery, refraining from trying to do too much, too soon is vital. A specialist at Boston University's Center for the Study of Traumatic Encephalopathy believes that someone who suffers a second concussion while still recovering from the first risks an even longer recovery.

GO ON TO THE NEXT PAGE

Full recovery from concussions is possible. Problems are seldom permanent, and for most people who have had a concussion, the long-term prognosis is typically excellent. The first baseball player recently returned to his team. And though he was told by his physician that he has no greater risk than anyone else of suffering another concussion, other physicians believe that suffering one sports-related concussion increases the likelihood of suffering another.

9. Which of the following is *not* listed as a detail in the passage?

   A. Football and lacrosse players suffer the most concussions.
   B. More than a million Americans a year suffer concussions.
   C. Concussions may result in diminished alertness.
   D. It may take longer to recover from a second concussion.

10. What is the meaning of the word *diminished* as used in the first paragraph?

   A. Miniature
   B. Reduced
   C. Recurrent
   D. Hollow

11. Choose the best summary of the passage.

   A. No two concussions are alike. Some people may recover easily from concussion, while others may take weeks or months. In any case, receiving a second concussion too soon may mean a lengthy recovery.
   B. When baseball players receive concussions, some take a long time to recover. Some may try to return to play too soon and receive a second concussion that ends their careers.
   C. Although most athletes shrug off concussions, they would be wise to take them seriously. Multiple concussions can cause serious harm to the brain, which is rattled around in the skull with each injury.
   D. Recovery from concussion is possible, but it is not always a good idea to return to play too soon. Some head injuries are called concussions but do not really qualify as such.

GO ON TO THE NEXT PAGE

12. What is the author's primary purpose in writing this essay?

     A. To entertain
     B. To analyze
     C. To reflect
     D. To inform

13. Which statement would *not* be inferred by the reader?

     A. Athletes should be careful after a first concussion.
     B. Severe headache after a fall may be a sign of concussion.
     C. Sports-related concussions are riskier than other kinds.
     D. Symptoms of concussion may linger for more than six months.

Sickle-Cell Anemia

Healthy red blood cells are shaped like a disc. Each cell contains the protein hemoglobin, which carries oxygen throughout the body. In some people, a crescent-shaped cell forms instead of the normal disc-shaped cell. The crescent-shaped cells contain abnormal hemoglobin. These sickle-shaped cells are fragile and are unable to carry oxygen properly throughout the body.

Sickle-cell anemia is an inherited disease that affects about 72,000 people in the United States. It is more common among people of South American or African descent. The genes for sickle-cell anemia are inherited from both parents. When both parents carry a gene for the trait for sickle-cell, there is a one in four chance that they will pass the disease on to their children.

Symptoms of sickle-cell anemia can include sudden occurrences of extreme abdominal and back pain, bone pain, fever, fatigue, and a rapid heart rate. One patient compared the pain in his back to a jackhammer and said the pain could take over his entire body. Another patient, an eight-year-old girl, described fevers and the feeling of someone squeezing her arms and legs.

GO ON TO THE NEXT PAGE

Cycles of symptoms are often unpredictable and can occur infrequently or almost constantly. Some people who are affected report weekly occurrences of persistent pain, while others report occurrences once a month. Some report that relief comes only by using powerful painkillers. For others, relief comes with bed rest and a hot-water bottle. Most agree that while the challenges of managing sickle-cell anemia are great, with diligent care, it can be managed.

14. What is the main idea of the passage?

    A. Bone pain is a typical sign of sickle-cell anemia.

    B. Without enough oxygen, the body can break down.

    C. Genetically inherited diseases affect thousands.

    D. Sickle-cell anemia is a painful, inherited disease.

15. What is the meaning of the word *diligent* as used in the last paragraph?

    A. Dispersed

    B. Incensed

    C. Painstaking

    D. Demanding

16. Identify the overall tone of the essay.

    A. Informal

    B. Insensitive

    C. Grim

    D. Uplifting

17. Which of the following is *not* listed as a detail in the passage?

    A. People of African descent may be prone to sickle-cell anemia.

    B. Symptoms of sickle-cell anemia may include abdominal pain.

    C. The red blood cells of sickle-cell patients are unusually shaped.

    D. Vitamin and mineral deficiencies may result in some anemia.

GO ON TO THE NEXT PAGE

Toxins and Your Health

Lie out in the sun too much today—and get skin cancer 20 years from now. Smoke too many cigarettes now—and get lung cancer decades down the road. Now there is potentially a third danger to add to this list: be exposed to too much lead, pesticides, or mercury now and have your aging brain become seriously confused during your senior years.

"We're trying to offer a caution that a portion of what has been called normal aging might in fact be due to ubiquitous environmental exposures like lead," says Dr. Brian Schwartz of Johns Hopkins University. "The fact that it's happening with lead is the first proof of the principle that it's possible."

A new area of medical research is one that studies how exposure to toxic elements in younger years can result in serious health problems in senior years. It is difficult to research these problems because the only way to do so is to observe people over many years.

Physicians test for lead amounts by seeing how much has accumulated in a person's shinbone. Testing the blood also often reveals amounts of lead, but that is a sign of recent, not lifelong, exposure. The higher the lifetime lead dose, according to the study, the worse the performance of mental functions, including verbal and visual memory and language ability.

18. A reader might infer from this passage that _____.
    A. most dangerous lead exposure happens later in life
    B. doctors are concerned about what happens to the brain during aging
    C. shinbones are good indicators of many health ailments or conditions
    D. blood tests are the best way to measure individuals' lifetime lead exposure

19. Which of the following statements is an opinion?

    A. Smoking cigarettes today may lead to lung cancer later.
    B. Doctors are studying the results of exposure to toxic elements.
    C. People with dementia should be tested for lead exposure.
    D. Researchers test the shinbone to look for built-up toxins.

GO ON TO THE NEXT PAGE

20. What is the meaning of the word *exposed* as used in the first paragraph?

   A. Uncovered
   B. Subjected
   C. Visible
   D. Divulged

21. What is the main idea of the passage?

   A. Environmental toxins may have dire health effects over time.
   B. Of three toxins studied, lead has the worst effect on health.
   C. Toxins may accumulate in the bones of older patients.
   D. Johns Hopkins University has discovered a new use for lead.

Yoga

Yoga is an exercise that everyone should try. Yoga was first practiced thousands of years ago. It helps connect the mind and body by taking a person through a series of poses while emphasizing controlled breathing and meditation. Every year hundreds of thousands of people enjoy the benefits of yoga by treating the movements and postures as exercise.

Yoga works by safely stretching muscles, ligaments, and tendons. This helps release the buildup of lactic acid in the muscles that can often cause stiffness, tension, and even pain. Yoga helps develop the body's range of mobility and increases the ease of everyday movements. Many participants report improved flexibility, especially in the trunk and shoulders, after only two months of practice. Yoga improves posture, balance, and sleep, and it also helps with weight control.

Physically, many yoga poses help build upper-body strength, which is increasingly important as the body ages. Other poses help strengthen the muscles in the lower back, and when properly practiced, nearly all of the poses strengthen the body's abdominal, or core, muscles. This helps improve the circulation of blood that increases the delivery of nutrients and oxygen to the body and also removes wastes produced by the body. When combined with yoga's benefit of lowering a person's heart rate, the result is increased cardiovascular endurance.

GO ON TO THE NEXT PAGE

The University of Maryland School of Nursing recently published a study that showed yoga was especially effective at reducing stress. In addition, researchers found that yoga surpassed traditional aerobic exercise, often significantly, in improving flexibility, pain tolerance, and daily energy levels. One enthusiast says that her advice to skeptics is simple, "Take a deep breath, stretch, and indulge in a few poses. You'll feel better."

22. Identify the overall tone of the essay.
    A. Earnest
    B. Negative
    C. Self-satisfied
    D. Skeptical

23. What is the meaning of the word *tolerance* as used in the last paragraph?
    A. Open-mindedness
    B. Approval
    C. Endurance
    D. Generosity

24. The passage lists all of these benefits of yoga EXCEPT
    _____.

    A. improved circulation
    B. strengthening of core muscles
    C. stress reduction
    D. fortification of immune system

25. What is the author's primary purpose in writing this essay?
    A. To persuade
    B. To entertain
    C. To analyze
    D. To reflect

GO ON TO THE NEXT PAGE

Super Foods

Super foods are whole, unprocessed foods such as blueberries, walnuts, beans, oats, and broccoli. Spinach, yogurt, and pomegranates are also super foods. They are classified as such because they contain high levels of essential nutrients, are low in calories, and can often help prevent—and even reverse—some of the common effects of aging, including cardiovascular disease, type 2 diabetes, high blood pressure, and certain types of cancer. Super foods help lower cholesterol levels in the blood and, some researchers believe, even improve a person's mood.

High on the list of super foods are blueberries, fresh or frozen, which are loaded with vitamin C, antioxidants, and potassium. Blueberries are also an anti-inflammatory, which many researchers and nutritionists believe is beneficial.

Lentils are a super food that helps prevent a spike in insulin levels that can increase body fat. Lentils are high in both fiber and protein, each of which contributes to stabilizing blood sugar levels and reducing excess fat, especially in the stomach area. Walnuts are a plant-based source of essential unsaturated omega-3 fatty acids, which can improve cholesterol and lower the risk of heart disease by as much as 50 percent. All oats are healthful. Oats, even instant oatmeal, are digested slowly while providing up to five grams of fiber per serving.

As physicians and nutritionists continue to study super foods and their effects, consumers continue to educate themselves about the variety of benefits. In an era when consumers question the origin and nutritional value of much of the food on store shelves, super foods are some of the most healthful and natural whole foods available.

26. The passage mentions all of the following claims for the health benefits of super foods EXCEPT _____.

    A. lowering cholesterol
    B. stabilizing insulin levels
    C. building muscle mass
    D. reducing blood pressure

GO ON TO THE NEXT PAGE

27. What is the meaning of the word *unprocessed* as used in the first paragraph?

    A. Natural and untreated
    B. Made of vegetable matter
    C. Home grown
    D. Uncirculated or undigested

28. Which statement would *not* be inferred by the reader?

    A. Instant oatmeal can be part of a healthful breakfast.
    B. Blueberries are an especially healthful food.
    C. Certain grains and dairy products are super foods.
    D. Super foods are more expensive than processed foods.

29. Which of the following statements is an opinion?

    A. Walnuts contain omega-3 fatty acids.
    B. Lentils are high in both protein and fiber.
    C. Pomegranates are delicious and healthful.
    D. Oats move slowly through the digestive tract.

30. What is the main idea of the passage?

    A. Super foods are low in calories but provide essential nutrients that have enormous health benefits.
    B. US supermarkets should make a point of stocking up on powerful super foods.
    C. Blueberries are a super food that contains a natural inflammatory as well as important vitamins and minerals.
    D. Doctors now believe that daily inclusion of super foods in the diet can reverse the aging process.

GO ON TO THE NEXT PAGE

Aromatherapy—Fact or Fiction?

For years, aromatherapy has been touted as a safe and natural way to relax and even heal. Essential oils from a variety of scents have been added to candles and sprays to help people feel better. However, a recent study performed at Ohio State University says that these smells, as nice as they may be, do not do a thing to improve people's health.

To find out if aromatherapy actually works, the researchers tested two of the most popular scents: lemon and lavender. First, test subjects had their heart rate, blood pressure, stress hormones, and immune function measured and noted. Next, they were subjected to mild stressors and then told to sniff one of the scents to see if the scent would help them relax. Finally, all the subjects were tested again to look for improvement. No significant changes were noted—even in people who had previously stated they were true believers in the power of aromatherapy.

Of course, this does not necessarily prove that aromatherapy is worthless, either. It was just one small study, pitted against the opinions of thousands of consumers who swear by peppermint on their pillow for an upset stomach or vanilla for a headache. More tests will be done, but in the meantime, a whiff of lavender, lemon, or other scents will certainly do no harm—and can be quite pleasant at the same time.

31. Which of the following is a conclusion that a reader can draw from this passage?

    A. Aromatherapy is not a legitimate therapy by anyone's standards.
    B. Lemon and lavender are not healthy scents to inhale or use.
    C. More studies are needed to determine if aromatherapy is truly beneficial.
    D. Adding aromatherapy to regular treatment will help speed healing.

32. What is the meaning of the word *touted* as used in the first paragraph?

    A. Revealed
    B. Glorified
    C. Overcome
    D. Deceived

GO ON TO THE NEXT PAGE

33. Identify the overall tone of the essay.

    A. Congratulatory

    B. Uncertain

    C. Annoyed

    D. Distressed

34. Which of the following is *not* listed as a detail in the passage?

    A. Subjects were given mild stressors.

    B. Lemon and lavender scents were tested.

    C. Vanilla worked better than lemon for stress.

    D. The study took place at Ohio State University.

An Old Form of Running Is New Again

Barefoot running is a rapidly growing movement that encourages people to leave their shoes at home and take to the streets in only their bare feet. Barefoot running advocates are quick to point out that while shoe technology has advanced significantly since the advent of the modern running shoe, there has been little decline in the number of injuries that occur from running.

Humankind has been running for millions of years, and modern running shoes have existed for less than 50 years. By wearing larger shoes with excessive cushioning we are changing the biomechanics of how we run, thereby increasing the likelihood for injury. Early humans ran with a "forefoot strike," landing closer to the balls of their feet and using their foot's natural arch as a spring to store and release energy. Modern shoe designs encourage a "heel strike," landing on the heel and rolling forward to the toe. Barefoot running advocates believe "heel striking" replaces your reliance on the natural mechanics of your feet with the cushioning provided by your shoes, and that this is what causes many of the injuries affecting runners today.

Critics assert that while our feet may have been designed for bare-foot running, our road surfaces were not. Concrete and asphalt are much firmer than any surface where our human ancestors would have been running. Broken glass and debris also may make barefoot running a significant challenge.

GO ON TO THE NEXT PAGE

There is little consensus when it comes to the safety and effectiveness of barefoot running, but even the most skeptical of podiatrists will agree that wearing heavily padded shoes too often can result in a weaker foot and leg structure. Spend some extra time walking barefoot around your house; aside from building up the muscles and tendons that strengthen your feet, you may just find yourself tempted to go for a run.

35. Which might be a good title for this passage?

    A. "Everyone Should Run Barefoot"

    B. "How to Prevent Running Injuries"

    C. "Modern Road Surfaces Versus Barefoot Running"

    D. "The Debate over Barefoot Running"

36. What is the meaning of the word *consensus* as it is used in the last paragraph?

    A. Investigation

    B. Purpose

    C. Trepidation

    D. Unanimity

37. Which statement would *not* be inferred by the reader?

    A. Runners who take their shoes off may face some hazards.

    B. Modern running shoes may increase the odds for injury.

    C. Walking barefoot is good for the muscles and tendons.

    D. Before 1950, even Olympic runners ran barefoot.

38. Which of the following statements is an opinion?

    A. Running barefoot is natural and advantageous.

    B. The cost of modern running shoes keeps increasing.

    C. Concrete sidewalks are harder than dirt paths.

    D. The arch of the foot gives a spring to the step.

GO ON TO THE NEXT PAGE

The Sleep Workout

Developing muscle growth is an effective way to stay healthy as we get older, but many people find it difficult to develop this muscle growth, even after modifying their exercise routine and food intake. What many people may not realize is that getting the proper amount of uninterrupted sleep plays a major role in the development of muscle.

The hard work of developing muscle is done in the gym, on a track, or on the court, but the actual growth takes places during the rest periods that follow a workout. Your body immediately begins rebuilding the muscle fibers that were broken down during the course of your workout. Much of this process is carried out while you are sleeping, so without a full night of sleep, muscle fibers will not have the opportunity to rebuild.

Human growth hormone (HGH) is an amino acid that is central to regulating metabolism, building muscle, facilitating calcium retention, and stimulating the immune system. The amount of HGH in your body spikes significantly during deep sleep, which makes getting at least 7 to 10 hours of sleep every night imperative to anyone hoping to develop additional muscle growth.

Recent studies have linked inadequate amounts of sleep to lowered levels of leptin, a hormone in the brain that controls appetite. Test subjects who received less sleep, or frequently interrupted sleep, would crave carbohydrates even after their caloric needs reached satiety. This can contribute to obesity and negatively affect any good habits people may have developed with regard to food intake.

39. What is the main idea of the passage?

A. Insufficient sleep can lead to obesity.

B. Insufficient sleep inhibits the natural release of human growth hormone in the human body.

C. Getting the proper amount of uninterrupted sleep plays a major role in the development of muscle.

D. Developing muscle growth is an effective way to stay healthy as we get older.

GO ON TO THE NEXT PAGE

40. The term *satiety*, as used in the last paragraph, can best be defined as _____.

    A. a state of tiredness

    B. a state of being satisfied

    C. a state of being overloaded

    D. a state of confusion

41. In this passage, which of the following is *not* mentioned as a role of HGH in the human body?

    A. Regulating the metabolism

    B. Stimulating the immune system

    C. Regulating leptin, an appetite-controlling hormone

    D. Facilitating calcium retention

42. What conclusion can the reader draw after reading this passage?

    A. Getting uninterrupted sleep is more important than getting enough sleep.

    B. Insufficient sleep may result in an increased risk for obesity.

    C. Human growth hormone is not essential for muscle development.

    D. Leptin is essential for building muscle.

GO ON TO THE NEXT PAGE

Sunny-Side Up

Most people are familiar with the damaging effects of the sun on unprotected skin, but not enough attention is paid to the many positive effects of receiving direct exposure to sunlight on a regular basis.

The most compelling argument for increased exposure to sunlight is the need for vitamin D in the human body. Vitamin D is integral for maintaining healthy bones and preventing diseases like rickets and osteoporosis. It is synthesized by the skin when it comes into contact with the UVB rays found in sunlight. In order to ensure you are receiving the proper amount of vitamin D, it is recommended to get 15 minutes of direct exposure to sunlight at least two or three times a week. UVB rays are made less intense when passing through clouds and pollution, and they will not transmit through glass or sunscreen. UVB rays are also less effective the farther you are from the equator. People with darker skin require more exposure to the sun to receive the same amount of vitamin D.

In addition to vitamin D, sunlight will help regulate the circadian rhythms that ensure you get a good night's sleep. Sunlight helps prevent an overactive immune system, which may prove useful in preventing autoimmune diseases like psoriasis and lupus. Recent studies have even shown that sunlight can help lessen the symptoms of Alzheimer's disease.

The negative impacts of excess exposure to sunlight should not be ignored; cancers resulting from skin damage are a real concern that must be taken seriously. But the importance of vitamin D and the other positive impacts of sunlight make a compelling argument for making sure we are spending enough time every week in direct sunlight.

43. What is the main idea of the passage?
    A. There are many positive effects of receiving direct exposure to sunlight.
    B. The negative impacts of sunlight should not be ignored.
    C. Vitamin D is integral for maintaining healthy bones and preventing diseases.
    D. Vitamin D is synthesized by our bodies in reaction to direct sunlight.

GO ON TO THE NEXT PAGE

44. The term *compelling*, as used in the second paragraph, can best be defined as _____.

A. reasonable
B. convincing
C. common
D. worthwhile

45. What is the author's primary purpose in writing this essay?

A. To persuade
B. To reflect
C. To entertain
D. To analyze

46. Identify the overall tone of the essay.

A. Confused
B. Confident
C. Disheartened
D. Disapproving

47. Choose the best summary of the passage.

A. Light-skinned people need a maximum of 15 minutes a day in direct sunlight to achieve the benefits of the sun's rays. Dark-skinned people may need far more time in the sun to reap the same benefits.
B. Spending too much time indoors can wreak havoc with your circadian rhythms, leach vitamin D from your bones, and damage your immune system. Exercising outdoors in direct sunlight or in a room with clear glass is recommended.
C. Although negative effects of sunlight are well known, people should be aware that some sunlight is necessary and beneficial. Exposure to sunlight increases vitamin D, improves sleep, and prevents hyperactivity of the immune system.
D. You can avoid direct sunlight but still reap the benefits of a day in the sun by using sunscreen or tinted glass. The effects of vitamin D are beneficial, so it is wise to spend some time outdoors while being fully protected from the dangerous rays.

GO ON TO THE NEXT PAGE

A Short History of the CDC

The Centers for Disease Control and Prevention started in 1946 as the Communicable Disease Center (CDC). Its original goal was to stop malaria in the United States. From a small office in Atlanta, health workers spread out over the South, spraying mosquitoes and using shovels to eliminate low spots of standing water. At that time, most of the CDC's workers were not doctors; the need was for entomologists and engineers.

The founder of the CDC, Dr. Joseph Mountin, enlarged the organization's mission to fight communicable diseases of all kinds, and over the next 20 years, the CDC would focus on smallpox, measles, and polio. In 1970, the name was changed to the Center for Disease Control, but the mission continued to expand.

By 1980, the CDC was working not only on eradication of existing diseases, but also on disease prevention. By this point, it had hundreds of doctors and researchers looking into health problems such as depression and addiction. The name changed again, to the Centers for Disease Control and Prevention.

Today, the CDC has thousands of employees and coordinates research activities with public health agencies worldwide. It is especially known for its work to protect people from epidemics and unexpected health threats, but its everyday work in the areas of environmental health, injury prevention, birth defects, healthy schools and workplaces, and health education is just as important and beneficial to all Americans.

48. What is the overall tone of the essay?

    A. Appreciative
    B. Awestruck
    C. Somber
    D. Disheartened

49. Which of the following is *not* listed as a detail in the passage?

    A. Where the organization began
    B. Who first ran the organization
    C. When the organization changed its name
    D. What divisions make up the current CDC

GO ON TO THE NEXT PAGE

50. A reader might infer from this passage that the organization _____.

    A. succeeded in eradicating malaria
    B. has always been led by a medical doctor
    C. no longer studies communicable diseases
    D. changed its name to match its mission

**STOP. IF YOU HAVE TIME LEFT OVER,
CHECK YOUR WORK ON THIS SECTION ONLY.**

VOCABULARY AND GENERAL KNOWLEDGE

| 50 items | Suggested time: 45 minutes |

1. Select the meaning of the underlined word in the following sentence.

   Due to his <u>mercurial</u> temperament, Justin did not work well with others.

   A. Continuous
   B. Unpredictable
   C. Mercenary
   D. Miraculous

2. What is another word for *elated*?

   A. Delighted
   B. Confused
   C. Flabbergasted
   D. Edified

3. What is the meaning of *disregard*?

   A. Have no opinion about
   B. Pay attention to
   C. Care for
   D. Ignore

4. Select the meaning of the underlined word in the following sentence.

   People with weakened immune systems should avoid <u>exposure</u> to flu.

   A. Disclosure
   B. Pretense
   C. Contact
   D. Display

GO ON TO THE NEXT PAGE

5. If a patient's condition is deteriorating, he is _____.

    A. getting worse

    B. improving gradually

    C. resisting medication

    D. failing to eat or drink

6. *Precipitous* is best defined as being _____.

    A. damp

    B. gentle

    C. swift

    D. dull

7. Select the meaning of the underlined word in the following sentence.

    Being overweight may <u>predispose</u> a person to diabetes.

    A. Make susceptible

    B. Bring to light

    C. Save from harm

    D. Pass over

8. A condition that is ongoing is _____.

    A. rapid

    B. continuous

    C. partial

    D. complete

9. A paroxysm is a sudden spasm. Another word for this might be _____.

    A. convulsion

    B. symptom

    C. efficacy

    D. embolism

GO ON TO THE NEXT PAGE

10. A restricted diet is _____.

   A. low in fat

   B. vegetarian

   C. banned

   D. limited

11. What is another word for *cicatrix*?

   A. Beetle

   B. Scalpel

   C. Antidote

   D. Scar

12. Select the meaning of the underlined word in the following sentence.

      Calcium pills may be used to <u>supplement</u> your diet.

   A. Replace

   B. Add to

   C. Reflect

   D. Parallel

13. Select the meaning of the underlined word in the following sentence.

      The patients are under <u>quarantine</u> until further notice.

   A. A specialist's care

   B. Experimental drug therapy

   C. Imprisonment in a rehabilitation unit

   D. Confinement away from the general population

14. Which word names a medicine whose purpose is to induce vomiting?

   A. Opiate

   B. Narcotic

   C. Emetic

   D. Prophylactic

GO ON TO THE NEXT PAGE

15. What is another word for *panacea*?

   A. Clinician
   B. Painkiller
   C. Vista
   D. Cure

16. What is the meaning of *principally*?

   A. Mostly
   B. Clearly
   C. In our opinion
   D. Royally

17. What is the best description for the term *selected plants* in the following sentence?

> Saturated fat comes principally from animal food products and selected plants.

   A. Plants that have been chosen
   B. Particular plants
   C. Top quality plants
   D. Restricted plants

18. What is the best description for the abbreviation LDL?

   A. A group of denominations
   B. A type of lipoprotein
   C. Self-care mobility skills
   D. A certain digital value

19. The outer bone in the lower leg is the _____.

   A. fascia
   B. fibrous
   C. filial
   D. fibula

GO ON TO THE NEXT PAGE

20. Select the meaning of the underlined word in the following sentence.

    It <u>disintegrates</u> in the mouth within seconds after placement on the tongue, allowing its contents to be swallowed with or without water.

    A. Evaporates
    B. Fizzes
    C. Deviates
    D. Fragments

21. The jawbone may be called the _____.

    A. mantis
    B. mantua
    C. mandible
    D. manganite

22. Select the meaning of the underlined word in the following sentence.

    Step-by-step, the doctor explained the <u>rationale</u> for the treatment.

    A. Reasoning
    B. Prescription
    C. Procedure
    D. Necessity

23. What is the meaning of *qualms*?

    A. Misgivings
    B. Habits
    C. Serenity
    D. Dispatches

GO ON TO THE NEXT PAGE

24. Select the meaning of the underlined word in the following sentence.

    The capsule remains <u>intact</u> even when placed in water.

    A. Viable
    B. Operational
    C. Tinted
    D. Whole

25. *Anterior* refers to which part of the human body?

    A. Top
    B. Bottom
    C. Front
    D. Back

26. What is the best description for the term *gravid*?

    A. Deadly serious
    B. Expecting a child
    C. Germ-free
    D. Diseased

27. Select the meaning of the underlined word in the following sentence.

    The cavity, once opened, proved to be <u>riddled</u> with infection.

    A. Challenged
    B. Overrun
    C. Separated
    D. Complete

28. What does *alimentary* mean?

    A. Related to nourishment
    B. Related to outflow
    C. Related to simplicity
    D. Related to protection

GO ON TO THE NEXT PAGE

29. Select the meaning of the underlined word in the following sentence.

    A single dose will <u>suppress</u> even the nastiest cough.

    A. Subdue
    B. Cure
    C. Restore
    D. Affect

30. What is the best description for the term *septic*?

    A. Infected
    B. Odorous
    C. Terminal
    D. Vigorous

31. Another word for the kneecap is the _____.

    A. patina
    B. patella
    C. pastel
    D. pathogen

32. What is another word for *paltry*?

    A. Insignificant
    B. Punitive
    C. Prolonged
    D. Economical

33. Select the meaning of the underlined word in the following sentence.

    A tube is used to <u>vent</u> the gases to the outside.

    A. Block
    B. Trade
    C. Emit
    D. Inhale

GO ON TO THE NEXT PAGE

34. Medicine that is given in inhalant form is _____.

    A. dissolved

    B. breathed in

    C. taken orally

    D. injected

35. Select the meaning of the underlined word in the following sentence.

    This medication works by <u>inhibiting</u> the action of a certain enzyme.

    A. Occupying

    B. Speeding

    C. Hindering

    D. Enhancing

36. A symptom that is exacerbated is _____.

    A. not dangerous

    B. disfiguring

    C. painful

    D. made worse

37. To critique something is to _____.

    A. appraise it

    B. condemn it

    C. extol it

    D. berate it

38. The abbreviation YOB on a medical form refers to a patient's _____.

    A. weight

    B. birthdate

    C. symptoms

    D. ethnicity

GO ON TO THE NEXT PAGE

39. Select the meaning of the underlined word in the following sentence.

    This is a disease that is likely to recur in a patient's <u>progeny</u>.

    A. Chest
    B. Hormones
    C. Offspring
    D. Lifetime

40. The crystalline compound that is a product of protein metabolism is known as _____.

    A. uracil
    B. urine
    C. ureter
    D. urea

41. Select the meaning of the underlined word in the following sentence.

    Too many potential job choices put Martin in a <u>quandary</u>.

    A. A place where rocks are mined
    B. A journey of discovery
    C. A state of uncertainty
    D. A major attempt or trial

42. What is a diagnostic test?

    A. One that locates a cure
    B. One that looks for a cause
    C. One that examines the skin
    D. One that is performed on doctors

GO ON TO THE NEXT PAGE

43. What is the best description for the word *establish* in the following sentence?

> Physicians use patch tests to establish the specific causes of contact dermatitis.

A. Determine
B. Introduce
C. Endorse
D. Launch

44. Contact dermatitis occurs through the sense of _____.

A. smell
B. taste
C. touch
D. sight

45. A UTI is likely to involve the _____.

A. bones
B. throat
C. stomach
D. bladder

46. Select the meaning of the underlined word in the following sentence.

> Treatment is <u>projected</u> to last three months or more.

A. Protruded
B. Guaranteed
C. Estimated
D. Alleged

47. To cauterize a wound is to _____.

A. soothe it
B. cover it
C. stitch it
D. burn it

GO ON TO THE NEXT PAGE

48. A patient who is heedless is _____.

    A. unlucky

    B. careless

    C. no longer in care

    D. hard of hearing

49. When directions are convoluted, what is wrong with them?

    A. They are erroneous.

    B. They are incomplete.

    C. They are confusing.

    D. They are unethical.

50. Select the meaning of the underlined word in the following sentence.

    Children not <u>adequately</u> responding to 55 mcg may use 110 mcg once daily.

    A. Without delay

    B. Willingly

    C. Satisfactorily

    D. Expectantly

STOP. IF YOU HAVE TIME LEFT OVER, CHECK YOUR WORK ON THIS SECTION ONLY.

GRAMMAR

50 items	Suggested time: 45 minutes

1. Which sentence is written correctly?

   A. Because she was uncertain of her abilities, Renee asked for help.

   B. Because she was uncertain of her abilities; Renee asked for help.

   C. Because she was uncertain of her abilities Renee asked for help.

   D. Because she was, uncertain of her abilities, Renee asked for help.

2. Select the phrase that will make the following sentence grammatically correct.

   Three days from now, the horses _____.

   A. performing in a show
   B. performed in a show
   C. will perform in a show
   D. have performed in a show

3. Which word in the following sentence is an adverb?

   The itinerant teacher moved continually from one school to another within the large district.

   A. itinerant
   B. another
   C. district
   D. continually

GO ON TO THE NEXT PAGE

4. Which sentence is grammatically correct?

   A. When I noticed Dave coming inside with a bundle in his arms, I ran to help him.
   B. Dave, coming inside with a bundle in his arms, was noticed and helped by me.
   C. Having noticed Dave coming inside, I ran to help him with a bundle in his arms.
   D. After Dave came inside with a bundle in his arms, I ran to help him, having noticed him.

5. Which word is used incorrectly in the following sentence?

   Dr. Leo lay the paperwork out upon the table for us to view.

   A. lay
   B. upon
   C. us
   D. view

6. Select the correct word for the blank in the following sentence.

   Nurse Junko and _____ will review the patient's chart.

   A. me
   B. she
   C. them
   D. him

7. What word is best to substitute for the underlined words in the following sentence?

   The nurse told Silvio's family that visiting hours were over, but <u>Silvio's family</u> could come back early tomorrow morning.

   A. them
   B. us
   C. they
   D. those

GO ON TO THE NEXT PAGE

8. Which word is used incorrectly in the following sentence?

For who was that email intended?

A. For
B. who
C. that
D. intended

9. Which of the following words fits best in the following sentence?

The meteorologist had forecast rain, _____ Sheila brought her umbrella to work.

A. because
B. yet
C. so
D. nor

10. What punctuation is needed in the following sentence to make it correct?

Harvey please make sure that the patient is resting comfortably.

A. Period
B. Question mark
C. Comma
D. Colon

11. Which of the following is spelled correctly?

A. Embarassing
B. Embarrasing
C. Embarrassing
D. Emberassing

GO ON TO THE NEXT PAGE

12. Select the word or phrase that makes the following sentence grammatically correct.

> The wheelchair started _____ down the corridor without assistance.

A. roll
B. will roll
C. rolled
D. to roll

13. Select the word in the following sentence that is *not* used correctly.

> Collecting personal and vital datum is one of the roles of an intake nurse.

A. personal
B. vital
C. datum
D. roles

14. Select the word or phrase that makes the following sentence grammatically correct.

> After _____ for an entire afternoon, the resident felt revitalized.

A. having rest
B. resting
C. rested
D. rest

15. Which sentence is grammatically correct?

A. We quickly consumed the picnic lunch she had made.
B. We consumed the picnic lunch she had made quickly.
C. We consumed the picnic lunch quickly she had made.
D. Quickly the picnic lunch she had made we consumed.

GO ON TO THE NEXT PAGE

16. Select the word that makes the following sentence grammatically correct.

> The nursing staff _____ to serve their patients well.

    A. hope

    B. hopes

    C. hoping

    D. does hope

17. What word is best to substitute for the underlined word in the following sentence?

> Roseanne was sent to the lab to collect <u>Roseanne's</u> results.

    A. she

    B. their

    C. her

    D. hers

18. Which of the following is *not* a coordinating conjunction?

    A. And

    B. So

    C. For

    D. Although

19. What punctuation is needed in the following sentence to make it correct?

> Have you finished reading the lab results so we can schedule an appointment with the patient

    A. Period

    B. Question mark

    C. Comma

    D. Semicolon

GO ON TO THE NEXT PAGE

20. What is the *dependent* clause in the following sentence?

> I like the boy who lives in the house next door because he's funny.

A. I like the boy
B. lives in the house
C. in the house next door
D. because he's funny

21. Which sentence is written correctly?

A. Whenever we meet at a party or dance he invariably kisses my hand.
B. Whenever we meet, at a party, or dance, he invariably kisses my hand.
C. Whenever we meet at a party or dance, he, invariably, kisses my hand.
D. Whenever we meet at a party or dance, he invariably kisses my hand.

22. Select the word that makes the following sentence grammatically correct.

> The intern had to select _____ three specialties.

A. among
B. between
C. with
D. along

23. Which word is *not* spelled correctly in the context of the following sentence?

> Their chairs were stationery, but the interns seated in them were agitated.

A. Their
B. stationery
C. seated
D. agitated

GO ON TO THE NEXT PAGE

24. Select the word that makes the following sentence grammatically correct.

    It is important that one is able to self-motivate and work by

    _____.

    A. oneself
    B. oneselves
    C. hisself
    D. themselves

25. Which sentence is the clearest?
    A. At the age of seven, my mother moved me to a new school.
    B. When I was seven, my mother moved me to a new school.
    C. At the age of seven, I moved my mother to a new school.
    D. My mother, at the age of seven, moved me to a new school.

26. Select the word or phrase that is misplaced in the following sentence.

    The book is in my locker at school that is long overdue.

    A. The book
    B. in my locker
    C. at school
    D. that is long overdue

27. Select the word or phrase that makes the following sentence grammatically correct.

    Miguel and I are waiting to _____ with the doctor.

    A. be met
    B. meeting
    C. met
    D. meet

GO ON TO THE NEXT PAGE

28. Select the phrase in the following sentence that is *not* used correctly.

    He had never had to been on his own in the past.

    A. had never
    B. never had
    C. to been
    D. on his own

29. Select the word that makes the following sentence grammatically correct.

    If you are _____ uncomfortable, I will bring you another pillow.

    A. to
    B. too
    C. much
    D. lesser

30. What punctuation is needed in the following sentence to make it correct?

    Follow my lead I have been performing this procedure for years.

    A. Period
    B. Comma
    C. Exclamation point
    D. Semicolon

31. Select the phrase that will make the following sentence grammatically correct.

    When the lecture was over, two students _____.

    A. raise their hands to ask questions
    B. raised their hands to ask questions
    C. have raised their hands to ask questions
    D. are raising their hands to ask questions

GO ON TO THE NEXT PAGE

32. Which word is used incorrectly in the following sentence?

    He received an oral dose initial, followed by an IV drip.

    A. received
    B. dose
    C. initial
    D. followed

33. Select the sentence that is grammatically correct.

    A. Dr. Chu told me and her to take a break for lunch.
    B. Dr. Chu told her and me to take a break for lunch.
    C. Dr. Chu told her and I to take a break for lunch.
    D. Dr. Chu told she and I to take a break for lunch.

34. What word is best to substitute for the underlined words in the following sentence?

    Francesca, Bill, and I enjoy using the hospital pool.

    A. They
    B. We
    C. Them
    D. Us

35. Which sentence is grammatically correct?

    A. Hector helped me complete my application.
    B. Hector helped myself complete my application.
    C. Hector helped me complete mine application.
    D. Hector helped me complete myself application.

36. What punctuation is needed in the following sentence to make it correct?

    After you complete your rounds please check in at the station.

    A. Period
    B. Comma
    C. Colon
    D. Semicolon

GO ON TO THE NEXT PAGE

37. In the following sentence, what part of speech is the word *with*?

> The pharmacist seemed to disagree with the prescription designated by the physician.

A. Preposition
B. Conjunction
C. Adverb
D. Article

38. Which word is used incorrectly in the following sentence?

> Jack practices piano while Sidney study for the exam.

A. practices
B. while
C. study
D. exam

39. Which of the following words or phrases fits best in the following sentence?

> The radiology department sends Troy to pick up lunch _____ it isn't too busy at the office.

A. as long as
B. as if
C. after
D. unless

40. Which word is *not* spelled correctly in the context of the following sentence?

> The counselor expected me to accept her advise without question.

A. counselor
B. expected
C. accept
D. advise

GO ON TO THE NEXT PAGE

41. Which sentence is grammatically correct?

    A. Having finished the meal, the check was called for by
       Mr. Innes.

    B. The check, having finished the meal, was called for by
       Mr. Innes.

    C. Having finished the meal, Mr. Innes called for the check.

    D. Mr. Innes called for the check, having finished the meal.

42. Select the word that makes the following sentence grammatically
correct.

    The hockey team _____ traveling to Albany for the
    semifinals.

    A. is

    B. are

    C. be

    D. were

43. What punctuation is needed in the following sentence to make it
correct?

    She purchased a notebook and a small handmade coffee mug.

    A. Period

    B. Comma

    C. Colon

    D. Hyphen

44. Which of the following is a compound sentence?

    A. Carolyn and Preston sit in the back of the class.

    B. Kathy sighs at Britt while he tells a story.

    C. Randy swept the driveway and brought in the empty trash
       cans.

    D. Cassie likes to read, but she doesn't have a library card.

GO ON TO THE NEXT PAGE

45. What word is best to substitute for the underlined words in the following sentence?

   Stu often regarded <u>his roommates'</u> housekeeping as sloppy and careless.

   A. his
   B. hers
   C. them
   D. their

46. Which word is used incorrectly in the following sentence?

   If you calculate too speedy, you may possibly fail to get the right answer.

   A. calculate
   B. speedy
   C. possibly
   D. right

47. Which sentence is the clearest?

   A. Resting in its well-built cage, I admired the lovely parrot.
   B. Resting in its well-built cage, the lovely parrot was admired by me.
   C. I admired the lovely parrot resting in its well-built cage.
   D. I admired in its well-built cage the lovely parrot that was resting.

48. Select the phrase or clause that is misplaced in the following sentence.

   I did not see the open carton of orange juice on the shelf standing with the refrigerator door open.

   A. I did not see
   B. of orange juice
   C. on the shelf
   D. standing with the refrigerator door open

GO ON TO THE NEXT PAGE

49. Select the word that will make the following sentence grammatically correct.

Do not be afraid to consult _____ your peers.

A. with

B. from

C. by

D. in

50. Which sentence is grammatically correct?

A. The soup was hot and made of tomatoes; Dan burned his tongue and gulped some cold water.

B. After burning his tongue on the hot tomato soup, Dan gulped some cold water.

C. Dan gulped some cold water when the tomato soup that was hot burned his tongue.

D. Gulping some cold water, Dan burned his tongue on the hot tomato soup.

STOP. IF YOU HAVE TIME LEFT OVER, CHECK YOUR WORK ON THIS SECTION ONLY.

BASIC MATH SKILLS

50 items │ Suggested time: 45 minutes

1. Multiply and simplify: $3\frac{1}{4} \times \frac{1}{16} =$

A. $\frac{5}{8}$

B. $\frac{13}{16}$

C. $\frac{13}{64}$

D. $3\frac{3}{16}$

2. How many ounces are in 17.5 pounds?

A. 70 ounces

B. 140 ounces

C. 210 ounces

D. 280 ounces

3. If a train travels 270 miles in 3 hours, how far will it travel in 4.5 hours?

A. 300 miles

B. 350 miles

C. 405 miles

D. 425 miles

4. If $3x + 7 = 4$, what is the value of x?

A. -1

B. 0

C. 1

D. 4

5. Express 20% as a fraction in lowest terms.

A. $\frac{1}{20}$

B. $\frac{1}{10}$

C. $\frac{1}{5}$

D. $\frac{1}{2}$

| | GO ON TO THE NEXT PAGE |

6. How many pounds are there in 8 kilograms?

 A. 3.6 pounds
 B. 16 pounds
 C. 16.6 pounds
 D. 17.6 pounds

7. What is 0.036 expressed as a percent?

 A. 36%
 B. 3.6%
 C. 0.36%
 D. 0.036%

8. Kim wants to run a 5-kilometer race. Approximately how many yards is that?

 A. 16,350 yards
 B. 5,450 yards
 C. 1,817 yards
 D. 545 yards

9. Mrs. Castanon wants to give each child in her class three markers. If there are 21 students in her class and markers are sold in boxes of 12, what is the minimum number of boxes she will need?

 A. 3
 B. 4
 C. 5
 D. 6

10. A farmer has a flock of sheep. He has 15 white sheep, 4 brown sheep, and 1 black sheep. What is the percentage of brown sheep in his flock? (Enter numeric value only. If rounding is necessary, round to the whole number.)

 _____

11. If $x = 12y$, what is the value of x when $y = 8$? (Enter numeric value only.)

 _____

GO ON TO THE NEXT PAGE

12. What is the least common denominator of ⅛ and ¹⁄₁₂? (Enter numeric value only.)

_____

13. The nurse told Laura that she weighed 264 kilograms. Approximately how many pounds is that?

A. 110 pounds

B. 120 pounds

C. 132 pounds

D. 206 pounds

14. Solve for _x_. 3 : 5 :: 81 : _x_

A. 48

B. 123

C. 135

D. 405

15. Divide and simplify: 4⅛ ÷ 1½ =

A. 4½

B. 4¼

C. 2¾

D. 2¼

16. During his lunch break, Noah withdraws $100 from the bank. He spends $11 on lunch, goes to the bookstore where he spends $20 on a new book, and buys a coffee for $2 on his way back to the office. How much does he have left from the original $100?

A. 67

B. 57

C. 46

D. 33

17. Frederica worked 7 hours on Monday and 6½ hours each day from Tuesday through Friday. If she makes $10.45 an hour, what was her gross income for the week? (Enter numeric value only. If rounding is necessary, round to the whole number.)

_____

GO ON TO THE NEXT PAGE

18. If $42 = 12 + 6k$, what is the value of k?

A. 5

B. 18

C. 24

D. 30

19. How many millimeters are there in 25 centimeters? (Enter numeric value only.)

_____

20. A plan for a house is drawn on a 1:40 scale. If the length of the living room on the plan measures 4.5 inches, what is the actual length of the built living room?

A. 45 feet

B. 25 feet

C. 15 feet

D. 12 feet

21. Add: 2.34 + 23.4 + 234 =

A. 70.2

B. 230.72

C. 234.74

D. 259.74

22. Seven gallons is approximately how many liters?

A. 1.85 liters

B. 10.79 liters

C. 17.46 liters

D. 26.53 liters

23. Add and simplify: $4\frac{2}{3} + 6\frac{1}{2} =$

A. 11⅙

B. 10⅓

C. 9⅙

D. 9

GO ON TO THE NEXT PAGE

24. Tamison bought 20 stamps for 29¢ each and 40 stamps for 42¢ each. If she gave the postal worker $25, how much change did she receive?

    A. $2.40
    B. $2.80
    C. $3.20
    D. $3.60

25. Convert this military time to regular time: 0705 hours.

    A. 7:05 A.M.
    B. 7:05 P.M.
    C. 5:07 A.M.
    D. 5:07 P.M.

26. Teresa began collecting baseball cards exactly 8 months ago, and in that time she has collected 144 cards. On average, how many baseball cards has she collected per month?

    A. 12
    B. 16
    C. 18
    D. 22

27. If the standard dose of a liquid cough medication is 74 mL, approximately how many ounces is that dose?

    A. 1.25 ounces
    B. 2.50 ounces
    C. 3.47 ounces
    D. 19.53 ounces

28. Divide: $5{,}117 \div 31 =$

    A. 109 r3
    B. 115 r14
    C. 133 r5
    D. 165 r2

GO ON TO THE NEXT PAGE

29. Gus is making a chili recipe that calls for three parts beans to five parts ground beef. If he is using 8 cups of ground beef for a big family dinner, how many cups of beans will Gus need?

    A. 3.6 cups

    B. 4 cups

    C. 4.6 cups

    D. 4.8 cups

30. Solve for b: $2b+1 = b+3$. (Enter numeric value only.)

_____

31. Express ¼ as a decimal.

    A. 1.25

    B. 1.45

    C. 1.75

    D. 1.95

32. How many feet are in 6 meters?

    A. 1.83 feet

    B. 18.48 feet

    C. 18.8 feet

    D. 19.68 feet

33. Express the ratio of 25:80 as a percentage.

    A. 31.25%

    B. 34%

    C. 41.25%

    D. 43.75%

GO ON TO THE NEXT PAGE

34. A package of 10 pencils is divided between every 2 students in class. If there are 20 students in class, then how many pencils are needed?

A. 20
B. 40
C. 80
D. 100

35. What date in Arabic numerals is Roman numeral MCCIV? (Enter numeric value only.)

_____

36. A certain number is 7 less than the product of 18 and 4. What is the value of that number?

A. 63
B. 65
C. 72
D. 79

37. Express 1.4 as a fraction in simplest terms.

A. $\frac{7}{5}$
B. $\frac{10}{14}$
C. $\frac{1}{4}$
D. $\frac{14}{100}$

38. Erlene is making a drink that calls for 3 ounces of orange juice and 5 ounces of lemon-lime soda. What is the ratio of lemon-lime soda to orange juice?

A. 3:8
B. 3:5
C. 5:8
D. 5:3

GO ON TO THE NEXT PAGE

39. If the outside temperature on a sunny day is 82 degrees on the Fahrenheit scale, what is the approximate temperature on the Celsius scale?

A. 18°C

B. 24°C

C. 28°C

D. 50°C

40. In a scale drawing for a garden, 2 cm = 1 m. If the garden measures 8 cm by 10 cm in the drawing, how large will it be in reality?

A. 2 m by 3 m

B. 4 m by 5 m

C. 8 m by 10 m

D. 16 m by 20 m

41. Express $13/4$ as a percent.

A. 32.5%

B. 52%

C. 325%

D. 520%

42. Divide: 8.11 ÷ 5 =

A. 1.424

B. 1.622

C. 1.672

D. 1.724

43. Subtract and simplify: $5/9 - 2/5 =$

A. $7/15$

B. $2/45$

C. $7/45$

D. $11/15$

GO ON TO THE NEXT PAGE

44. The Soap Factory is selling 3 bars of almond-scented soap for $2.58. What would it cost to buy 5 bars of soap?

    A. $4.80

    B. $4.30

    C. $3.80

    D. $3.30

45. Subtract and simplify $4\frac{1}{5} - 2\frac{2}{3}$.

    A. $2\frac{1}{15}$

    B. $1\frac{1}{5}$

    C. $1\frac{2}{3}$

    D. $1\frac{8}{15}$

46. Express 20% as a decimal.

    A. 0.2

    B. 0.25

    C. 0.4

    D. 2.5

47. In a group of people, four are children and six are adults. What is the ratio of adults to the total number of people?

    A. 2:5

    B. 3:5

    C. 2:3

    D. 3:2

48. Callie makes 2% interest quarterly on a deposit of $100. After a year, about how much is in her account?

    A. $102

    B. $104

    C. $106

    D. $108

49. Patient X usually ingests about 2,000 calories daily. If Patient X is placed on a regimen that cuts that daily intake by 20%, how many calories will Patient X consume in a week? (Enter numeric value only.)

_____

GO ON TO THE NEXT PAGE

50. How many teaspoons are there in 3 tablespoons?

    A. 9 teaspoons

    B. 10.5 teaspoons

    C. 12 teaspoons

    D. 18 teaspoons

**STOP. IF YOU HAVE TIME LEFT OVER,
CHECK YOUR WORK ON THIS SECTION ONLY.**

BIOLOGY

25 items | Suggested time: 21 minutes

1. Which organelle is responsible for protein synthesis?

   A. Mitochondrion
   B. Vacuole
   C. Cell membrane
   D. Ribosome

2. Why is yeast used to make bread rise?

   A. It engages in photosynthesis, which produces oxygen gas.
   B. Carbon dioxide forms while yeast carries out photosynthesis.
   C. Yeast carries out fermentation, producing ethanol and carbon dioxide.
   D. Yeast breathes in oxygen and produces carbon dioxide through aerobic respiration.

3. How is mitosis different from meiosis?

   A. Mitosis is the process by which sex cells are formed.
   B. Meiosis creates cells with half the chromosomes of the parent cell.
   C. Telophase does not take place in mitosis.
   D. Spermatogenesis and oogenesis occur via mitosis.

4. Which statement is untrue?

   A. RNA is single-stranded.
   B. RNA contains uracil.
   C. DNA codes for proteins.
   D. DNA cannot be altered.

GO ON TO THE NEXT PAGE

5. Imagine that two parents both carry the recessive gene for cystic fibrosis. Any homozygous recessive offspring will manifest the disease. What percentage of the offspring is predicted to be carriers but not manifest the disease?

   A. 0%
   B. 25%
   C. 50%
   D. 100%

6. A cell is in a solution in which the concentration of solutes is higher inside the cell than outside the cell. What would you expect to happen to the cell?

   A. It will swell and possibly burst.
   B. It will shrivel and shrink.
   C. It will maintain its current size.
   D. It will grow a supportive cell wall.

7. In a cell, where is most of the energy needed by the cell produced?

   A. Mitochondria
   B. Endoplasmic reticulum
   C. Ribosomes
   D. Cytoplasm

8. Physical factors such as temperature and pH can alter enzyme activity because they have an effect on the enzyme's _____.

   A. acidity
   B. shape
   C. chemistry
   D. substrate

9. Which part of a plant's reproductive system is of a different "gender" than the others?

   A. Stamen
   B. Pistil
   C. Stigma
   D. Style

GO ON TO THE NEXT PAGE

10. What kind of symbiosis exists between a pneumonia bacterium and a human?

A. Mutualism
B. Parasitism
C. Commensalism
D. Competition

11. The scientific name for a house cat is *Felis catus*. This indicates the house cat's _____ and _____.

A. kingdom; family
B. order; subspecies
C. phylum; class
D. genus; species

12. Beeswax is an example of what kind of molecule?

A. Lipid
B. Carbohydrate
C. Protein
D. Nucleic acid

13. What takes place in a lysosome?

A. Ribosomes are made.
B. Food is produced.
C. Water is stored.
D. Food is digested.

14. Which organism reproduces via binary fission?

A. Mushroom
B. Blue whale
C. Rainbow trout
D. Salmonella

15. In which phase of cell division do the chromosomes replicate?

A. Interphase
B. Prophase
C. Anaphase
D. Telophase

GO ON TO THE NEXT PAGE

16. In a strand of DNA, you would expect to see adenine paired with
_____.

    A. cytosine

    B. uracil

    C. thymine

    D. guanine

17. Hemophilia is a sex-linked trait carried on the X chromosome. In an example of a male with hemophilia and a female carrier, what ratio of the offspring is predicted to have the disease?

    A. 0 female : 2 male

    B. 1 female : 0 male

    C. 1 female : 2 male

    D. 2 female : 1 male

18. What is represented by this formula: $6CO_2 + 6H_2O \rightarrow C_6H_{12}O_6 + 6O_2$?

    A. Glycolysis

    B. Cellular respiration

    C. Photosynthesis

    D. Electronic transport

19. What type of bonding do water molecules exhibit?

    A. Polar covalent

    B. Ionic

    C. Hydrogen

    D. Metallic

20. Which statement regarding energy content is true?

    A. Decomposers > secondary consumers

    B. Primary consumers > producers

    C. Producers > secondary consumers

    D. Secondary consumers > primary consumers

GO ON TO THE NEXT PAGE

21. How should a researcher test the hypothesis that eating chocolate leads to acne in teenagers?

   A. Take 100 teenagers and feed each one a different amount of chocolate daily for 60 days; then test for acne.
   B. Take 100 teenagers and feed 50 two bars of chocolate daily for 60 days while the other 50 eat no chocolate; then test for acne.
   C. Take 1 teenager and feed him or her two bars of chocolate for 30 days and no chocolate for 30 days; then test for acne.
   D. Take 100 teenagers and feed them no chocolate for 30 days and two bars of chocolate apiece for 30 days; then test for acne.

22. Which is *not* a step in the water cycle?

   A. Condensation
   B. Transpiration
   C. Nitrification
   D. Absorption

23. Why do we perceive chlorophyll as green?

   A. It absorbs yellow and blue light.
   B. It primarily absorbs green light.
   C. It fails to absorb green light.
   D. It primarily absorbs red light.

24. Why are bacteria and blue-green algae often classified together?

   A. Both are gymnosperms.
   B. Both are prokaryotes.
   C. Both are autotrophs.
   D. Both are pathogens.

25. Which of these molecules contains glucose?

   A. Proteins
   B. Lipids
   C. Nucleic acids
   D. Carbohydrates

STOP. IF YOU HAVE TIME LEFT OVER, CHECK YOUR WORK ON THIS SECTION ONLY.

CHEMISTRY

25 items | Suggested time: 21 minutes

1. Carbon-12 and carbon-14 are isotopes. What do they have in common?

   A. Number of nuclear particles
   B. Number of protons
   C. Number of neutrons
   D. Mass number

2. A substance with a pH of 3 is how many times more acidic than a substance with a pH of 5?

   A. 8
   B. 2
   C. 100
   D. 1,000

3. Radioactive isotopes are frequently used in medicine. What kind of half-life would a medical isotope probably have?

   A. Seconds long
   B. Days long
   C. Year long
   D. Many years long

4. When an acid is added to a base, water and a salt form. What kinds of bonds form in these two compounds?

   A. Liquid and metallic
   B. Polar and nonpolar covalent
   C. Polar covalent and ionic
   D. Ionic only

5. $Al(NO_3)_3 + H_2SO_4 \rightarrow Al_2(SO_4)_3 + HNO_3$ is an example of which kind of reaction?

   A. Decomposition reaction
   B. Synthesis reaction
   C. Single replacement reaction
   D. Double replacement reaction

GO ON TO THE NEXT PAGE

6. B, Si, As, Te, At, Ge, and Sb form a staircase pattern on the right side of the periodic table. How can these elements be classified?

    A. As metals

    B. As semimetals

    C. As nonmetals

    D. As ultrametals

7. If gas A has four times the molar mass of gas B, you would expect it to diffuse through a plug _____.

    A. at half the rate of gas B

    B. at twice the rate of gas B

    C. at a quarter the rate of gas B

    D. at four times the rate of gas B

8. Which of the following is *not* an allotrope of carbon?

    A. Diamonds

    B. Graphite

    C. Fluorine

    D. Buckminsterfullerene

9. Which of these factors would *not* affect rates of reaction?

    A. Temperature

    B. Surface area

    C. Pressure

    D. Time

10. You would expect an amino acid to contain which two functional groups?

    A. R-NH2 and R-COOH

    B. R-CHO and $R\text{-}CO\text{-}NH_2$

    C. R-OH and R-COOR

    D. R-O-R and R-COOH

GO ON TO THE NEXT PAGE

11. What is the coefficient of O_2 after the following equation is balanced?

_____CH_4 + _____O_2 → _____CO_2 + _____H_2O

A. 1
B. 2
C. 3
D. 4

12. Which element would you expect to be least reactive?

A. Li
B. Cr
C. Nd
D. Xe

13. Which is a property of an ionic compound?

A. Crystalline shape
B. Poor conductivity
C. Shared electrons
D. Low melting point

14. How many neutrons are in an atom of uranium-235?

A. 92
B. 125
C. 143
D. 235

15. What is the correct electron configuration for lithium?

A. $1s^2 2s^1$
B. $1s^2 2s^2$
C. $1s^2 2s^1 2p^1$
D. $1s^1 2s^1 2p^2$

GO ON TO THE NEXT PAGE

16. The molar mass of glucose is 180.0 g/mol. If an IV solution contains 5 g glucose in 100 g water, what is the molarity of the solution?

    A. 0.28 M
    B. 1.8 M
    C. 2.8 M
    D. 18 M

17. Which ion would you expect to dominate in water solutions of bases?

    A. $MgCl_2$
    B. 2HCl
    C. H^+
    D. OH^-

18. To the nearest whole number, what is the mass of one mole of water?

    A. 16 g/mol
    B. 18 g/mol
    C. 20 g/mol
    D. 22 g/mol

19. What is the charge of an alpha particle?

    A. −1
    B. +1
    C. +2
    D. No charge

20. What is the correct name of $AgNO_3$?

    A. Argent nitrous
    B. Argent oxide
    C. Silver nitrite
    D. Silver nitrate

GO ON TO THE NEXT PAGE

21. What is the oxidation state of the chlorine atom in the compound HCl?

    A. +1
    B. −1
    C. +2
    D. −2

22. Which of these types of intermolecular force is strongest?

    A. Hydrogen bonding
    B. London dispersion force
    C. Keesom interaction
    D. Dipole-dipole interaction

23. A salt solution has a molarity of 1.5 M. How many moles of this salt are present in 2.0 L of this solution?

    A. 0.75
    B. 1.5
    C. 2.0
    D. 3.0

24. What is the correct formula for silver hydroxide?

    A. AgO_2
    B. AgOH
    C. $AgOH_2$
    D. AgH_2O

25. Which gives the number of protons in the atomic nucleus of an alkali metal?

    A. 9
    B. 10
    C. 11
    D. 12

STOP. IF YOU HAVE TIME LEFT OVER, CHECK YOUR WORK ON THIS SECTION ONLY.

ANATOMY AND PHYSIOLOGY

25 items │ Suggested time: 21 minutes

1. Which is an anterior muscle?

    A. Quadriceps femoris
    B. Gluteus maximus
    C. Biceps femoris
    D. Adductor magnus

2. How might the headrest on a car prevent traumatic injury?

    A. By limiting hyperflexion of the neck
    B. By limiting hyperextension of the neck
    C. By reducing vertebral compression
    D. By preventing disc degeneration

3. Which might you expect to see in a whiplash injury?

    A. Cardiopulmonary problems
    B. Side-to-side spinal curvature
    C. Eventual herniation of discs
    D. Traumatic injury to ligaments

4. Muscle contractions that normally move food along the human digestive system are known as _____.

    A. defecation
    B. osmosis
    C. peristalsis
    D. circulation

5. Which type of nutrient does *not* provide the body with energy?

    A. Vitamin
    B. Carbohydrate
    C. Fat
    D. Protein

GO ON TO THE NEXT PAGE

6. Where would you be likely to find a Schwann cell?

    A. In the digestive system

    B. In the nervous system

    C. In the skeletal system

    D. In the muscular system

7. How does the nervous system work with the muscular system?

    A. The muscles of the body produce chemicals that feed the nerves.

    B. The nervous system tells the muscles how to respond to the environment.

    C. The nervous system releases chemicals that remove excess waste from the muscles.

    D. The muscular system provides input that allows the nerves to make decisions.

8. Which part of the nervous system includes the femoral, radial, and ulnar nerves?

    A. Somatic

    B. Autonomic

    C. Sympathetic

    D. Parasympathetic

9. Where might a herniated lumbar disc be most likely to create pain?

    A. Along the radial nerve

    B. Within the spinal cord

    C. Along the sciatic nerve

    D. Along the tibial nerve

10. What is the name of the bone in the human thigh?

    A. Ulna

    B. Femur

    C. Radius

    D. Humerus

GO ON TO THE NEXT PAGE

11. The ovaries are part of the _____.

    A. skeletal system

    B. nervous system

    C. lymphatic system

    D. reproductive system

12. Of the following processes, which one is a different level of defense from the others?

    A. A low pH in the stomach

    B. Cilia present in the trachea

    C. Body cells recognizing a pathogen

    D. Mucus present in the nasal cavity

13. Which organ system is primarily responsible for regulating muscle growth?

    A. The endocrine system

    B. The skeletal system

    C. The nervous system

    D. The reproductive system

14. Which parts of the heart are separated by the mitral valve?

    A. Left atrium and right atrium

    B. Right atrium and right ventricle

    C. Left ventricle and right ventricle

    D. Left atrium and left ventricle

15. How might vitamin D deficiency present?

    A. As bleeding gums

    B. As swollen extremities

    C. As red patches

    D. As crooked bones

GO ON TO THE NEXT PAGE

16. How does the lymphatic system work with the circulatory system?

    A. The circulatory system produces red blood cells for the lymphatic system.

    B. Lymph draws excess fluid from the cells and deposits it into the blood vessels.

    C. The heart regulates the production of lymph in the lymph glands.

    D. White cells from the lymphatic system eliminate excess red blood cells.

17. What is the function of parathyroid hormone?

    A. Increasing energy levels

    B. Stimulating cell reproduction

    C. Speeding up metabolism

    D. Activating vitamin D

18. Which feature of the ear is most medial?

    A. Pinna

    B. Tympanic membrane

    C. Cochlea

    D. Outer canal

19. Which of the following are considered normal values for the measure of a person's pulse and blood pressure?

    A. 55 beats per minute and 75 over 60 mm Hg

    B. 72 beats per minute and 120 over 80 mm Hg

    C. 100 beats per minute and 140 over 100 mm Hg

    D. 160 beats per minute and 100 over 70 mm Hg

20. How does a sagittal section divide the body?

    A. Into right and left regions

    B. Into upper and lower regions

    C. Into front and back regions

    D. Between the dorsal and ventral cavities

GO ON TO THE NEXT PAGE

21. How is pepsin used by the body?

   A. To break down proteins
   B. To break down starches
   C. To emulsify fats and oils
   D. To absorb water and nutrients

22. The esophagus is part of the _____.

   A. endocrine system
   B. respiratory system
   C. digestive system
   D. nervous system

23. Which mineral supports the function of the thyroid?

   A. Manganese
   B. Iodine
   C. Phosphorus
   D. Zinc

24. The cheekbones are _____ to the nose.

   A. anterior
   B. proximal
   C. deep
   D. lateral

25. Which organ system is primarily responsible for generating antibodies?

   A. The endocrine system
   B. The digestive system
   C. The lymphatic system
   D. The nervous system

**STOP. IF YOU HAVE TIME LEFT OVER,
CHECK YOUR WORK ON THIS SECTION ONLY.**

PHYSICS

25 items | Suggested time: 50 minutes

1. When a junked car is compacted, which statement is true?

   A. Its mass increases.
   B. Its mass decreases.
   C. Its density increases.
   D. Its density decreases.

2. A car travels 3 miles north, 6 miles south, 2 miles east, 2 miles west, and then 3 miles north. Which of the following is true?

   A. The displacement of the car is 16 miles, and the distance traveled is 0 miles.
   B. The displacement of the car is 16 miles, and the distance traveled is 16 miles.
   C. The displacement of the car is 0 miles, and the distance traveled is 0 miles.
   D. The displacement of the car is 0 miles, and the distance traveled is 16 miles.

3. Why doesn't a raindrop accelerate as it approaches the ground?

   A. Gravity pulls it down at a constant rate.
   B. Air resistance counteracts the gravitational force.
   C. Its mass decreases, decreasing its speed.
   D. Objects in motion decelerate over distance.

4. An object moves 100 m in 10 s. What is the velocity of the object over this time?

   A. 10 m/s
   B. 90 m/s
   C. 110 m/s
   D. 1,000 m/s

GO ON TO THE NEXT PAGE

5. Which of these objects has the greatest momentum?

   A. An 80-kg person running at 4 m/s
   B. A 1,250-kg car moving at 5 m/s
   C. A 10-kg piece of meteorite moving at 600 m/s
   D. A 0.5-kg rock moving at 40 m/s

6. Sublimation is the change in matter from solid to gas or gas to solid without passing through a liquid phase. Outside of the laboratory, which solid provides the best example of this?

   A. Iron
   B. Silver
   C. Salt crystal
   D. Dry ice

7. A 1.0-kg block on a table is given a push so that it slides along the table. If the block is accelerated at 6 m/s^2, what was the force applied to the block?

   A. 0 N
   B. 3 N
   C. 6 N
   D. The answer cannot be determined from the information given.

8. A 60-watt lightbulb is powered by a 110-volt power source. What is the current being drawn?

   A. 0.55 amperes
   B. 1.83 amperes
   C. 50 amperes
   D. 6,600 amperes

9. A wave moves through its medium at 20 m/s with a wavelength of 4 m. What is the frequency of the wave?

   A. 5 s^{-1}
   B. 16 s^{-1}
   C. 24 s^{-1}
   D. 80 s^{-1}

GO ON TO THE NEXT PAGE

10. An electromagnet is holding a 1,500-kg car at a height of 25 m above the ground. The magnet then experiences a power outage, and the car falls to the ground. Which of the following is false?

    A. The car had a potential energy of 367.5 kJ.

    B. 367.5 kJ of potential energy is converted to kinetic energy.

    C. The car retains potential energy of 367.5 kJ when it hits the ground.

    D. The car's potential energy converts to kinetic energy and then to sound energy.

11. Why does potential energy increase as particles approach each other?

    A. Attractive forces increase.

    B. Repulsive forces increase.

    C. Attractive forces decrease.

    D. Repulsive forces decrease.

12. A transverse wave does *not* have _____.

    A. an amplitude

    B. a compression

    C. a frequency

    D. a wavelength

13. How do a scalar quantity and a vector quantity differ?

    A. A scalar quantity has both magnitude and direction, and a vector does not.

    B. A scalar quantity has direction only, and a vector has only magnitude.

    C. A vector has both magnitude and direction, and a scalar quantity has only magnitude.

    D. A vector has only direction, and a scalar quantity has only magnitude.

14. Which one has the highest density?

    A. Mist

    B. Water

    C. Steam

    D. Ice

GO ON TO THE NEXT PAGE

15. Two objects attract each other with a gravitational force of 12 units. If you double the distance between the objects, what is the new force of attraction between the two?

    A. 3 units
    B. 6 units
    C. 24 units
    D. 48 units

16. What is the purpose of a switch in a circuit?

    A. To reverse the direction of alternating current
    B. To increase the voltage of the batter or cell
    C. To increase the resistance of wires in the circuit
    D. To allow the circuit to open and close

17. When a car is driven for a long time, the pressure of air in the tires increases. This is best explained by which of the following gas laws?

    A. Boyle's law
    B. Charles' law
    C. Gay-Lussac's law
    D. Dalton's law

18. A 5-cm candle is placed 20 cm away from a concave mirror with a focal length of 15 cm. About what is the image height of the candle in the mirror?

    A. 30.5 cm
    B. 15.625 cm
    C. −15 cm
    D. −30.5 cm

19. A plucked guitar string makes 80 vibrations in one second. What is the period?

    A. 0.0125 s
    B. 0.025 s
    C. 0.125 s
    D. 0.25 s

GO ON TO THE NEXT PAGE

20. A 2,000-kg car travels at 15 m/s. For a 1,500-kg car traveling at 15 m/s to generate the same momentum, which would need to happen?

   A. It would need to accelerate to 20 m/s.

   B. It would need to add 500 kg in mass.

   C. Both A and B

   D. Either A or B

21. Given the four wires described here, which would you expect to have the greatest resistance?

   A. 1 km of American wire gauge 1; diameter 7.35 mm

   B. 1 km of American wire gauge 2; diameter 6.54 mm

   C. 1 km of American wire gauge 3; diameter 5.83 mm

   D. 1 km of American wire gauge 4; diameter 5.19 mm

22. A 5-kg block is suspended from a spring, causing the spring to stretch 10 cm from equilibrium. What is the spring constant for this spring?

   A. 4.9 N/cm

   B. 9.8 N/cm

   C. 49 N/cm

   D. 50 N/cm

23. A 1,000-kg car drives at 10 m/s around a circle with a radius of 50 m. What is the centripetal acceleration of the car?

   A. 2 m/s^2

   B. 4 m/s^2

   C. 5 m/s^2

   D. 10 m/s^2

24. A 3-volt flashlight uses a bulb with 60-ohm resistance. What current flows through the flashlight?

   A. 18 amp

   B. 1.8 amp

   C. 0.5 amp

   D. 0.05 amp

GO ON TO THE NEXT PAGE

25. A balloon with a charge of 5 μC is placed 25 cm from another balloon with the same charge. What is the magnitude of the resulting repulsive force?

A. 0.18 N

B. 1.8 N

C. 10^{-3} N

D. 5×10^{-3} N

STOP. IF YOU HAVE TIME LEFT OVER, CHECK YOUR WORK ON THIS SECTION ONLY.

ANSWER KEY

Reading Comprehension

1. B	18. B	35. D
2. D	19. C	36. D
3. A	20. B	37. D
4. B	21. A	38. A
5. C	22. A	39. C
6. D	23. C	40. B
7. C	24. D	41. C
8. B	25. A	42. B
9. A	26. C	43. A
10. B	27. A	44. B
11. A	28. D	45. A
12. D	29. C	46. B
13. C	30. A	47. C
14. D	31. C	48. A
15. C	32. B	49. D
16. C	33. B	50. D
17. D	34. C	

Vocabulary and General Knowledge

1. B	19. D	37. A
2. A	20. D	38. B
3. D	21. C	39. C
4. C	22. A	40. D
5. A	23. A	41. C
6. C	24. D	42. B
7. A	25. C	43. A
8. B	26. B	44. C
9. A	27. B	45. D
10. D	28. A	46. C
11. D	29. A	47. D
12. B	30. A	48. B
13. D	31. B	49. C
14. C	32. A	50. C
15. D	33. C	
16. A	34. B	
17. B	35. C	
18. B	36. D	

Grammar

1. A	18. D	35. A
2. C	19. B	36. B
3. D	20. D	37. A
4. A	21. D	38. C
5. A	22. A	39. A
6. B	23. B	40. D
7. C	24. A	41. C
8. B	25. B	42. A
9. C	26. D	43. B
10. C	27. D	44. D
11. C	28. C	45. D
12. D	29. B	46. B
13. C	30. D	47. C
14. B	31. B	48. D
15. A	32. C	49. A
16. A	33. B	50. B
17. C	34. B	

Basic Math Skills

1. C	18. A	35. 1204
2. D	19. 250	36. B
3. C	20. C	37. A
4. A	21. D	38. D
5. C	22. D	39. C
6. D	23. A	40. B
7. B	24. A	41. C
8. B	25. A	42. B
9. D	26. C	43. C
10. 20	27. B	44. B
11. 96	28. D	45. D
12. 36	29. D	46. A
13. B	30. 2	47. B
14. C	31. C	48. D
15. C	32. D	49. 11,200
16. A	33. A	50. A
17. 345	34. D	

Biology

1. D	5. C	9. A
2. C	6. A	10. B
3. B	7. A	11. D
4. D	8. B	12. A

13. D	18. C	23. C
14. D	19. A	24. B
15. A	20. C	25. D
16. C	21. B	
17. B	22. C	

Chemistry

1. B	10. A	19. C
2. C	11. B	20. D
3. B	12. D	21. B
4. C	13. A	22. A
5. D	14. C	23. D
6. B	15. A	24. B
7. A	16. A	25. C
8. C	17. D	
9. D	18. B	

Anatomy and Physiology

1. A	10. B	19. B
2. B	11. D	20. A
3. D	12. C	21. A
4. C	13. A	22. C
5. A	14. D	23. B
6. B	15. D	24. D
7. B	16. B	25. C
8. A	17. D	
9. C	18. C	

Physics

1. C	12. B	23. A
2. D	13. C	24. D
3. B	14. B	25. B
4. A	15. A	
5. B	16. D	
6. D	17. C	
7. C	18. C	
8. A	19. A	
9. A	20. D	
10. C	21. D	
11. B	22. A	

EXPLANATORY ANSWERS

Reading Comprehension

1. (B) The main idea is the most important theme, one that carries throughout the passage. If someone asked you what the passage was about, you would be most likely to answer "the connection between high fructose corn syrup and obesity," making B the best answer.

2. (D) Detail A is in paragraph 3, detail B is in paragraph 2, and detail C is in paragraph 2. Detail D is never mentioned.

3. (A) The author is not trying to convince you of anything, as a persuasive essay might do (choice B). The basic purpose here is to provide information on a topic.

4. (B) A summary cannot go beyond the information given in the passage, as summaries A, C, and D seem to do. Only summary B focuses on what is suggested by the passage.

5. (C) If the blood vessels "lose elasticity and stiffen," that means that they were not stiff before, eliminating choices A and D as reasonable possibilities. You might also use what you know about the word *elastic* to guess that elasticity is stretchiness, or flexibility.

6. (D) A question that asks you to suggest a title is really asking you to identify the main idea of a passage. Here, the passage provides a brief introduction to the causes of hypertension. It also gives information about the symptoms and complications of the condition and provides insight into some of the ways blood pressure can be lowered, such as through weight loss or medication.

7. (C) A statement of fact can be proved or checked. A statement of opinion is what someone thinks or believes. In this case, statements A, B, and D could be proved scientifically, but statement C is simply a suggestion.

8. (B) If a statement cannot be inferred by the reader, either there is not enough information to draw conclusions about it or the passage contradicts the inference. In this case, it's the latter—the passage makes clear that there are treatments for hypertension, so choice B cannot be inferred from the text. Statement A could be inferred from information given in paragraph 3, statement C from paragraph 1, and statement D from paragraph 2.

9. (A) Skim the passage to identify the detail that does not appear. The sports in choice A are never mentioned, so you do not even need to look at the other choices.

10. (B) Substitute the choices in place of the vocabulary word. Only *reduced* (choice B) fits the context.

11. (A) Find the summary that best fits the overall substance of the passage. Some choices may be too specific, as B is, or too subjective, as choice D is.

12. (D) This passage is primarily informational, providing facts and data about the topic.

13. (C) Choices A, B, and D relate directly to information given in the passage. Choice C, on the other hand, is never even hinted at by the author, who speaks of sports-related concussions but does not compare them to other types of concussions.

14. (D) What is the passage mostly about? It is about one particular disease, sickle-cell anemia.

15. (C) With what kind of care can you manage the disease? You can manage it with diligent care, or painstaking, attentive care.

16. (C) The passage's tone is the attitude of the author toward the material being discussed. The descriptions of persistent pain and difficulties make the overall tone fairly grim here.

17. (D) Detail A is found in paragraph 2, detail B is found in paragraph 3, and detail C is found in paragraph 1. The author does not speak of other types of anemia that may be caused by vitamin or mineral deficiencies, so choice D is correct.

18. (B) Lead exposure happens over a lifetime (choice A), the shinbone is simply a good way to test for lifetime toxic exposure (choice C), and blood tests don't look at lifetime exposure (choice D). The best choice is B.

19. (C) The word *should* is a clue that this is what someone thinks or believes. The other statements could be checked or proved.

20. (B) Look at the context: "to be exposed to lead." The only word that makes sense in context is choice B, *subjected*.

21. (A) Choice A is the only one that applies to every paragraph in the passage.

22. (A) The author's attitude toward yoga seems to be positive and sincere. *Earnest* (choice A) would be a good description of this tone.

23. (C) This question is all about context. The passage refers to the tolerance of pain, making choices A, B, and D illogical.

24. (D) Although statement D may be true, it is not a detail in the passage. Choices A and B are found in paragraph 3, and choice C is in paragraph 4.

25. (A) Although this passage is partly informative, that is not a choice here. The author does present the opinion that everyone should try yoga, making this a persuasive essay.

26. (C) The effects of super foods on cholesterol, insulin and blood sugar, and blood pressure are noted in paragraphs 1 and 3, but no mention is made of muscle mass.

27. (A) Since yogurt is a super food, not all super foods are vegetables (choice B), and since oats are a super food, they are not all home grown (choice C). The best answer is choice A.

28. (D) Skimming the passage should indicate that cost (choice D) is never mentioned. Each of the other inferences is easy to draw based on the material given.

29. (C) *Delicious* is a matter of opinion—one person may love blueberries or yogurt, while another does not. The other choices are testable facts.

30. (A) Choice B is an opinion that is not expressed by this author, choice C is just a small detail from the passage, and choice D goes beyond the scope of the passage. The best answer is A.

31. (C) The passage describes a single experiment that tends to belie choice D but does not nearly lead to the conclusions in choice A or B. The best choice is C—one study cannot be considered conclusive.

32. (B) Substituting the choices for *touted* in the first sentence should make it clear that choice B is best.

33. (B) Think about the author's overall attitude toward aromatherapy. The author does not dismiss it entirely, but she does raise questions about its efficacy. The best choice is B—she is uncertain about the topic.

34. (C) Choices A and D are in paragraph 1, and choice B is in paragraph 2. Choice C is never mentioned.

35. (D) The author does not conclude choice A, and the passage does not deal with choice B. Only one paragraph deals with the topic in choice C. The passage is mostly about the pros and cons of barefoot running, making D the best choice.

36. (D) Read the word in context: "There is little consensus when it comes to the safety and effectiveness of barefoot running." The author means that people do not agree on the safety and effectiveness; there is no unanimous opinion about it.

37. (D) All of the other choices have some support in the passage. Although modern running shoes have only been around for 50 years, there is no indication that people ran barefoot before that time.

38. (A) You can test the cost of running shoes (choice B), the hardness of roads and paths (choice C), and even the springiness of the arch (choice D). Whether running barefoot is natural and advantageous remains an opinion (choice A).

39. (C) The passage as a whole has to do with the connection between uninterrupted sleep and muscle development.

40. (B) Even if checking the word in context leaves you with a couple of possible choices, looking at the structural connection between *satisfied* and *satiety* should give you the clue you need.

41. (C) Choices A, B, and D are all mentioned as being affected by HGH levels in the human body. The passage mentions leptin levels in the body being affected by sleep deprivation, but not by HGH.

42. (B) Choice A is incorrect because the passage never compares the importance of uninterrupted sleep to the importance of getting adequate amounts of sleep. Choice C is the opposite of what was stated in the passage. Choice D is incorrect because leptin is never connected to muscle development, only to appetite and obesity.

43. (A) The main idea is the idea that applies to the passage as a whole.

44. (B) Although choice A is close, the word *compel* means "to force," so a compelling argument is one that forces the listener to a conclusion.

45. (A) There is much information here, too, but the author's main reason for writing is to encourage the reader to understand the importance of sun exposure. The first and last sentences in the passage help clarify this purpose.

46. (B) How does the author feel about the topic of sun exposure? The only reasonable answer is choice B, *confident*. Again, the first and last sentences in the passage clarify this tone.

47. (C) Choice C is the only one that sticks to the premise of the passage without focusing too closely on one detail or moving beyond the scope of the essay.

48. (A) Words such as *important* and *beneficial* indicate that the author appreciates the work of the CDC without showing the sort of astonishment that would lead to being awestruck (choice B).

49. (D) Ask yourself the questions and see whether you can answer them based on the passage. The answer to choice A is Atlanta, the answer to choice B is Dr. Joseph Mountin, and the answer to choice C is 1970 and 1980. Choice D has no answer in the passage.

50. (D) The passage never says whether or not the CDC succeeded in its original mission (choice A) or whether it continued to be led by doctors (choice B). Inferring either of those things would be a leap unsupported by the text. Choice C is countered by information in the final paragraph, but choice D is a logical inference based on the two name changes described in the text.

Vocabulary and General Knowledge

1. (B) *Mercurial* stems from the god Mercury, but is more closely related to the element, which has qualities of volatility.
2. (A) *Elated* comes from a root that means "to lift up."
3. (D) To disregard is to "not regard," or to pay no attention to.
4. (C) To expose yourself to something is to open yourself up to contact.
5. (A) *Deteriorate* is literally "to make or become worse." A patient whose condition deteriorates may fail to eat or drink (choice D), but that is a side effect of the overall deterioration, not a definition of the word.
6. (C) A precipice is a steep cliff; something that precipitates falls steeply or rushes rapidly, as rain or sleet might do. Something that is precipitous is steep or fast-moving.
7. (A) If you are predisposed to a condition, you are receptive or susceptible to it ahead of time.
8. (B) *Ongoing* denotes action in progress, no matter what the speed of that action might be.
9. (A) A convulsion is one sort of paroxysm, or spasm.
10. (D) A restricted diet comes in many forms. It may be low in fat (choice A) or vegetarian (choice B), but it is always somehow limited (choice D).
11. (D) *Cicatrix* is Latin for "scar," and it may refer to the scar on either a plant or an animal after a wound has begun to heal.
12. (B) Calcium would not replace (choice A) a diet, but it could be used to add to it.
13. (D) *Quarantine* comes from the word for "forty." It originally referred to the period of 40 days that a ship was detained in port if it was thought to harbor infectious diseases. Today quarantine is used to separate very contagious patients from the general population.
14. (C) You might give an emetic to a victim of poisoning.
15. (D) A panacea is literally a cure-all—a remedy for all illness.
16. (A) Plug the word into a sentence of your choice, and you will see that the best synonym is *mostly.*
17. (B) Although *selected* may mean many things, in this context, it simply means "particular" or "certain."
18. (B) *LDL* stands for "low-density lipoprotein." LDL cholesterol is often referred to as "bad cholesterol" because it collects in blood vessel walls and can put patients at risk.
19. (D) The fibula is the smaller of the two bones between the knee and the ankle; the larger bone is the tibia.
20. (D) To disintegrate is to fall into pieces.

21. (C) The lower jaw of vertebrates or either jaw of certain insects is the mandible.

22. (A) Looking at the root of the word should help you determine its meaning.

23. (A) If you have qualms about something, you have a feeling of uneasiness. The word can also refer to a brief feeling of sickness or nausea.

24. (D) Something that is intact has no part that is missing or damaged.

25. (C) *Anterior* is the opposite of *posterior*; something that is anterior is near the front.

26. (B) Although *gravid* comes from the same root as *grave* (choice A), it refers to the heaviness of pregnancy, not to seriousness.

27. (B) A wall might be riddled with bullet holes; an essay might be riddled with errors. Either meaning has to do with being affected throughout.

28. (A) You take in food through your alimentary canal.

29. (A) A cough suppressant does not cure a cough (choice B), but it does calm, or subdue it (choice A).

30. (A) A septic wound may indeed be odorous (choice B) or even terminal (choice C), but it is certainly infected (choice A).

31. (B) The patella is the kneecap, a small, movable bone at the front of the knee.

32. (A) *Paltry* comes from a root meaning "rag." It refers to something that is without value.

33. (C) If you think about the noun version of *vent*, you can probably determine that the verb means "to let out."

34. (B) Inhalants are inhaled, or breathed in.

35. (C) If the action is inhibited, it is held back, or hindered.

36. (D) The symptom may be disfiguring (choice B) or painful (choice C), but it is definitely made worse (choice D) or intensified.

37. (A) A critique may be positive (choice C) or negative (choices B and D), but it is always some form of assessment or appraisal (choice A).

38. (B) *YOB* stands for "year of birth."

39. (C) Your progeny are your children, just as your progenitor is your ancestor.

40. (D) Urea, or $CO(NH_2)_2$, is found in the urine and other bodily fluids.

41. (C) A quandary is a perplexing or confusing position or situation.

42. (B) Doctors use a diagnostic test to diagnose, or determine the cause of, a condition.

43. (A) *Establish* has several meanings, but only choice D makes sense here.

44. (C) The word *contact* should be a clue here. Contact dermatitis is a skin inflammation brought on by touching something that promotes sensitivity.

45. (D) A UTI is a urinary tract infection.

46. (C) A projection in this context is a prediction, or estimate.

47. (D) When you cauterize a wound, you use a flame, laser, or caustic agent to burn the skin and close the blood vessels.

48. (B) To heed is to pay attention; to be heedless is to fail to pay attention.

49. (C) Look at the roots of the word. To convolve is to roll or twist. Something convoluted is twisted and complicated.

50. (C) To be adequate is to be good enough, or satisfactory.

Grammar

1. (A) This question tests your knowledge of basic punctuation. A comma must appear between the dependent clause *Because she was uncertain of her abilities* and the independent clause *Renee asked for help*. No other commas are needed.

2. (C) The phrase *three days from now* places the action in the future, so the future-tense verb is required.

3. (D) *Continually* is an adverb that modifies the verb *moved*.

4. (A) Reading the choices aloud may help you determine which choice has a logical order of phrases and clauses. Choice B is passive rather than active, and the other choices misplace certain modifiers.

5. (A) The past-tense form of the intransitive verb *lie* is *lay*. That kind of verb does not take a direct object. The past tense form of the transitive verb *lay* is *laid*. Dr. Leo laid the paperwork out on the table.

6. (B) No matter who is working with Nurse Junko, the pronoun required must be a subject pronoun. Only *she* fulfills this requirement.

7. (C) The pronoun must be a plural, third-person, subject pronoun. When in doubt, test the choices in place of the underlined phrase.

8. (B) The correct sentence is "For whom was that email intended?"

9. (C) Pick the word that makes sense given the sentence as a whole. The meteorologist's prediction was not made because of Sheila's clever thinking (choice A), and her bringing of an umbrella was a reasonable consequence of the forecast, not a contrast to it (choice B). The best choice is C.

10. (C) *Harvey* is a noun of direct address and should be followed by a comma.

11. (C) The correct spelling has two *r*s and two *s*s.

12. (D) Substituting each choice in place of the blank should prove to you that the only answer that sounds correct is the infinitive phrase.

13. (C) *Datum* is singular; the intake nurse collects data.

14. (B) *Having rested* would be another possibility, but *resting* (choice B) is correct.

15. (A) Although choice B is possible if the lunch were made quickly rather than consumed quickly, choice A is far more logical and grammatically correct.

16. (A) The word *staff* may be singular or plural. Here, the pronoun *their* indicates that it is being used as a plural noun, which means that the verb that agrees is *hope* (choice A), not *hopes* (choice B).

17. (C) The pronoun should be singular, third-person, and possessive.

18. (D) The coordinating conjunctions are *for*, *and*, *nor*, *but*, *or*, *yet*, and *so*. Although is a subordinating conjunction.

19. (B) The sentence is missing its end punctuation. Since it is a question, it needs a question mark.

20. (D) *Because he's funny* is a dependent clause. It has a subject and a verb but cannot stand alone as a sentence.

21. (D) Only the introductory clause requires a comma to separate it from the independent clause it precedes.

22. (A) If you have two choices, you select between them (choice B). If you have three or more, you select among them (choice A).

23. (B) Stationery is paper for letter-writing. *Stationary* means "motionless."

24. (A) The pronoun must be reflexive and refer back to the pronoun already in the sentence—the pronoun *one*. The correct form of that reflexive pronoun is shown in choice A.

25. (B) Choices A and D make it seem as though the mother were age seven, and choice C is nonsensical. Only choice B eliminates the problem of misplaced modifiers.

26. (D) The school is not long overdue; the book is.

27. (D) The correct verb completes the infinitive phrase.

28. (C) The correct sentence would be "He had never had to be on his own in the past."

29. (B) *Too* means "overly" here. *Much uncomfortable* (choice C) is ungrammatical.

30. (D) Placing a semicolon between the clause *Follow my lead* and the rest of the sentence would make this sentence correct.

31. (B) In this type of question, you must make sure that the tense of verbs remains consistent. Because *was* is past tense, the correct answer contains another past-tense verb, *raised*.

32. (C) The construction of the sentence calls for an adverb, *initially*, not an adjective, *initial*.

33. (B) The pronouns should be object pronouns because they receive the action of the verb. Only choice B places the first-person pronoun last, which is correct in standard English.

34. (B) The correct pronoun is plural and first-person because it encompasses the first-person pronoun *I.*

35. (A) There are two pronouns in the sentence. The first should be an object pronoun, which is true in choices A, C, and D. The second should be a possessive pronoun that describes a noun, which is true in choice A. The possessive pronoun *mine* is only used after a verb, as in "The application is mine."

36. (B) A comma should follow *rounds* to separate the introductory dependent clause from the rest of the sentence.

37. (A) *With* is a preposition that begins the prepositional phrase *with the prescription.*

38. (C) The verb *study* does not agree with the singular noun *Sidney.* The word should be *studies.*

39. (A) Try reading the sentence aloud with each choice replacing the blank. Only choice A makes sense.

40. (D) There are several frequently confused words in this sentence, but only *advise* (choice D) is incorrect. The correct word would be *advice,* meaning "recommendation" or "guidance."

41. (C) To be clear and correct, the phrase *having finished the meal* must lie as close as possible to the name it modifies, *Mr. Innes.*

42. (A) The team is traveling as a unit, making the singular form of the verb correct here.

43. (B) A comma should separate the adjectives *small* and *handmade.*

44. (D) This compound sentence has two independent clauses joined with a comma and coordinating conjunction.

45. (D) The pronoun that replaces this plural noun should be plural, third-person, and possessive.

46. (B) You would calculate *speedily* (an adverb), not *speedy* (an adjective).

47. (C) Choice A misplaces the modifier, making it seem as though I were resting in a cage. Choice B is passive. Choice D is just confusing. The best choice is C.

48. (D) In questions like this one, try to find the phrase that, if moved around, would improve the sentence. In this case, *Standing with the refrigerator door open* should really begin the sentence. If it did, all phrases would appear properly next to the nouns that they modify.

49. (A) You consult *with* people, not from, by, or in them.

50. (B) Read the choices aloud if you are in doubt. The only one that contains phrases in logical order is choice B.

Basic Math Skills

1. (C) To multiply mixed numbers and fractions, first express mixed numbers as fractions. In this case, $3\frac{1}{4}$ may be expressed as $\frac{13}{4}$. Next, multiply numerators and denominators. $13 \times 1 = 13$. $4 \times 16 = 64$. The answer is $\frac{13}{64}$.

2. (D) There are 16 ounces in a pound, so there will be $16 \times 17.5 = 280$ ounces in 17.5 pounds.

3. (C) Set this up as a proportion: $\frac{270}{3} = \frac{x}{4.5}$. You may cross-multiply to solve: $270 \times 4.5 = 3x$. $1{,}215 = 3x$. $x = \frac{1{,}215}{3}$, or 405.

4. (A) $3x + 7 - 7 = 4 - 7$; $3x = -3$; $\frac{3x}{3} = \frac{-3}{3}$; $x = -1$

5. (C) 20% is the same as $\frac{20}{100}$. Reduce that to lowest terms by dividing numerator and denominator by 20: $\frac{1}{5}$.

6. (D) If 1 kilogram equals 2.2 pounds, 8 kilograms equal 2.2×8, or 17.6 pounds.

7. (B) Multiply by 100 to find the percent. $0.036 \times 100 = 3.6$.

8. (B) One meter is about 1.09 yards. A kilometer is 1,000 meters, so 5 kilometers would be 5,000 meters. $5{,}000 \times 1.09 = 5{,}450$ yards.

9. (D) $21 \times 3 = 63$ markers total. Since they come in boxes of 12, divide that by 12: $63 \div 12 = 5.25$, so she will need at least 6 boxes.

10. (20) Find the total number of sheep in the flock: $15 + 4 + 1 = 20$. Of those 20, 4 are brown. $\frac{4}{20} = \frac{x}{100}$; $x = 20$.

11. (96) Substitute 8 for y to calculate x: $12 \times 8 = 96$.

12. (36) The least common denominator is the smallest number into which both denominators can divide. Use the larger of the two denominators and a guess-and-check system: Multiplying 12 by 2 equals 24, but the other denominator, 9, does not divide into 24. Multiplying 12 by 3 equals 36, and 9 does divide into 36. Therefore, 36 is the least common denominator.

13. (B) 1 kilogram is about 2.2 pounds. $264 \div 2.2 = 120$.

14. (C) Think of the ratio this way: 3 is to 5 as 81 is to x. You may solve this by setting up an equation and cross-multiplying. $\frac{3}{5} = \frac{81}{x}$. $5 \times 81 = 3x$. $405 = 3x$. $x = 135$.

15. (C) Begin by expressing the mixed numbers as improper fractions: $4\frac{1}{8} = \frac{33}{8}$, and $1\frac{1}{2} = \frac{3}{2}$. To divide by a fraction, multiply by its reciprocal. Therefore, $\frac{33}{8} \div \frac{3}{2} = \frac{33}{8} \times \frac{2}{3}$, or $\frac{66}{24}$. Now reduce to lowest terms: $\frac{66}{24} \div \frac{6}{6} = \frac{11}{4}$. Finally, express $\frac{11}{4}$ as a mixed number: $2\frac{3}{4}$.

16. (A) Add up everything Noah spends and then subtract it from the $100: $11 + $20 + $2 = $33; $100 - $33 = $67.

17. (345) First figure out how many hours she worked all week.
    $7 + 6.5 + 6.5 + 6.5 + 6.5 = 33$ hours in all. Now multiply that by
    \$10.45 per hour: $\$10.45 \times 33 = \$344.85$. Since you must round to
    the nearest whole number, the answer is \$345.

18. (A) Do the subtraction first to remove the 12 that is added to $6k$:

    $$42 = 12 + 6k$$
    $$42 - 12 = 12 + 6k - 12$$
    $$30 = 6k$$

    Now divide both sides by 6: $\dfrac{30}{6} = \dfrac{6k}{6}$. $k = 5$.

19. (250) One centimeter = 10 millimeters, so 25 centimeters =
    250 millimeters.

20. (C) You can find the answer by setting up a proportion: $\dfrac{1}{40} = \dfrac{4.5}{x}$.
    Cross-multiplication leads to $x = 4.5(40)$, or $x = 180$ inches.
    Converting that to feet gets you an answer of $^{180}\!/_{12}$, or 15 feet.

21. (D) You should not need to compute if you estimate first. Your
    answer will be greater than 234 by around $23 + 2$. The only
    possible answer is D.

22. (D) 1 gallon is about 3.79 liters, so 7 gallons would be:
    $3.79 \times 7 = 26.53$ liters.

23. (A) To add mixed numbers, first express them as improper
    fractions. In this case, $4\frac{2}{3}$ may be expressed as $^{14}\!/_3$, and $6\frac{1}{2}$ may be
    expressed as $^{13}\!/_2$. Next, find the common denominator, 6. $^{14}\!/_3 = {}^{28}\!/_6$,
    and $^{13}\!/_2 = {}^{39}\!/_6$. Add the numerators: $28 + 39 = 67$. $^{67}\!/_6 = 11\frac{1}{6}$.

24. (A) Find the total amount she spent by multiplying number of
    stamps by cost: $20 \times \$0.29 = \$5.80$, and $40 \times \$0.42 = \$16.80$.
    $\$16.80 + \$5.80 = \$22.60$. $\$25.00 - \$22.60 = \$2.40$.

25. (A) 7:05 P.M. Choice B would be 1905 in military time.

26. (C) You can find the average by dividing her total by the number
    of months she has been collecting. $144 \div 8 = 18$.

27. (B) 1 ounce is about 29.6 mL, so divide 74 mL by 29.6 mL/oz:
    $74 \div 29.6 = 2.5$.

28. (D) The calculation would look like this:

    ```
          165 r2
    31)5117
       31
       201
       186
       157
       155
         2
    ```

29. (D) The ratio is 3:5 beans to beef. Gus is using x beans:8 beef. Make an equation and cross-multiply to find the answer: $\frac{3}{5} = \frac{x}{8}$. $3 \times 8 = 5 \times x$. $x = 24 \div 5 = 4.8$

30. (2) Subtract b from each side of the equation: $2b + 1 - b = b + 3 - b$ Now you have: $b + 1 = 3$. Subtract 1 from both sides: $b + 1 - 1 = 3 - 1 = 2$

31. (C) Decimals must have denominators of 10, 100, and so on. You can make $\frac{7}{4}$ into a fraction with a numerator of 100 by multiplying both numerator and denominator by 25: $\frac{7}{4} \times \frac{25}{25} = \frac{175}{100}$. $\frac{175}{100} = 1.75$.

32. (D) Because 1 meter = around 3.28 feet, 6 meters = 3.28×6 feet, or 19.68 feet.

33. (A) A percentage is equivalent to a fraction with a denominator of 100. Think $\frac{25}{80} = \frac{x}{100}$. Cross-multiply to get the answer: $2,500 = 80x$, so $x = 31.25$.

34. (D) If 10 pencils are divided between 2 students, each student gets 5 pencils. For 20 students, you need 20×5, or 100 pencils.

35. (1,204) M = 1,000, CC = 200, and IV = 4.

36. (B) You can think of this algebraically: The certain number, $x = (18 \times 4) - 7$. Therefore, $x = 65$.

37. (A) To convert a decimal to a fraction, first put the decimal number over 1: $\frac{1.4}{1}$. Now multiply the fraction by a factor of 10: $\frac{1.4}{1} \times \frac{10}{10} = \frac{14}{10}$ then reduce: $\frac{14}{10} = \frac{7}{5}$.

38. (D) If there are 5 ounces lemon-lime soda to 3 ounces orange juice, then the ratio of lemon-lime soda to orange juice is 5:3.

39. (C) The formula is $(F - 32) \times \frac{5}{9} = C$. So $(82 - 32) \times \frac{5}{9} = 27.777$, or around 28.

40. (B) The units don't matter here; the scale is 2:1. If 2 cm = 1 m, 8 cm = 4 m, and 10 cm = 5 m.

41. (C) First, divide to find the decimal: $13 \div 4 = 3.25$. Then multiply by 100 to find the percent: $3.25 \times 100 = 325$.

42. (B) Estimating may not get you close enough to the answer.

43. (C) First find the least common denominator. Then subtract the numerators. $\frac{25}{45} - \frac{18}{45} = \frac{7}{45}$.

44. (B) Think of this as a proportion: 3 bars/$2.58 = 5$ bars/x. Cross-multiply to solve: $5(\$2.58) = 3x$, so $\$12.90 = 3x$, so $\$4.30 = x$. You may also solve this by figuring out the unit cost: $\$2.58/3 = \$0.86$ per bar, so 5 bars would cost $\$0.86 \times 5 = \$4.30$.

45. (D) To subtract mixed numbers, first express them as improper fractions. In this case, $4\frac{1}{5}$ may be expressed as $\frac{21}{5}$, and $2\frac{2}{3}$ may be expressed as $\frac{8}{3}$. Next, find the common denominator—15. $\frac{21}{5} = \frac{63}{15}$, and $\frac{8}{3} = \frac{40}{15}$. Subtract the numerators: $63 - 40 = 23$. $\frac{23}{15} = 1\frac{8}{15}$.

46. (A) Percent means "per 100," so to change a percent to a decimal, divide the percent by 100. $\frac{20}{100} = 0.2$.

47. (B) Find the total: $4 + 6 = 10$. If there are 6 adults and 10 people total, then the ratio of adults to the total number of people is 6:10, which reduces to 3:5.

48. (D) If she gets 2% quarterly, she gets 2% calculated four times a year. The first quarter, she ends up with $102. The second quarter, she makes 2% on $102, for a total of $104.04. The third quarter, she makes 2% on $104.04, for a total of $106.12. The fourth quarter, she makes 2% on $106.12, for a total of $108.24.

49. (11,200) First find the number of calories daily: $2,000 - (0.2 \times 2,000) = 1,600$. Now multiply that by the number of days in a week: $1,600 \times 7 = 11,200$.

50. (A) There are 3 teaspoons in a tablespoon, so there are 9 teaspoons in 3 tablespoons.

Biology

1. (D) These beadlike organelles are located in the cytoplasm of nearly all cells, on the rough endoplasmic reticulum. They assemble the proteins that the cell uses to grow, repair itself, and control processes.

2. (C) The products of fermentation are ethanol and carbon dioxide. It is the latter that causes the dough to rise.

3. (B) Mitosis creates cells that are exact copies of each other, down to the number of chromosomes in the cell. Meiosis, which creates sex cells, forms cells with half the number of chromosomes in the original cell.

4. (D) DNA can mutate and change. The other choices are true statements.

5. (C) The gene for the disease is recessive, so only homozygous recessive offspring (*aa*) manifest the disease. An offspring that carries the recessive gene along with the dominant *A* gene (*Aa*) will carry but not manifest the disease. In a Punnett square, this would mean two out of four offspring.

6. (A) This describes a hypotonic situation—there are fewer dissolved particles outside the cell than inside. This may enable water to flow into the cell from the solution, swelling the cell, which may burst.

7. (A) Mitochondria produce most of the energy needed by a cell.

8. (B) The shape of an enzyme controls its fit with its substrate. Changes in temperature and/or pH can alter an enzyme's shape.

9. (A) The stamen (choice A) is the male reproductive organ in a flowering plant. The pistil (choice B) is the female reproductive organ. The stigma (choice C) is the top part of the pistil, and the style (choice D) is a slender stalk below the stigma.

10. (B) A parasitic relationship is one in which one organism benefits (in this case, the bacterium) to the detriment of another (in this case, the human).

11. (D) The Latin names by which we know certain animals are typically their genus and species names. In order, a house cat is from the kingdom Animalia, phylum Chordata, class Mammalia, order Carnivora, family Felidae, genus *Felis*, and species *catus*.

12. (A) Waxes, oils, and fats are lipids.

13. (D) The lysosome contains digestive enzymes. The job of a lysosome is to digest food for cells and break down cells' waste products.

14. (D) In the asexual process known as binary fission, one parent cell divides into two offspring cells with DNA identical to the parent cell's. Many bacteria, some algae, and some protozoa reproduce this way.

15. (A) During this active phase of a cell's reproductive life, the cell produces nucleic acids and proteins and doubles its number of chromosomes.

16. (C) In the twisted strand of DNA, the base adenine always pairs with thymine, and cytosine pairs with guanine. Uracil is found in RNA.

17. (B) Picture a Punnett square. Reading the chart clockwise from top left, the cross would yield one female carrier, one female hemophiliac, one male hemophiliac, and one normal male who neither carries nor manifests the disease. Only one of the four, a female X_hX, would be a carrier only.

18. (C) The formula represents carbon dioxide pairing with water to form a simple sugar and oxygen. This is what happens in the process of photosynthesis.

19. (A) Water molecules have polar covalent bonds. Oxygen atoms have a partial negative charge, and hydrogen atoms have a partial positive charge. The polarity of a water molecule allows it to easily attract other water molecules.

20. (C) The greatest energy content is at the base of the energy pyramid, where the producers of energy congregate; therefore, producers > primary consumers > secondary consumers > decomposers.

21. (B) Only this choice presents you with the control group and test group needed for a valid experiment.

22. (C) Nitrification (choice C) is a step in the nitrogen cycle. Condensation (choice A) is the change from gas to liquid that water vapor undergoes as it cools. Transpiration (choice B) is the loss of water through a plant's stomata. Absorption (choice D) is the intake of water from the water table by plant roots.

23. (C) Chlorophyll absorbs red and blue light but reflects green light.

24. (B) Bacteria and blue-green algae are prokaryotes, organisms whose cells have no true nucleus. They are not gymnosperms (vascular plants whose seeds have no protective covering). Of the choices, only blue-green algae are autotrophs (organisms that make their own food through photosynthesis), and only certain bacteria may be pathogens (infectious organisms that spread disease).

25. (D) Simple carbohydrates are simple sugars. Complex carbohydrates are simple sugars linked with covalent bonds.

Chemistry

1. (B) Isotopes of an element differ in the number of neutrons they have in an atom. Their mass number is also different, as is the number of particles in their nucleus.

2. (C) The pH scale is a logarithmic scale. Therefore, each number on the pH represents a tenfold increase or decrease in acidity. In this example, a difference in pH of 2 equals a 10 times 10, or 100 times increase in acidity.

3. (B) Radioactive isotopes have an extremely short half-life and would degrade too quickly to be useful. Too long a half-life would mean that the isotope would remain in the body for too long a period of time.

4. (C) There are polar covalent bonds in water and ionic bonds in a salt.

5. (D) This is an example of the double replacement reaction that occurs when aluminum nitrate and sulfuric acid react together.

6. (B) Metals make up about two-thirds of the periodic table and are mostly located on the left and center areas of the table. Nonmetals are located on the upper right side of the periodic table. Semimetals form a staircase that runs between metals and nonmetals on the periodic table.

7. (A) Set up a simple equation if it helps. Suppose that gas A has a molar mass of M_1, and gas B has a molar mass four times that, M_2. Now suppose that $M_1 = 1$ and $M_2 = 4$. The square root of $4/1 = 2/1$, so the rate of effusion for gas A is half that of gas B.

8. (C) Allotropes are different forms of the same element. Diamonds, graphite, and buckminsterfullerene are all allotropes of carbon. Fluorine is an atomic element of its own and is not an allotrope of carbon.

9. (D) Temperature, surface area, and pressure all affect the rate of a reaction. Time is simply used to measure the rate of reaction and is not a factor that would affect the rate.

10. (A) An amino acid has an amine and a carboxylic acid group present. These are represented by R-NH2 and R-COOH.

11. (B) Examination of the first substance shows that methane gas has one carbon atom. There is also one carbon atom on the right side of the equation, so there is no need to balance this. There are four hydrogen atoms on the left side. To balance this, change the coefficient on the right side so that there are four hydrogen atoms there as well:

$$\underline{\hspace{2cm}} CH_4 + \underline{\hspace{2cm}} O_2 \rightarrow \underline{\hspace{2cm}} CO_2 + 2H_2O$$

Now there are two atoms of oxygen on the left and four on the right (two from carbon dioxide and two from water). To balance, change the coefficient on the left to 2:

$$CH_4 + 2O_2 \rightarrow CO_2 + 2H_2O$$

12. (D) Reactivity is the tendency of an element to undergo chemical change, which in turn depends on its stability. Xenon, a noble gas, is extremely stable and thus nonreactive under normal conditions.

13. (A) Ionic compounds have high melting points, good connectivity, and a crystalline shape. An example is table salt, NaCl.

14. (C) Calculate the number of protons by subtracting the atomic number from the mass number. Uranium-235 is so named because its mass number is 235, and the atomic number for uranium is 92, so $235 - 92 = 143$.

15. (A) The electron distribution of an atom is divided into shells, which in turn contain subshells composed of the orbitals in which the electrons reside. In electron configuration, the symbols 1s, 2s, 2p, and so on are used to designate subshells, with superscripts indicating the number of electrons in each subshell. There is a maximum number of electrons per subshell. Lithium has atomic number 3, meaning that it has 3 protons, and in its balanced state, 3 electrons. Looking at the superscripts alone should tell you that only choice A offers a solution with 3 electrons—2 in the first subshell and 1 in the second.

16. (A) To perform this operation, you must know the number of moles of solute and the number of liters of solution, because molarity equals moles/liter. 100 grams of solution = 0.1 liters of solution. 5 grams of solute where the molar mass of the solute is 180.0 g/mol means a molarity of $5/180$, or $0.027777\ldots$ $0.028/0.1 = 0.28$, so the molarity of the solution is 0.28 M.

17. (D) As a general rule of thumb, for acid solutions $[H^+] > [OH^-]$, for basic solutions $[H^+] < [OH^-]$, and for neutral solutions or for pure water $[H^+] = [OH^-]$.

18. (B) The standard for a mole is based on a single isotope of carbon. It is the amount of a substance that contains the same number of chemical units as the number of atoms in exactly 12 g of that isotope of carbon. That number, known as Avogadro's number, has a value of 6.022×10^{23}. A mole of atoms consists of Avogadro's number of atoms and has a mass in grams numerically equal to the atomic weight of the element. So, one mole of H_2O has a mass in grams equal to the atomic weight of two atoms of hydrogen plus one atom of oxygen—about 1 + 1 + 16, or 18 g.

19. (C) Certain unstable atoms emit particles/rays and thus change into atoms with a different chemical identity, a process known as radioactivity. Alpha particles consist of particles that carry a +2 charge.

20. (D) Chemical compounds are named in the order of the elements shown. Ag is silver, and NO_3 is nitrate. Nitrates have three oxygen atoms; nitrites (choice C) have two.

21. (B) Oxidation numbers for atoms in a neutral molecule must add up to zero. Hydrogen has an oxidation number of +1 when combined with nonmetals and −1 when combined with metals. In this case, it is combined with a nonmetal, so to obtain a sum of 0, the chlorine atom must have an oxidation number of −1.

22. (A) Generally, the rule is

London dispersion < dipole-dipole < H-bonding < ion-ion

A Keesom interaction is one form of dipole-dipole interaction.

23. (D) If x = number of moles, then $x \div 2.0$ L = a concentration of 1.5 M, so x = 3.0 moles.

24. (B) Ag^+ is silver, and OH^- is hydroxide, forming a molecule of AgOH.

25. (C) The atomic number of an element equals the number of protons in its nucleus. Of the numbers given, only 11, Na (sodium), is an alkali metal.

Anatomy and Physiology

1. (A) An anterior muscle is located near the front of the body. Of those listed, the quadriceps (frontal thigh muscle) is the most anterior.

2. (B) The headrest prevents the head from moving too far backward or hyperextending the neck beyond its normal range.

3. (D) Because of the hyperflexion and hyperextension caused by such a collision, it is not uncommon to find tears or stretching of the ligaments of the spine. The injury is front-to-back, making choice B unlikely, and a herniated disc (choice C) is more of a compression injury.

4. (C) Defecation (choice A) is the elimination of waste. Osmosis (choice B) is the movement of molecules across a membrane. Circulation (choice D) is the movement of blood through the body. Peristalsis (choice C) is the involuntary, wavelike movement of muscles in the intestine and elsewhere that pushes food along.

5. (A) Some nutrients supply energy, and others support metabolism. Nutrients in the first set include carbohydrates, proteins, and fats. Those in the second set include vitamins, minerals, and water.

6. (B) Schwann cells wrap around the nerve fibers and form the myelin sheath in the peripheral nervous system.

7. (B) The nervous system is made up of the brain, spinal cord, and nerves. It receives and transmits signals from the environment that regulate voluntary and involuntary movement.

8. (A) The sympathetic and parasympathetic systems (choices C and D) are part of the autonomic nervous system (choice B), which controls involuntary actions of the smooth muscles, glands, and heart. The somatic nervous system (choice A) has to do with reception of external stimuli and voluntary control of the muscles.

9. (C) Damage to a disc in the lower back will most likely cause pain radiating downward along the sciatic nerve.

10. (B) The ulna (choice A), radius (choice C), and humerus (choice D) are arm bones.

11. (D) The ovaries are the egg-producing reproductive organs.

12. (C) A low pH in the stomach (choice A), cilia in the trachea (choice B), and mucus (D) are primary defenses. Cells recognizing a pathogen (choice C) are a third line of defense.

13. (A) Hormones from the endocrine system, particularly from the pituitary gland, regulate growth.

14. (D) The mitral valve opens to allow oxygenated blood collected in the left atrium to flow into the left ventricle.

15. (D) The disease known as rickets is a product of vitamin D deficiency and results in the softening and bending of bones.

16. (B) One of the jobs of the lymphatic system is to prevent excess fluid from accumulating in tissues by collecting it and moving it into the circulatory system via the brachiocephalic veins.

17. (D) The parathyroid hormone regulates calcium in the body through several means, one of which is increasing the production of activated vitamin D.

18. (C) The most medial feature is the one closest to the middle of the body.
19. (B) The average person in good health has a pulse of about 72 beats per minute and a blood pressure of 120 over 80 mm Hg.
20. (A) A sagittal section occurs along a longitudinal plane, dividing the body into right and left regions.
21. (A) Pepsin aids chemical digestion in the stomach by breaking down proteins.
22. (C) The esophagus is the passage that connects the pharynx to the stomach.
23. (B) Iodine is the key mineral in thyroid hormone production. Iodine deficiency can cause a goiter, swelling of the thyroid gland.
24. (D) The cheekbones are to the right and left of the nose, meaning that they are lateral to it, or away from the body's midline.
25. (C) Antibodies are formed when an antigen stimulates B cells, special lymphocytes, to produce specialized proteins that combat foreign substances or organisms.

Physics

1. (C) Since density = mass/volume, it should be obvious that the decrease in volume as a car is crushed should lead to an increase in density. Nothing happens to change the mass of the car.
2. (D) If a car travels 3 miles north, 6 miles south, 2 miles east, 2 miles west, and then 3 miles north, it has traveled a total distance of 16 miles. However, because of the directions it has traveled, it has ended up in the place where it started, giving it a displacement of 0.
3. (B) Gravity in fact causes acceleration, making choice A incorrect—unless air resistance counteracts that acceleration, which it may easily do for an object as small and lightweight as a raindrop. Raindrops may lose mass (choice C), but that would not decrease their acceleration. Choice D violates Newton's first law.
4. (A) Velocity is the change in distance over time. 100 m/10 s is the same as 10 m/s.
5. (B) Momentum is calculated by multiplying mass by velocity, $p = mv$. Although the meteorite seems intimidating, it is the car that has the greatest momentum, at 6,250 kg·m/s.
6. (D) Dry ice is frozen carbon dioxide. As it breaks down, it transforms directly into gas without passing through a liquid phase. Sublimation of metals is possible, but not "outside of the laboratory."

7. (C) Applying Newton's second law, $F = ma$, a 1.0-kg block accelerated at 6 m/s² requires a 6-N force to move it.

8. (A) The equation $P = IV$, power equals current times voltage, is the one to use. Dividing the power by the voltage gives you $I = P/V$, and 60 watts/110 volts equals approximately 0.55 amperes.

9. (A) According to the equation $v = f\lambda$, frequency is equal to the velocity of the wave divided by the wavelength. Dividing 20 m/s by 4 m gives you 5 s⁻¹.

10. (C) When the car is attached to the electromagnet, its potential energy (PE) is 367.5 kJ because PE = mgh, or (1,500 kg)(9.8 m/s²)(25 m). As the car falls, all 367.5 kJ of PE are converted to kinetic energy. On hitting the ground and making a sound, the car will no longer possess any PE.

11. (B) Unlike charges attract each other; like charges repel each other. As two like charges near each other, work is required to push them together, and potential energy increases.

12. (B) Transverse waves do not have areas of compression and expansion as they move perpendicular to the direction of the wave.

13. (C) A vector quantity, for example, 25 k/h N, has both magnitude and direction. A scalar quantity has only magnitude.

14. (B) Ice (choice D) floats on water (choice B) because its density is less, despite the fact that it is a solid. When water freezes, its volume increases, making its density (mass/volume) less.

15. (A) Increasing distance by a factor of 2 decreases the force by a factor of 2², or 4. The new force of attraction is the original force divided by 4, or 3 units.

16. (D) The switch interrupts the electrical circuit or allows the current to flow from one conductor to another.

17. (C) Gay-Lussac's law states that temperature and pressure are directly proportional. Heat from friction caused as tires rub on the road increases the temperature of the air in the tire, causing an increase in pressure. This is why you are advised to measure the pressure in your tires when they are cold—before starting a trip.

18. (C) You are looking first at the relationship between the object distance (d_o), the image distance (d_i), and the focal length (f). Start out with $1/f = 1/d_o + 1/d_i$ where $f = 15$ cm and $d_o = 20$ cm. In this case, $1/15 = 1/20 + 1/d_i$. Use equivalent fractions to solve:

$4/60 = 3/60 + 1/60$, so $d_i = 60$ cm

Now you can use what you know to calculate the image height (h_i), using $h_i/h_o = -d_i/d_o$ where $h_o = 5$ cm, $d_o = 20$ cm, and $d_i = 60$ cm. So $h_i/5 = -60/20$, meaning that the image height is -15 cm. The negative value indicates an inverted image.

19. (A) The period is the reciprocal of the frequency. Here, the frequency is 80 vibrations per second. The period is 1/80, or 0.0125 s.

20. (D) Momentum is the product of velocity and mass. The first car's momentum is $2,000 \times 15 = 30,000$ kg·m/s. The second car's momentum is $1,500 \times 15 = 22,500$ kg·m/s. For its momentum to equal that of the first car, it could either accelerate to 20 kg/s or add 500 kg to its mass.

21. (D) Resistance of a wire depends on length, material, and cross-sectional area. Given four wires of the same length and material, the thinnest wire would have the highest resistance.

22. (A) The equation to use is $K = f/x$, where K is the spring constant, f is force, and x is distance. First, find the force in Newtons. Since the gravitational constant on Earth is 9.8, multiply the mass, 5, by that constant to find the force: $9.8 \times 5 = 49$ N. Now calculate the spring constant: $K = 49$ N/10 cm. $K = 4.9$ N/cm.

23. (A) Determine the acceleration by dividing the speed squared by the radius of the track: $a = v^2/R$. In this case, $a = 100/50$, or 2 m/s^2.

24. (D) According to Ohm's law, current (I) equals voltage (ΔV) divided by resistance (R), or $I = \Delta V/R$. In this case, you know voltage and resistance, so $I = 3/60$, or 0.05 amp.

25. (B) Use Coulomb's law to find the force. The equation to use is this:

$$F_{elect} = \frac{k \times Q_1 \times Q_2}{d^2}$$

Remember that 1 coulomb = 10^6 microcoulombs. Both balloons in this problem have the same charge, so Q_1 and Q_2 in this case equal 5×10^{-6} C, and d, distance, = 25 cm, or 0.25 m. Now, you must recall Coulomb's constant, $k = (9.0 \times 10^9$ N·m^2/C^2). From this point, it's all about computation:

$$\frac{9.0 \times 10^9 \, \text{N·m}^2 \times (5 \times 10^{-6} \, \cancel{C}) \times (5 \times 10^{-6} \, \cancel{C})}{\cancel{C^2} \, (0.25 \, \cancel{m})^2} = \frac{225 \times 10^{-3}}{0.0125} = 1.8 \, \text{N}$$

CHAPTER 4

A2 Practice Test 2

READING COMPREHENSION

50 items | Suggested time: 55 minutes

Microbes and Health

There are 10 times more microbes than human cells in the human body. Scientists have long known that the human body is host to a staggering number of microorganisms, but recent information is shedding light on just how pivotal a role these bacteria play in the development of the human immune system.

The human body plays host to a wide array of microorganisms that are specially adapted to survive in particular portions of the human body. There is such a great amount of variation in these microorganisms that few people will share the same strains of bacteria in the same quantities. This process begins at birth: a newborn infant emerges from the womb, a germ-free environment, and is immediately coated with germs from its mother's birth canal. These germs immediately begin to breed and colonize the human body that will now be its new host.

GO ON TO THE NEXT PAGE

The most intriguing discovery is not that the body's immune system tolerates these millions of harmless organisms, but that it may rely upon their presence to function properly. Scientists recently found that with laboratory mice that could not produce a particular inflammation-reducing molecule, upon being injected with a particular strain of bacteria that was then allowed to breed, their immune system quickly developed the ability to synthesize that molecule. Simply put, the mice needed the bacteria for their immune systems to function properly.

This same basic concept is also being used with humans. A relatively experimental process known as fecal bacteriotherapy is now being used to reintroduce healthy bacteria into a colon that lacks the capability to defend itself against pathogenic agents. Scientists are just beginning to understand the important role that these microorganisms play in the body of a healthy human being, but early tests have yielded remarkable discoveries.

1. What is the main idea of the passage?

   A. Recent discoveries are revealing just how critical microorganisms are to maintaining a properly functioning immune system.
   B. The human body is host to a wide array of microorganisms.
   C. Bacteriotherapy is being used to reintroduce healthy bacteria into a colon that lacks the capability to defend itself against pathogenic agents.
   D. Early tests have shown remarkable potential for the possibilities of bacteriotherapy.

2. Which of the following is *not* listed as a detail in the passage?

   A. Babies are born coated with germs from the birth canal.
   B. Mice and humans respond to microbes similarly.
   C. Few people share the same microbes in the same quantities.
   D. Human bodies contain far more microbes than they do cells.

3. What is the author's primary purpose in writing this essay?

   A. To inform
   B. To persuade
   C. To entertain
   D. To analyze

GO ON TO THE NEXT PAGE

4. Choose the best summary of the passage.

A. Scientists have used experiments on mice to prove the body's need for certain microorganisms. Instead of damaging the immune system, it turns out that bacteria of certain types may in fact support immunity, at least in lower organisms.

B. Bacteriotherapy was originally tried on mice, and the results were positive enough that it now is being used in human trials as well. The essential theory states that introducing bacteria into a damaged colon can help with reconstruction and immune response.

C. Although scientists have known for years that the body tolerates certain microorganisms, experiments now show that some bacteria may be required for a healthily functioning immune system. For example, introducing harmless bacteria seems to help the colon defend itself against pathogens.

D. Humans are born germ-free, but it does not take long for pathogens to find their way into the body, often destroying an otherwise healthy immune system. Replacing these harmful bacteria with harmless ones is a new and exciting process known as bacteriotherapy.

MRSA

Methicillin-resistant *Staphylococcus aureus* (MRSA) is a form of the *Staphylococcus aureus* bacterium that is resistant to antibiotics and as a result is very difficult to treat. MRSA now kills more Americans every year than HIV/AIDS, and the rates of infection are rising.

Methicillin is an antibiotic that was introduced in the 1960s as a way of combating the *Staphylococcus aureus* bacterium that is ubiquitous in hospitals. Within a year, doctors began finding strains of bacteria that had already developed immunity to methicillin. By the 1990s, MRSA had become the leading hospital-acquired skin infection in the United States. At the same time MRSA started appearing outside of hospitals. These were different strains of the bacteria, but just as dangerous, and spreading just as quickly. In the past 15 years, MRSA bacteria have become ubiquitous not only in hospitals, but in gyms, locker rooms, swimming pools, and any other settings where human contact is common.

GO ON TO THE NEXT PAGE

Researchers in Ireland are developing a technology that may significantly halt the spread of the hospital-associated MRSA bacteria. They have developed a textile consisting of nanomaterials 1,000 times smaller than a human hair; these textiles are shown to halt the spread of infection and can be used for linens, drapes, and upholstery in hospitals. The potential for this technology to reduce the instances of hospital-associated MRSA is staggering.

You can reduce your risk for community-associated MRSA infection by regularly washing your hands, covering all open wounds with a clean bandage, and not sharing any personal items like razors or towels.

5. As used in the second paragraph, what does the term *ubiquitous* mean?

   A. Indigenous
   B. Often ignored
   C. Found everywhere
   D. Dangerous

6. What is the main idea of the passage?

   A. Methicillin may prove to be the best way to keep MRSA from killing more hospital patients.
   B. A new textile is the best bet to protect hospital patients against the dangers of MRSA.
   C. There are many different strains of MRSA, but only one is potentially fatal.
   D. MRSA is a scourge both in and out of hospitals, but there may be ways to reduce the risk.

7. Which of the following statements is an opinion?

   A. Hand-washing stations are one means of combating MRSA infection.
   B. Not all *Staphylococcus* bacteria are resistant to antibiotics.
   C. Hospitals in the United States should quickly adopt the use of new germ-fighting textiles.
   D. MRSA infection kills more people in the United States than does HIV/AIDS.

GO ON TO THE NEXT PAGE

8. Which statement would *not* be inferred by the reader?

    A. Hospitals may soon limit the spread of infection with a new textile.

    B. MRSA begins by infecting the skin.

    C. You are most likely to contract MRSA in a crowded location.

    D. Used clothing stores may harbor MRSA.

Fat for Fitness

After years of bad publicity it may sound absurd, but many dietitians are now extolling the virtues of consuming fat. According to Laurie Tansman, a nutritionist at Mt. Sinai Medical Center in New York, fat "not only plays a vital role in the health of the membrane of every cell in our body, it also helps protect us from a number of key health threats." Fat is a critical part of your necessary food intake, and it is generally recommended that 30 percent of your daily calories should come from fat. Without it, your body would not be able to absorb or transport vitamins A, D, E, and K. Body temperature, hair follicles, and skin cells are all reliant upon the consumption of fats to function properly.

There is near-universal agreement that the healthiest fats are unsaturated fats. This list of healthy fats includes olive oil, sesame oil, walnut oil, avocado oil, and omega-3 fatty acids. These fats, when eaten in moderation, can lower cholesterol levels, thereby reducing your risk for heart disease.

Saturated fats are considered less healthy than unsaturated fats and should be consumed more sparingly. Most saturated fats are found in animal products, such as beef, pork, and chicken. The least healthy of all fats are trans-fatty acids, or trans fats. These fats can occur in small amounts naturally in animal products, but they are more commonly found as artificially produced oils used for frying foods or softening prepackaged snacks. These fats will increase your risk for heart disease; the U.S. Dietary Guidelines recommend that you consume as few trans fats as possible.

GO ON TO THE NEXT PAGE

9. Which statement is *not* a detail from the passage?

   A. Nearly one-third of your calories should come from fat.
   B. Canola oil is one source of unsaturated fat.
   C. Most saturated fats are derived from animal products.
   D. Trans fatty acids put you at risk for heart disease.

10. What is the meaning of the word *moderation* as used in the second paragraph?

    A. Adequate amounts
    B. Intervals of time
    C. Excess
    D. Variation

11. Choose the best summary of the passage.

    A. We often think of all fat as bad, but it is clear that certain fats, especially the more healthful unsaturated fats, are important for bodily function.
    B. If you must consume some fat, be sure to choose unsaturated fats such as oils rather than saturated fats found in prepackaged snacks or animal products.
    C. Doctors and researchers have discovered that without the calories found in fat, people would not have functioning metabolisms.
    D. Some intake of saturated fat is necessary, but you should stay away from the kind of fat found in fried food, which can lead to heart disease.

12. What is the author's primary purpose in writing this essay?

    A. To entertain
    B. To analyze
    C. To reflect
    D. To persuade

13. What is a conclusion that a reader could draw from this passage?

    A. It is advisable to choose unsaturated fats over saturated fats.
    B. Saturated fats are more calorically dense than unsaturated fats.
    C. Trans fats are more calorically dense than saturated fats.
    D. Unsaturated fats are mostly found in animal products.

GO ON TO THE NEXT PAGE

Food for Seniors

The food pyramid is a visual representation of how the different food groups can be combined to form a healthy diet. Although it was a vital part of dietary guidelines for years before being replaced by the "MyPlate" model, the pyramid was constantly analyzed and revised as additional study was done in nutritional fields. A few years ago, the pyramid underwent a change regarding the unique dietary needs of seniors.

Modifications in the pyramid for older adults included an emphasis on fiber and calcium, as well as on vitamins D and B_{12}. By incorporating these changes, the pyramid indicated that the nutrients found in a person's routine daily consumption typically are not enough for seniors. Seniors need supplementation.

As people age, they tend to move less and thus need fewer calories to maintain their weight. Because seniors tend to eat a more limited amount, dietitians urge them to choose wisely. They are urged to eat nutrient-rich meals featuring such food as fruits, vegetables, low-fat dairy products, and high-fiber whole grains.

The revised pyramid also focused on the importance for older people of ingesting adequate amounts of fluids daily. This helps to ensure proper digestion and prevent dehydration.

Finally, the revised pyramid included information on incorporating exercise and other physical activities into the lives of older adults. Suggestions included swimming, walking, or simple yard work. Because recent reports have stated that obesity levels for people older than 70 years of age are climbing, performing some type of regular exercise is more essential than ever.

14. What is the main idea of the passage?

    A. Senior citizens need to increase their calcium and vitamin D intake.

    B. Physical activity is a new addition to the food pyramid.

    C. The food pyramid was revised to reflect the needs of seniors.

    D. The revised food pyramid looks more like a food square.

GO ON TO THE NEXT PAGE

15. What is the meaning of the word *supplementation* as used in the second paragraph?

    A. Extra

    B. Organization

    C. Attachment

    D. Revision

16. Identify the overall tone of the essay.

    A. Idealistic

    B. Theatrical

    C. Unconcerned

    D. Pragmatic

17. Which of the following is *not* mentioned as being important for seniors?

    A. Vitamin B_{12}

    B. Calcium

    C. Nitrates

    D. Exercise

You're Getting Sleepy . . .

Most people get a little grumpy when they do not get enough sleep, but when it comes to children, the problem may be more than just some extra irritation. Lack of sleep may also affect their weight as well as their overall behavior.

A study conducted in New Zealand at the University of Auckland and published in the medical journal *Sleep* followed almost 600 children from infancy through seven years of age. Researchers observed the children's sleep patterns and found that generally they slept less on the weekends than during the week and even less during the summer months. According to the findings, the children who tended to sleep the least were at greater risk for being overweight and/or experiencing behavioral problems. In fact, those who regularly slept less than nine hours a night were three times more likely than longer sleepers to be obese and to show signs of attention deficit disorder (ADD) and attention deficit hyperactivity disorder (ADHD). These results were based on questionnaires completed by the children's parents and teachers.

GO ON TO THE NEXT PAGE

How does sleep affect weight? The answer to that is still not clear, but experts suspect that chronic sleep deprivation somehow alters the hormones involved in appetite control and metabolism. This is a connection that still needs to be explored to be better understood.

How much sleep is enough for a child? Experts recommend that preschoolers get 11 to 13 hours of sleep each night, whereas school-age children should get between 10 and 11 hours per night. Many children average only 8 hours. The study concluded that sleep duration is one risk factor that can be fairly easily altered to prevent future health problems for today's young people.

18. What conclusion can a reader draw about the connection between sleep and young children?

   A. Lack of sleep causes children to fail in school.
   B. Inadequate rest raises the risk of behavioral and physical problems.
   C. Sleeping less than 10 hours a night is guaranteed to result in obesity.
   D. Eight hours of sleep each night meets the requirements of most children.

19. Which of the following statements is an opinion?

   A. The connection between sleep and weight should be explored.
   B. Many young children average only eight hours of sleep a night.
   C. People who sleep less are more likely to be obese.
   D. Researchers in New Zealand studied almost 600 children.

20. What is the meaning of the word *duration* as used in the last paragraph?

   A. Basis
   B. Extent
   C. Cure
   D. Solidity

GO ON TO THE NEXT PAGE

21. What is the main idea of the passage?

A. Researchers disagree on the optimum amount of sleep for children.

B. Bad sleep habits may result in attention deficit disorders.

C. Lack of sleep may have negative effects on weight and behavior.

D. Sleep deprivation appears to alter certain hormones in children.

Killer Cosmetics

In recent years, there have been frightening headlines about harmful ingredients such as mercury and lead in ordinary cosmetics. However, these are hardly the first examples of people paying a heavy price to conform to cultural ideals of beauty. That is a tradition that has been around for centuries.

Ancient Egyptians decorated their eyes with malachite (a green ore of copper), galena (a lead sulfide), and kohl (a paste made from soot, fat, and metals such as lead). This may have made them look more beautiful, but it also led to health problems such as insomnia and mental confusion.

The ancient Greeks went even further. They applied lead to their entire faces, supposedly to clear their complexions of any blemishes and improve the coloration of the skin. Health problems that resulted ranged from infertility to insanity. The lead ointment whitened their faces—a sure sign of beauty—and they then added some red lead to their cheeks for that rosy glow. As if that toxic mess were not enough, they also used hair dyes that contained lead. The Romans adopted these practices, and some historians suspect that lead poisoning was part of what later led to the fall of the Roman Empire.

As recently as 2007, lipsticks for sale were found to contain lead, and mascara was found to contain mercury. An additional concern is phthalates, industrial chemicals that can cause birth defects and infertility. They are found in personal care products such as shampoos, lotions, perfume, and deodorants.

An old saying states that beauty has a price. Sometimes that price may be much higher than consumers realize. Know what you are putting on your face.

GO ON TO THE NEXT PAGE

22. What is the author's attitude toward the use of cosmetics?

A. Sympathetic
B. Mocking
C. Tolerant
D. Disapproving

23. What is the meaning of the word *conform* as used in the first paragraph?

A. Authorize
B. Fit in
C. Hand over
D. Bewilder

24. The author describes cosmetics in each of the following cultures EXCEPT _____.

A. Greek
B. Egyptian
C. Roman
D. Native American

25. What is the author's primary purpose in writing this essay?

A. To persuade
B. To analyze
C. To entertain
D. To reflect

Lifewings

What do pilots, astronauts, physicians, and risk managers have in common? In this case, they are all part of an organization based in Memphis, Tennessee, called Lifewings Partners. This unusual group focuses on finding ways to eliminate mistakes and accidents in medical settings within the United States.

GO ON TO THE NEXT PAGE

Lifewings Partners emphasizes the need for a watchdog in various medical settings. According to the Institute of Health, approximately 98,000 patients die each year in US health care settings due to nothing more than medical error. Examples of medical errors include the man who had the wrong testicle removed in a Los Angeles hospital, a young boy who went in for a typical hernia surgery and ended up with brain damage from the anesthesia, and a hospital in Rhode Island that performed brain surgery on the wrong side of the brain—three times on three different patients in less than a year.

In addition to making internal changes in medical settings by changing procedures and establishing checklists, Lifewings Partners also works to educate patients on safety before they even enter the hospital. The company suggests that all consumers do the following: go online to obtain public information on a hospital's safety, talk to their doctors to see what safety standards are in place already, and ask professionals about which facilities tend to have the best safety records. Founder Steve Harden says, "Just because a hospital has a great reputation for cutting-edge medicine doesn't necessarily mean the hospital is the safest place to go for routine procedures." After all, some mistakes are too big and too irrevocable to risk.

26. Which of the following is *not* listed as a detail in the passage?

    A. Many patients die each year from medical error.
    B. Lifewings Partners educates patients on consumer safety.
    C. Steve Harden is the founder of Lifewings Partners.
    D. The most common medical error is overmedication.

27. The word *watchdog* as used in the second paragraph of the passage can best be defined as _____.

    A. companion
    B. guard
    C. manager
    D. punisher

GO ON TO THE NEXT PAGE

28. Which statement could be inferred by the reader from the last paragraph of the passage?

    A. Medical mistakes can happen at even the best hospitals.

    B. Procedures that Lifewings Partners recommends are always effective.

    C. City hospitals know more than others about cutting-edge medicine.

    D. Medical mistakes will one day be completely eradicated.

29. Which statement about Lifewings Partners is a fact?

    A. Everyone should have access to Lifewings.

    B. The people in Lifewings are modern heroes.

    C. Steve Harden was clever to found Lifewings.

    D. Lifewings is based in Memphis, Tennessee.

30. What is the main idea of the passage?

    A. Medical mistakes are made in health centers every day.

    B. Lifewings Partners is made up of an eclectic mix of people.

    C. Lifewings Partners is working hard to prevent medical errors.

    D. Consumers should talk to their doctors about hospital safety.

A New Use for Acupuncture

Over the years, acupuncture has become a more widely accepted type of alternative medicine. It is used for a wide variety of ailments, and if a recent study from Germany is valid, relieving menstrual pain can be added to the continuously growing list.

Traditionally nonsteroidal anti-inflammatory drugs (NSAIDs) are the typical treatment for menstrual discomfort. However, as many consumers and physicians are aware, NSAIDs have a number of side effects, including nausea, vomiting, rash, dizziness, headache, and drowsiness. Acupuncture rarely has any kind of side effects other than the occasional stinging sensation when the needle is inserted or a deep ache around it after it is in place.

GO ON TO THE NEXT PAGE

Acupuncture has proven helpful with relieving a number of kinds of pain, so researchers at Charité University Medical Center in Berlin wanted to find out how effective it might be in combating cramps and other menstrual discomforts.

More than 200 women were enrolled in the study, and after three months and approximately 10 sessions, the women who were treated with acupuncture reported significantly less pain than those in the control group who received no treatment at all. They also reported a 33 percent improvement in their symptoms. Because of these findings, the researchers came to the conclusion that "acupuncture should be considered as a viable option in the management of these patients."

31. What conclusion is suggested by this study from Germany?

   A. So far, acupuncture does not have much credibility as a treatment option.
   B. Acupuncture can relieve women of all menstrual discomfort.
   C. NSAIDs are generally more effective than acupuncture for treating cramps.
   D. Acupuncture is a reasonable treatment choice for cramps.

32. What is the meaning of the word *viable* as used in the last paragraph?

   A. Reasonable
   B. Unresolved
   C. Contemporary
   D. Consistent

33. Identify the overall tone of the essay.

   A. Cautionary
   B. Unconvinced
   C. Optimistic
   D. Insensitive

34. Which detail is *not* given as a side effect of NSAIDs?

   A. Nausea
   B. Headache
   C. Weight loss
   D. Dizziness

GO ON TO THE NEXT PAGE

Caffeine and Pregnancy

The health risks of coffee have long been debated, but a recent study has added another argument against too much coffee consumption. This study looked at the effect of drinking coffee on pregnant women. Conducted by physicians at Kaiser Permanente, the study explored the connection between caffeine and the risk of miscarriage.

This study followed more than 1,000 women who became pregnant within a two-year period. The amount of caffeine they drank was logged, as well as which women experienced a miscarriage. The results, as published in the January 2008 issue of the *American Journal of Obstetrics and Gynecology*, stated that the risk of miscarriage more than doubled in women who consumed 200 mg or more of caffeine per day—about what is found in two cups of coffee.

Why does caffeine carry this risk? Researchers are not sure, but they theorize that the caffeine restricts blood flow to the placenta. This, in turn, can harm the developing fetus.

Does this mean the physicians will start advising women to quit drinking coffee while pregnant? Yes and no. Some doctors will certainly take this report to heart and encourage their patients to stay away from more than one cup of coffee a day, just as they recommend not drinking alcohol or smoking cigarettes. Others are not so convinced and doubt that this single study is enough to overturn the established guidelines of the American College of Obstetricians and Gynecologists. Instead, they believe that a lot more research needs to be done.

35. What is the main idea of the passage?

    A. Coffee carries some obvious health risks for people.

    B. Two cups of coffee a day may be enough to raise the risk of miscarriage.

    C. There is a link between miscarriages and morning sickness.

    D. Miscarriage rates are on the rise internationally.

36. What is the meaning of the word *overturn* in the last paragraph of the passage?

    A. Justify

    B. Invalidate

    C. Support

    D. Review

GO ON TO THE NEXT PAGE

37. Based on this passage, what can the reader infer about the advice physicians will give their pregnant patients about coffee consumption?

    A. Almost all of them will advise women to stop drinking any caffeine until after the baby is born.

    B. The majority will ignore the study altogether and continue to advise caffeine in moderation as before.

    C. All of them will demand additional research be done before they change what they tell their patients.

    D. Some will continue to make their normal recommendations about caffeine, while others will be more cautious than before.

38. Which of the following statements is an opinion?

    A. People continue to debate the risks of caffeine.

    B. Doctors studied the link between caffeine and miscarriage.

    C. To be safe, pregnant women must avoid coffee.

    D. Two cups of coffee hold about 200 mg of caffeine.

A New Vision for PE

In some schools around the country, physical education classes look a lot different than they did a generation or two ago. Kids are still in motion, stretching, running, lifting, and sweating. But instead of everyone doing the same activity at the same time as a team, they are exercising independently. They are being taught movements and activities that their teachers hope they will incorporate into their lives rather than just perform long enough to get a good grade.

By teaching kids the pleasure of exercise, gym teachers hope to instill important lessons about maintaining good health, staying fit, and keeping weight under control. Students can also participate in low-impact sports like yoga, martial arts, and weight lifting. Instead of playing basketball or baseball, they can focus on more general skills like passing the ball.

GO ON TO THE NEXT PAGE

A growing number of physical education (PE) teachers are also putting more of an emphasis on general nutrition and health. With the continual increase in the number of children who are obese, there is greater pressure to teach students how to stay fit. To do this, gym teachers have to look at new ways to introduce exercise to their students that will not intimidate or overwhelm them but instead intrigue and engage them.

One other difference found in some modern gym classes is the grading system. Instead of being graded on their ability to run laps in a set time or make a certain number of baskets, the students are graded simply on the effort they make in the class. Some even get extra credit if they are the sweatiest students in the room!

39. What would be the best title for this passage?

    A. "Being a Team in PE"
    B. "A New Kind of Grade"
    C. "Learning Martial Arts"
    D. "PE for School and Life"

40. What is the meaning of the word *instill* as used in the second paragraph of the passage?

    A. Impart
    B. Propagandize
    C. Demand
    D. Create

41. Which is *not* listed as an example of a low-impact sport?

    A. Martial arts
    B. Basketball
    C. Yoga
    D. Weight lifting

42. What can the reader infer about the "sweatiest students" referred to in the last sentence in the passage?

    A. These students are more overweight than anyone else.
    B. These students do not need extra credit.
    C. These students have worked harder during class.
    D. These students are behind all of their classmates.

GO ON TO THE NEXT PAGE

Studying Alzheimer's

Years of research have proven that Alzheimer's disease, along with other types of dementia, elevates the risk of dying early in the majority of patients. In a recent study performed by the Institute of Public Health at the University of Cambridge, scientists set out to determine exactly how long people were likely to survive following the onset of dementia.

Currently, approximately 24 million people throughout the world suffer from the memory loss and orientation confusion that comes with Alzheimer's disease and other forms of dementia. That number appears to double every 20 years, and experts predict that by the year 2040, there will be 81 million people living with some level of the condition. The more researchers and doctors can learn about what causes the problem, as well as how to treat it, the better prepared they will be to handle these millions of future patients.

To determine how people's life spans are affected by this medical condition, the scientists studied 13,000 seniors for a period of 14 years. During that time, 438 people developed dementia, the vast majority of whom died. The factors of age, disability, and gender were analyzed to see how they affected longevity as well.

Conclusions from the study showed that women tended to live slightly longer than men, averaging 4.6 years from the onset of dementia, as opposed to 4.1 years for men. The patients who were already weak or frail at the onset of the dementia died first, regardless of age. Marital status, living environment, and degree of mental decline, although relevant factors, were not shown to be influential.

Researchers from the University of Cambridge hope that this new information will help patients, clinicians, care providers, service providers, policy makers, and others who deal with dementia. The more they know, the better they will be able to respond to this heartbreaking condition.

43. What is the main idea of the passage?

    A. More than 24 million people suffer from some form of dementia.

    B. A recent study looked at the longevity of dementia sufferers.

    C. Women with dementia live slightly longer than men do.

    D. Dementia is a heartbreaking disease that is hard on families.

GO ON TO THE NEXT PAGE

44. What is the meaning of the word *onset* as used in the first paragraph?

    A. Cure rate

    B. Incubation period

    C. Remainder

    D. Commencement

45. What is the author's primary purpose in writing this essay?

    A. To persuade

    B. To entertain

    C. To inform

    D. To analyze

46. Identify the overall tone of the essay.

    A. Anxious

    B. Irate

    C. Indifferent

    D. Sympathetic

47. Choose the best summary of the passage.

    A. Marital status, age, and gender seem not to be issues in the longevity of patients who suffer from dementia. Out of 438 people with dementia, the vast majority were dead within a few years.

    B. In hopes of discovering information that can assist with care for dementia patients, Cambridge researchers studied 13,000 seniors. They found that dementia sufferers lived on average slightly longer than four years.

    C. Alzheimer's is just one form of dementia, a medical condition that affects millions and whose prevalence is expected to increase greatly over the next few decades.

    D. Researchers at Cambridge University have discovered that men with dementia live longer than women with the condition, but frailty is a definite indicator of an early death in patients with dementia.

GO ON TO THE NEXT PAGE

Comparative Life Expectancy

Where would you expect the United States to rank in life expectancy, the average number of years a person is expected to live? Near the top in the world, right? Well, surprise—we rank number 31, after Costa Rica and right before Cuba.

World Health Organization data from 2015 indicate that the average life expectancy worldwide is 71 years—slightly more for females and slightly less for males. In the United States, we beat that average by around eight years. Yet we are several years behind Japan, with a female life expectancy of 86.8 years, or Switzerland, with a male life expectancy of 81.3 years. Even relatively poor European countries, such as Slovenia, Cyprus, and Malta, do better than we do.

There are a number of indicators that lead to our low score among wealthy nations. Those include obesity and its accompanying heart disease and diabetes, car crash deaths, gun violence, and embarrassingly high infant mortality rates. We eat more, drive more, have more guns, and allow poor women to go through pregnancies unattended by regular physicians. There are many other health indicators that separate us from other developed nations, but most correspond to the extreme wealth inequities in the United States.

It is too soon to tell whether an increase in insured Americans will help to turn this distasteful data around. Certainly those nations with universal health care have better numbers than we do. Much of our problem has to do with lifestyles that will not be easy to alter. We continue to build living spaces that are not walkable, to work long hours and drive long distances, to overeat—and we love our Second Amendment right to bear arms. It is difficult to imagine how we will overcome these realities and improve our longevity status.

48. What is the overall tone of the essay?

A. Apathetic
B. Fascinated
C. Discouraged
D. Hopeful

49. Which of the following is *not* listed as a detail in the passage?

   A. Malta beats the United States in life expectancy.

   B. Japan's male life expectancy is 80.5 years.

   C. Heart disease contributes to low life expectancy.

   D. US infant mortality rates are quite high.

50. A reader might infer from this passage that _____.

   A. obesity can be detrimental to a long life

   B. car crashes are most frequent in the United States

   C. the Second Amendment should be overturned

   D. people in Asia and Africa have the shortest life spans

**STOP. IF YOU HAVE TIME LEFT OVER,
CHECK YOUR WORK ON THIS SECTION ONLY.**

VOCABULARY AND GENERAL KNOWLEDGE

50 items | Suggested time: 45 minutes

1. Select the meaning of the underlined word in the following sentence.

   The chemicals in plastic containers may be <u>deleterious</u> to children's health.

   A. Harmful
   B. Deleting
   C. Delightful
   D. Inoffensive

2. What is another word for *deferentially*?

   A. Imperfectly
   B. Respectfully
   C. Competently
   D. Energetically

3. What is the meaning of *perused*?

   A. Passed judgment on
   B. Engaged in
   C. Read thoroughly
   D. Took notes about

4. Select the meaning of the underlined word in the following sentence.

   What is the <u>prognosis</u> for those accident victims?

   A. Expected outcome
   B. Treatment option
   C. Fabrication
   D. Hindsight

| GO ON TO THE NEXT PAGE |

5. If a patient's condition is upgraded, he is _____.

  A. getting worse
  B. improving in status
  C. released from the hospital
  D. approved for surgery

6. *Concise* is best defined as being _____.

  A. exact
  B. brief
  C. accurate
  D. assembled

7. Select the meaning of the underlined word in the following sentence.

  The night nursing staff is <u>accountable</u> for those records.

  A. Receptive
  B. Notorious
  C. Responsible
  D. Preoccupied with

8. A blood vessel that is distended is _____.

  A. overturned
  B. swollen
  C. twisted
  D. overlong

9. Something that is viscous is thick and sticky. Another word for this might be _____.

  A. gelatinous
  B. molten
  C. fluid
  D. malleable

10. An overt symptom is _____.

  A. dangerous
  B. hidden
  C. obvious
  D. controlled

GO ON TO THE NEXT PAGE

11. What is another word for *toxin*?

    A. Impurity
    B. Element
    C. Remedy
    D. Poison

12. Select the meaning of the underlined word in the following sentence.

    The pain of childbirth may often be <u>acute</u>.

    A. Escalating
    B. Emergent
    C. Eased
    D. Intense

13. Select the meaning of the underlined word in the following sentence.

    We will do more tests, as the data so far are <u>inconclusive</u>.

    A. Unsettled
    B. Convincing
    C. Unfavorable
    D. Bewildering

14. Which word names an infected swelling with liquid inside?

    A. Blast
    B. Gash
    C. Hive
    D. Boil

15. What is another word for *asymmetric*?

    A. Uneven
    B. Impartial
    C. Proportionate
    D. Magnified

GO ON TO THE NEXT PAGE

16. What is the meaning of *counterfeit*?

  A. Over-the-counter
  B. Foreign
  C. Fake
  D. Unidentified

17. What is the best description for the word *efficacy* in the following sentence?

  The quality, safety, and efficacy of counterfeit medicines are not known.

  A. Effectiveness
  B. Significance
  C. Corollary
  D. Conclusion

18. If illegal operators are *posing* as licensed pharmacists, what are they doing?

  A. Modeling
  B. Inquiring
  C. Positioning
  D. Pretending

19. One muscle in the shoulder is the _____.

  A. dendrite
  B. delphic
  C. deltoid
  D. dentate

20. Select the meaning of the underlined word in the following sentence.

  It is a clear, yellowish liquid having a peculiar <u>ethereal</u>, fruity odor.

  A. Aerated
  B. Incapacitating
  C. Delicate
  D. Distinctive

| GO ON TO THE NEXT PAGE |

21. The voice box may be called the _____.

    A. larynx

    B. lynx

    C. pharynx

    D. phalanx

22. Select the meaning of the underlined word in the following sentence.

    The interns observed the <u>contour</u> of the patient's rash.

    A. Shape

    B. Answers

    C. Amount

    D. Extension

23. What is the meaning of *incorrigible*?

    A. Clever

    B. Potential

    C. Undistinguished

    D. Incurable

24. Select the meaning of the underlined word in the following sentence.

    The patient will need to <u>undergo</u> additional testing.

    A. Fail

    B. Offer

    C. Experience

    D. Succumb

25. *Ventral* refers to which part of the body?

    A. Front

    B. Bottom

    C. Top

    D. Back

GO ON TO THE NEXT PAGE

26. What is the best description for the term *anodyne*?

    A. Emulsified

    B. Liquefied

    C. Contaminated

    D. Painkilling

27. Select the meaning of the underlined word in the following sentence.

    At this point, we are providing mainly <u>palliative</u> care.

    A. Scientific

    B. Surgical

    C. Soothing

    D. Serious

28. What does *plastic* mean?

    A. Mechanical

    B. Durable

    C. Authentic

    D. Flexible

29. Select the meaning of the underlined word in the following sentence.

    The patient is lying <u>prone</u> next to the monitor.

    A. Face down

    B. Immovable

    C. Face up

    D. Asleep

30. What is the best description for the term *euphoric*?

    A. Disease-ridden

    B. High-spirited

    C. Pretentious

    D. Understated

GO ON TO THE NEXT PAGE

31. Another word for the gonads might be the _____.

    A. sperm

    B. vagina

    C. testes

    D. pelvis

32. What is another word for *deluge*?

    A. Earthquake

    B. Dimness

    C. Downpour

    D. Chasm

33. Select the meaning of the underlined word in the following sentence.

    In children with high fevers, the use of aspirin is underlined contraindicated.

    A. Banned

    B. Inadvisable

    C. Anticipated

    D. Expedient

34. A sore with disintegration of tissue might be called an _____.

    A. allergy

    B. erythema

    C. alopecia

    D. ulcer

35. Select the meaning of the underlined word in the following sentence.

    Quick action kept the disease from permeating the general population.

    A. Conquering

    B. Wounding

    C. Deterring

    D. Infiltrating

GO ON TO THE NEXT PAGE

36. A treatment that is detrimental is _____.

    A. risk-free

    B. destructive

    C. agonizing

    D. effective

37. To censure something is to _____.

    A. inspect it

    B. denounce it

    C. admire it

    D. overlook it

38. The abbreviation *DTs* on a patient's chart stands for _____.

    A. deep tendon reflex

    B. descending thorax

    C. delirium tremens

    D. dextrose in water

39. Select the meaning of the underlined word in the following sentence.

    He made a <u>posthumous</u> donation to the clinic.

    A. Generous

    B. Immense

    C. Postmortem

    D. Time-honored

40. Pulse, temperature, and respiration are known as _____.

    A. vital signs

    B. vital statistics

    C. vital force

    D. vital capacity

GO ON TO THE NEXT PAGE

41. Select the meaning of the underlined word in the following sentence.

> The children became <u>bellicose</u> after too much time in the moving car.

A. Beautiful
B. Selfless
C. Tolerant
D. Quarrelsome

42. In the world of pharmaceuticals, a recall policy is a policy involving the _____.

A. ability to remember
B. the withdrawal of products
C. manufacture of cosmetics
D. effectiveness of customers

43. What is the best description for the phrase *monitor progress* in the following sentence?

> The agency will monitor progress of the pilot program, reviewing reports and conducting our own inspections if necessary.

A. Watch over modernization
B. Take charge of expansion
C. Keep an eye on improvement
D. Pore over succession

44. What is the best description of an *audit check*?

A. A restraint on appraisals
B. A payment for inventory
C. A test of hearing
D. A review or inspection

45. HPV is likely to involve the _____.

A. skull and spine
B. mucous membranes
C. kidneys
D. heart

GO ON TO THE NEXT PAGE

46. Select the meaning of the underlined word in the following sentence.

All <u>volatile</u> liquids should be stored and labeled correctly.

   A. Unstable
   B. Abnormal
   C. Lethal
   D. Blended

47. To vivify someone is to _____.

   A. belittle him
   B. animate him
   C. alarm him
   D. spoil him

48. A truculent patient is _____.

   A. exhausted
   B. irresponsible
   C. supportive
   D. argumentative

49. If patients are being counseled, what is happening?

   A. They are being comforted.
   B. They are being advised.
   C. They are being deceived.
   D. They are being healed.

50. Select the meaning of the underlined word in the following sentence.

Apply the gel on the gingival <u>margin</u> around the selected teeth using the blunt-tipped applicator included in the package.

   A. Edge
   B. Grease
   C. Incisor
   D. Cavity

**STOP. IF YOU HAVE TIME LEFT OVER,
CHECK YOUR WORK ON THIS SECTION ONLY.**

GRAMMAR

| 50 items | Suggested time: 45 minutes |

1. Which sentence is written correctly?

   A. Having finished the exam early Rudy checked it over for errors.

   B. Having finished the exam early Rudy checked, it over for errors.

   C. Having finished the exam early, Rudy checked it over for errors.

   D. Having finished, the exam early, Rudy checked it over for errors.

2. Select the phrase that will make the following sentence grammatically correct.

   Before I had finished supper, James _____.

   A. is texting me on my cell phone
   B. had texted me on my cell phone
   C. texts me on my cell phone
   D. texting me on my cell phone

3. In the following sentence, what part of speech is the word *four*?

   Everyone in the fraternity found the four boys' pranks sophomoric.

   A. Adverb
   B. Conjunction
   C. Adjective
   D. Noun

| **GO ON TO THE NEXT PAGE** |

4. Which sentence is grammatically correct?

    A. The geese were flying south in a V formation with hikers on the mountain spotting them.

    B. As the geese flew south, hikers were on the mountain, spotting the geese in a V formation.

    C. Hikers on the mountain spotted geese flying south in a V formation.

    D. In a V formation, geese flying south spotted hikers on the mountain.

5. Which word is used incorrectly in the following sentence?

The professor was formally an intern in this very hospital back in the 1980s.

    A. professor
    B. formally
    C. intern
    D. very

6. Select the correct word for the blank in the following sentence.

The children and _____ performed a skit for the elderly patients.

    A. he
    B. me
    C. them
    D. her

7. What word is best to substitute for the underlined words in the following sentence?

The nurse left the room to look for the paperwork <u>the nurse</u> had misplaced.

    A. her
    B. he
    C. his
    D. it

GO ON TO THE NEXT PAGE

8. Which word is used incorrectly in the following sentence?

    That is the doctor who's diploma is hung on the partition.

    A. That
    B. who's
    C. hung
    D. partition

9. Which of the following words fits best in the following sentence?

    _____ the emergency room was not busy last night, the head nurse still did not let anyone end her shift early.

    A. Because
    B. Provided that
    C. As if
    D. Although

10. What punctuation is needed in the following sentence to make it correct?

    Nurse Henry requisitioned a number of items, including pens, pencils, and paper

    A. Period
    B. Question mark
    C. Comma
    D. Colon

11. Which of the following is spelled correctly?

    A. Amature
    B. Amerture
    C. Amateur
    D. Ameteur

GO ON TO THE NEXT PAGE

12. Select the word or phrase that makes the following sentence grammatically correct.

Kalinda spends part of her day _____ data from the lab.

A. inputs
B. input
C. having input
D. inputting

13. Select the word in the following sentence that is *not* used correctly.

On departing, the patient complimented her therapist and councilor.

A. departing
B. complimented
C. therapist
D. councilor

14. Select the word that makes the following sentence grammatically correct.

Having _____ one pill at bedtime, the patient was able to sleep for eight hours.

A. took
B. take
C. taking
D. taken

15. Which sentence is grammatically correct?

A. Tapping the beat, Ms. Schuster led the chorus in song.
B. Ms. Schuster led the chorus in song tapping the beat.
C. Ms. Schuster led the chorus, tapping the beat, in song.
D. Tapping the beat, the chorus was led in song by Ms. Schuster.

GO ON TO THE NEXT PAGE

16. Select the word that makes the following sentence grammatically correct.

    One out of four doctors _____ to this plan.

    A. subscribe
    B. subscribes
    C. subscribing
    D. are subscribed

17. What word is best to substitute for the underlined words in the following sentence?

    The doctor and I went over <u>the doctor's and my</u> notes.

    A. his
    B. their
    C. our
    D. mine

18. Which word is *not* spelled correctly in the context of the following sentence?

    The principle role of this clinic has to do with the provision of convenient care.

    A. principle
    B. role
    C. provision
    D. convenient

19. What punctuation is needed in the following sentence to make it correct?

    Dr. Levine could not answer all of our questions she promised to research the topic and return with a recommendation the next day.

    A. Colon
    B. Question mark
    C. Comma
    D. Semicolon

GO ON TO THE NEXT PAGE

20. What type of sentence is shown below?

    The bird's mangled wing would keep it from flying for many months.

    A. Simple
    B. Compound
    C. Complex
    D. Compound-complex

21. Which sentence is written correctly?

    A. Since completing the technical course Jasper has had several offers.
    B. Since completing the technical course, Jasper has had several offers.
    C. Since completing, the technical course, Jasper has had several offers.
    D. Since completing the technical course; Jasper has had several offers.

22. Select the phrase that makes the following sentence grammatically correct.

    There is a fountain _____ the driveway and the main entrance.

    A. among
    B. between
    C. by way of
    D. in conjunction with

23. Which is a past tense verb in the sentence below?

    Last year, Robert played football and ran track, but this year, he will be on the debate team and play soccer.

    A. played
    B. will be
    C. play
    D. debate

GO ON TO THE NEXT PAGE

24. Select the word that makes the following sentence grammatically correct.

> Mary Ann gave _____ credit for studying so hard and passing the test.

A. oneself
B. itself
C. herself
D. themselves

25. Which sentence is the clearest?

A. In the mailbox there was a note from her boyfriend.
B. From her boyfriend, there was a note in the mailbox.
C. There was in the mailbox a note from her boyfriend.
D. In the mailbox there was from her boyfriend a note.

26. Select the word or phrase that is misplaced in the following sentence.

> In the apartment house, the car with the white roof and new tires belongs to our friends.

A. In the apartment house
B. with the white roof
C. and new tires
D. to our friends

27. Select the word or phrase that makes the following sentence grammatically correct.

> The students promised _____ themselves with quiet dignity.

A. conduct
B. conducting
C. to conduct
D. to be conducted

GO ON TO THE NEXT PAGE

28. Select the phrase in the following sentence that is *not* used correctly.

     Before their hospitalization, the children had rarely eat three meals a day.

     A. Before their
     B. children had
     C. had rarely
     D. rarely eat

29. Select the word or phrase that makes the following sentence grammatically correct.

     If Angela attends the seminar tomorrow, she _____ the employee discount.

     A. gave
     B. gives
     C. will given
     D. will be given

30. What punctuation is needed in the following sentence to make it correct?

     Because of a major accident on the freeway the emergency room was overcrowded.

     A. Period
     B. Comma
     C. Exclamation point
     D. Semicolon

31. Select the phrase that will make the following sentence grammatically correct.

     Dr. Johnson had a serious look when he _____.

     A. spoke to the patient's parents
     B. is speaking to the patient's parents
     C. will speak to the patient's parents
     D. has spoken to the patient's parents

GO ON TO THE NEXT PAGE

32. Which word is used incorrectly in the following sentence?

    The boys leapt up happy to assist their favorite teacher.

    A. leapt
    B. happy
    C. assist
    D. their

33. Select the sentence that is grammatically correct.

    A. Nurse Lin asked she and I for our opinion.
    B. Nurse Lin asked me and her for our opinion.
    C. Nurse Lin asked her and me for our opinion.
    D. Nurse Lin asked her and I for our opinion.

34. What word is best to substitute for the underlined words in the following sentence?

    Mr. Menotti's wife collected <u>Mr. Menotti's</u> belongings for the ride home.

    A. her
    B. him
    C. he
    D. his

35. Which sentence is grammatically correct?

    A. The professor explained the chemical reaction to me.
    B. The professor explained the chemical reaction to I.
    C. The professor explained the chemical reaction to myself.
    D. The professor explained the chemical reaction to mine.

36. What punctuation is needed in the following sentence to make it correct?

    In addition to the hospitals regularly scheduled festivities, the custodians celebrate with a party of their own.

    A. Period
    B. Comma
    C. Apostrophe
    D. Semicolon

GO ON TO THE NEXT PAGE

37. Which of the following is spelled correctly?

    A. Perseptable
    B. Perseptible
    C. Perceptable
    D. Perceptible

38. Which word is used incorrectly in the following sentence?

    Everybody pretends to do so, but few truly understands the essay.

    A. pretends
    B. truly
    C. understands
    D. essay

39. Which word or phrase fits best in the following sentence?

    Cathy asked many questions the first time she _____ at the hospital.

    A. volunteered
    B. volunteering
    C. was volunteered
    D. volunteer

40. Which word is *not* used correctly in the context of the following sentence?

    Does your grimace infer that you loathed the performance?

    A. grimace
    B. infer
    C. loathed
    D. performance

41. Which sentence is grammatically correct?

    A. We saw a car parked behind the building with silver tires.
    B. Behind the building, we saw a car parked with silver tires.
    C. Parked behind the building, we saw a car with silver tires.
    D. We saw a car with silver tires parked behind the building.

GO ON TO THE NEXT PAGE

42. Select the word that makes the following sentence grammatically correct.

One of the students _____ completed the course.

A. have
B. has
C. are
D. is

43. What punctuation is needed in the following sentence to make it correct?

The days seem long but the nights seem even longer.

A. Period
B. Comma
C. Colon
D. Apostrophe

44. What is the simple predicate of the sentence below?

Too many potential job choices put Elba Dean in a quandary.

A. too
B. potential
C. put
D. quandary

45. What word is best to substitute for the underlined words in the following sentence?

You can hear <u>the nurses'</u> laughter all the way down the hallway.

A. his
B. hers
C. them
D. their

GO ON TO THE NEXT PAGE

46. Which word is used incorrectly in the following sentence?

> Moving stealthy, the sneaky little boy reached for the cookie jar on the topmost shelf.

A. stealthy
B. sneaky
C. reached
D. topmost

47. Which sentence is the clearest?

A. I saw the criminals who were arrested on the TV news.
B. I saw the criminals on the TV news who were arrested.
C. On the TV news, the criminals who were arrested were seen by me.
D. On the TV news, I saw the criminals who were arrested.

48. Select the phrase or clause that is misplaced in the following sentence.

> At a presentation he informed us about the dangers of drugs and alcohol in the auditorium.

A. At a presentation
B. about the dangers
C. of drugs and alcohol
D. in the auditorium

49. Select the word that will make the following sentence grammatically correct.

> The lounge needs a thorough cleaning, _____ the windows must be washed.

A. or
B. and
C. but
D. yet

GO ON TO THE NEXT PAGE

50. Which sentence is grammatically correct?

A. Maria planted a pear tree in her orchard of apple trees; it was small.

B. The pear tree in Maria's apple orchard was planted when it was small.

C. Maria planted a small pear tree among the apple trees in her orchard.

D. Having planted a small pear tree, apple trees grew in Maria's orchard.

STOP. IF YOU HAVE TIME LEFT OVER, CHECK YOUR WORK ON THIS SECTION ONLY.

BASIC MATH SKILLS

50 items | Suggested time: 45 minutes

1. Multiply and simplify: $\frac{2}{3} \times 2\frac{1}{8} =$

   A. $1\frac{7}{24}$
   B. $1\frac{5}{12}$
   C. $1\frac{11}{12}$
   D. $2\frac{1}{24}$

2. Emma Lee is 65 inches tall. How many meters is that?

   A. 1.65 meters
   B. 1.98 meters
   C. 5.42 meters
   D. 6.50 meters

3. If a party planner assumes 2 bottles of sparkling water per 5 guests, how many bottles must she purchase for a party of 145?

   A. 27
   B. 36
   C. 49
   D. 58

4. Stu purchased a set of 6 cups and 6 plates at a garage sale. The cups were 25 cents apiece, and the plates were 75 cents apiece. If Stu paid with a $10 bill, how much change was he owed?

   A. $4
   B. $4.50
   C. $5
   D. $5.50

5. Express 1.25 as a fraction in lowest terms.

   A. $1\frac{1}{25}$
   B. $1\frac{2}{5}$
   C. $1\frac{1}{2}$
   D. $1\frac{1}{4}$

GO ON TO THE NEXT PAGE

6. Zane wants to put a border along one side of his 17-foot-long driveway. The border material is sold by the whole yard. How many yards will he need to purchase?

    A. 2 yards

    B. 6 yards

    C. 20 yards

    D. 51 yards

7. Mr. Voelkle has to order supplies for his class to do a science project. Each student needs a pumpkin, a small bottle of vinegar, and a box of baking soda. Pumpkins are $5 each, a bottle of vinegar is $2, and a box of baking soda is $1. Mr. Voelkle has 23 students in his class. How much will the supplies cost? (Enter numeric value only.) _____

8. In an electrical panel with 30 circuit breakers, 4 of them are off. What is the ratio of breakers that are on to breakers that are off?

    A. 13:2

    B. 4:13

    C. 2:15

    D. 2:13

9. If $\dfrac{2}{x}+5=6$, what is the value of x? (Enter numeric value only.)

_____

10. Approximately how many ounces are in 60 mL?

    A. 0.49 ounces

    B. 2.03 ounces

    C. 29.6 ounces

    D. 30.4 ounces

11. Express 204% as a mixed number.

    A. $2\frac{1}{25}$

    B. $2\frac{4}{25}$

    C. $2\frac{2}{5}$

    D. $2\frac{4}{5}$

GO ON TO THE NEXT PAGE

12. What is the least common denominator of $\frac{1}{6}$ and $\frac{1}{15}$? (Enter numeric value only.)

   _____

13. Lights out on the base is at 10:30 P.M. What would that be in military time?

   A. 1030
   B. 1300
   C. 1230
   D. 2230

14. A recent census of visitors to a popular beach showed that there was a ratio of 6:16 surfers to swimmers. Which of the following is a possible actual number of surfers and swimmers at the beach?

   A. 60:165
   B. 72:210
   C. 120:300
   D. 210:560

15. Divide and simplify: $3\frac{1}{2} \div 1\frac{1}{10} =$

   A. $3\frac{1}{20}$
   B. $3\frac{2}{11}$
   C. $3\frac{1}{5}$
   D. $3\frac{2}{23}$

16. Lenore's weekly paycheck is $434.79. Of that, she puts $\frac{1}{3}$ aside for her share of rent and utilities and spends $75 on groceries. What is left from her weekly paycheck?

   A. $219.93
   B. $214.86
   C. $204.26
   D. $192.76

17. Nurse Morgan ordered 6 reams of paper at $8.99 per ream and 10 boxes of envelopes at $3.99 a box. How much did she spend in all? (Enter numeric value only. If rounding is necessary, round to the dollar.)

   _____

GO ON TO THE NEXT PAGE

18. Of the 1,525 homes sold by Homestyle Realty last year, Clara sold 244. What percentage of the homes did she sell?

A. 16%

B. 18%

C. 22%

D. 24%

19. How many centimeters are there in 1 foot?

A. 4.72 centimeters

B. 10 centimeters

C. 25.4 centimeters

D. 30.48 centimeters

20. In a scale drawing for a toy rocket, 1 inch = 6 inches. If the rocket is 6 inches tall on the drawing, how tall will it be in reality?

A. 1 foot

B. 6 feet

C. 1 yard

D. 2 yards

21. Add: 7.34 + 3.74 + 4.37 =

A. 14.45

B. 14.55

C. 15.45

D. 15.55

22. Three cups are approximately how many liters?

A. 0.71 liters

B. 0.75 liters

C. 1.06 liters

D. 1.35 liters

23. Add and simplify: $2/15 + 1/12 =$

A. $1/9$

B. $13/60$

C. $7/15$

D. $11/12$

GO ON TO THE NEXT PAGE

24. If Dr. Bumguardner's class has 75 students and 30 of them are women, what is the ratio of women to the total number of students in the class?

   A. 2:5

   B. 2:3

   C. 1:4

   D. 3:5

25. Which of the following is a solution to $|x-1| = 3$?

   A. −4

   B. −3

   C. −2

   D. 2

26. A gross is equal to 12 dozen. If Lanyard Farms sells 15 gross of eggs a week and packages them in one dozen egg containers, how many containers do they need for a week's worth of eggs?

   A. 15

   B. 150

   C. 180

   D. 2,160

27. Andy weighs 154 pounds. Approximately how many kilograms does he weigh? (Enter numeric value only.) _____

28. Divide: $727 \div 6 =$

   A. 120 r1

   B. 120 r3

   C. 121 r1

   D. 127 r3

GO ON TO THE NEXT PAGE

29. If Latoya spends 15 minutes every day practicing her flute, how much time does she spend practicing over a period of two weeks?

    A. 1 hour 45 minutes
    B. 2 hours 30 minutes
    C. 3 hours 30 minutes
    D. 3 hours 45 minutes

30. What is 35% of 70?

    A. 17.5
    B. 24.5
    C. 35
    D. 50

31. Express $^{17}/_5$ as a decimal.

    A. 0.034
    B. 0.34
    C. 3.4
    D. 34

32. How many ounces are in 14.25 pounds?

    A. 228 ounces
    B. 171 ounces
    C. 114 ounces
    D. 57 ounces

33. Express the ratio of 13:60 as a percentage.

    A. 19.5%
    B. 22%
    C. 25.5%
    D. 31%

34. If blank CDs cost 36 cents for two, how much does it cost to buy 10 blank CDs?

    A. $0.90
    B. $1.35
    C. $1.80
    D. $3.60

GO ON TO THE NEXT PAGE

35. What date in Arabic numerals is Roman numeral MCMLV? (Enter numeric value only.)

_____

36. Lulu is 5 years younger than her sister, who is 7 years older than their 15-year-old cousin. How old is Lulu?

A. 27
B. 22
C. 19
D. 17

37. Express 0.05 as a percent.

A. 0.05%
B. 0.5%
C. 5%
D. 50%

38. At a used book store, Nicholle paid $2 each for 7 paperbacks and $6 each for 3 hardcover books. She gave the cashier a $50 bill. How much change did she receive? (Enter numeric value only.)

_____

39. If the outside temperature is currently 22 degrees on the Celsius scale, what is the approximate temperature on the Fahrenheit scale?

A. 56°F
B. 62°F
C. 66.5°F
D. 71.6°F

GO ON TO THE NEXT PAGE

40. If $\frac{2x}{3} - 6 = 17$, what is the value of x?

A. 34.5
B. 23.0
C. 16.5
D. 15.3

41. A team from the highway department can replace 14 streetlights in 7 hours of work. If they work a 30-hour week at this job, in how many weeks will they replace all 120 downtown streetlights?

A. 1½ weeks
B. 2 weeks
C. 2½ weeks
D. 3 weeks

42. Divide: $4.5 \div 0.9 =$

A. 0.05
B. 0.5
C. 5
D. 50

43. Subtract and simplify: $\frac{4}{10} - \frac{1}{4} =$

A. $\frac{5}{20}$
B. $\frac{3}{10}$
C. $\frac{3}{20}$
D. $\frac{9}{40}$

44. At Bethesda Elementary, the student to teacher ratio is 20:1. If there are 360 students, how many teachers are there? (Enter numeric value only.) _____

GO ON TO THE NEXT PAGE

45. Subtract and simplify: $5\frac{1}{4} - 3\frac{5}{6} =$

   A. $2\frac{1}{6}$

   B. $1\frac{1}{2}$

   C. $1\frac{7}{24}$

   D. $1\frac{5}{12}$

46. Express 18.3% as a decimal.

   A. 183

   B. 18.3

   C. 1.83

   D. 0.183

47. If $2x + 1 = y$, what is the value of x when $y = 7$?

   A. 3

   B. 9

   C. 14

   D. 15

48. If a crate weighs 68 kilograms, how many pounds does it weigh?

   A. 217.6 pounds

   B. 149.6 pounds

   C. 136.0 pounds

   D. 30.9 pounds

49. The nursing staff is currently composed of 20 female and 5 male nurses. Over the next year, the clinic hopes to increase the male nursing staff to equal at least 25% of the total nursing staff. If everyone now working retains his or her job, what is the least number of people the clinic will need to hire? (Enter numeric value only.)

_____

50. How many ounces are there in 4 cups?

   A. 16 ounces

   B. 24 ounces

   C. 28 ounces

   D. 32 ounces

STOP. IF YOU HAVE TIME LEFT OVER, CHECK YOUR WORK ON THIS SECTION ONLY.

BIOLOGY

| 25 items | Suggested time: 21 minutes |

1. Which organelle is the site of protein synthesis?

    A. Mitochondrion
    B. Vacuole
    C. Cell membrane
    D. Ribosome

2. What happens to glucose during glycolysis?

    A. Its energy is entirely lost.
    B. It splits into molecules of pyruvic acid.
    C. It is stored in NADH.
    D. It joins with molecules of citric acid.

3. What process do cells in the tip of a plant's root undergo to increase in number?

    A. Meiosis
    B. Cytokinesis
    C. Fractioning
    D. Mitosis

4. How do RNA and DNA derive their names?

    A. From the sugar each contains
    B. From the structure of their nucleotides
    C. From the information they transfer
    D. From their formative processes

5. Huntington's disease is carried on the dominant allele. In a situation where two heterozygous parents have the disease, what percentage of their offspring are predicted to be disease-free?

    A. 0%
    B. 25%
    C. 50%
    D. 100%

GO ON TO THE NEXT PAGE

6. If bacteria are placed in a strong solution of salt water, they will shrink as water moves out of the bacteria. What is this process called?

   A. Dehydration synthesis
   B. Hydrolysis
   C. Osmosis
   D. Isotonic transport

7. Which animal has an open transport system?

   A. Grasshopper
   B. Earthworm
   C. Dolphin
   D. Chicken

8. How does an enzyme work on a chemical reaction that occurs in a substrate?

   A. An enzyme slows down the chemical reaction.
   B. An enzyme speeds up the chemical reaction.
   C. An enzyme has no effect on the chemical reaction.
   D. An enzyme stops most chemical reactions.

9. Where is the ovary located in a flowering plant?

   A. Anther
   B. Stamen
   C. Pistil
   D. Calyx

10. Two organisms live in a relationship from which both benefit. What is this called?

    A. Competition
    B. Parasitism
    C. Commensalism
    D. Mutualism

GO ON TO THE NEXT PAGE

11. Which gives the order of four taxonomic categories from least to most specific?

A. Kingdom, phylum, class, order
B. Kingdom, phylum, order, class
C. Kingdom, order, phylum, class
D. Kingdom, class, order, phylum

12. Which molecules contain only carbon, hydrogen, and oxygen?

A. Lipids and proteins
B. Carbohydrates and lipids
C. Proteins and carbohydrates
D. Nucleic acids and proteins

13. Which structure is found in protists but not in monerans?

A. Golgi apparatus
B. Chromosome
C. Cytoplasm
D. Cell membrane

14. How does yeast reproduce?

A. Binary fission
B. Spore formation
C. Budding
D. Cloning

15. What takes place during anaphase?

A. Chromosomes move to opposite ends of the spindle.
B. Nuclear membrane and nucleoli disintegrate.
C. Chromatids line up at the center of the spindle.
D. Nuclear membrane and nucleoli form.

16. Which is *not* found in the nucleotide of DNA?

A. Simple sugar
B. Nitrogen base
C. Phosphate group
D. Citric acid

GO ON TO THE NEXT PAGE

17. Hemophilia is a sex-linked trait carried on the X chromosome. In an example of a male with hemophilia and a female carrier, what ratio of the offspring are predicted neither to carry nor to manifest the disease?

   A. 0 female : 1 male
   B. 1 female : 1 male
   C. 1 female : 0 male
   D. 2 female : 1 male

18. Which is *not* a product of the Krebs cycle?

   A. ATP
   B. Carbon dioxide
   C. Glucose
   D. NADH

19. A student was asked to count birds in a given location over a 24-hour period. Which count would make her data most valid?

   A. Count birds at one feeder every 6 hours.
   B. Count birds at three feeders at noon and 6:00 P.M.
   C. Count birds at one feeder at noon and 6:00 P.M.
   D. Count birds at three feeders every 6 hours.

20. Whose efficiency of energy is greater?

   A. Herbivore
   B. Carnivore
   C. Omnivore
   D. Decomposer

GO ON TO THE NEXT PAGE

21. How should a researcher test the hypothesis that radiation from cell phones is significant enough to raise the temperature of water in a test tube?

A. Dial a cell phone that rests beside a test tube of water, let it ring for two minutes, and record the temperature of the water before and after the two-minute interval.

B. Dial a cell phone that rests beside a test tube of water; let it ring for two, three, and four minutes; and record the temperature of the water before and after each interval.

C. Use three different brands of cell phone; dial each as it rests beside its own test tube of water, let it ring for two minutes, and record the temperature of the water before and after the two-minute interval.

D. Use three different brands of cell phone, dial each and let one ring for two minutes, one for three minutes, and one for four minutes; record the temperature of the water before and after each interval.

22. What is the function of decomposition in the carbon cycle?

A. To produce light energy
B. To convert carbon to fuel
C. To release carbon dioxide
D. To store food for consumers

23. What is the basal metabolic rate?

A. The number of calories burned at peak performance
B. The number of calories burned at rest
C. The amount of time needed to burn 100 calories
D. The amount of time needed for the body to turn glucose into energy

24. Which bacteria are spherical in shape?

A. Clostridia
B. Bacilli
C. Spirilla
D. Cocci

GO ON TO THE NEXT PAGE

25. What is the term for the breakdown of glycogen into glucose subunits?

A. Hydrolysis
B. Reduction
C. Metabolism
D. Transpiration

**STOP. IF YOU HAVE TIME LEFT OVER,
CHECK YOUR WORK ON THIS SECTION ONLY.**

CHEMISTRY

25 items | Suggested time: 21 minutes

1. The energy required to remove the outermost electron from an atom is called _____.

   A. covalent bonding
   B. electronegativity
   C. atomic radius
   D. ionization energy

2. In the presence of an acid, what color is phenolphthalein?

   A. Clear
   B. Blue
   C. Pink
   D. Red

3. Fifty-six kg of a radioactive substance has a half-life of 12 days. How many days will it take the substance to decay naturally to only 7 kg?

   A. 8 days
   B. 12 days
   C. 36 days
   D. 48 days

4. Which compound contains a polar covalent bond?

   A. O_2
   B. F_2
   C. Br_2
   D. H_2O

5. $AB \rightarrow A + B$ represents what type of chemical reaction?

   A. Synthesis
   B. Decomposition
   C. Single replacement
   D. Double replacement

GO ON TO THE NEXT PAGE

6. Among the following elements, which is a nonmetal?

A. Mercury

B. Magnesium

C. Sulfur

D. Potassium

7. You contain two odorous gases in vials with porous plugs. Gas A has twice the mass of Gas B. Which observation is most likely?

A. You will smell Gas A before you smell Gas B.

B. You will smell Gas B before you smell Gas A.

C. You will smell Gas A but not Gas B.

D. You will smell Gas B but not Gas A.

8. The three important allotrophic forms of phosphorus are red, white, and _____.

A. green

B. gray

C. silver

D. black

9. Here are the solubilities of four substances at 0°C, in grams of solute per 100 mL of water.

Solid citric acid	49
Solid potassium phosphate	44
Gaseous nitrogen	0.0030
Gaseous oxygen	0.0070

If the temperature increases to 20°C, what would you expect to happen to the solubility figures?

A. Citric acid and potassium phosphate will decrease; nitrogen and oxygen will increase.

B. Citric acid and potassium phosphate will increase; nitrogen and oxygen will decrease.

C. All four figures will increase.

D. All four figures will decrease.

GO ON TO THE NEXT PAGE

10. What is the name of the compound CH_3-CH_2-CH_2-CH_3?

    A. Cyclobutane

    B. Butane

    C. Butene

    D. Butyne

11. When balanced, the reaction $Fe + O_2 \rightarrow Fe_2O_3$ will be

    _____

    A. $2Fe + 2O_2 \rightarrow 3Fe_2O_3$

    B. $4Fe + 6O_2 \rightarrow 6Fe_2O_3$

    C. $2Fe + 3O_2 \rightarrow 2Fe_2O_3$

    D. $4Fe + 3O_2 \rightarrow 2Fe_2O_3$

12. Which two elements are most alike in reactivity?

    A. He and H

    B. K and Ar

    C. Cl and P

    D. Ba and Mg

13. How many electrons are shared in a single covalent bond?

    A. 1

    B. 2

    C. 3

    D. 4

14. How many neutrons are in an atom of carbon-12?

    A. 2

    B. 4

    C. 6

    D. 24

15. What is the correct electron configuration for magnesium?

    A. $1s^2 2s^2$

    B. $1s^2 2s^2 2p^6$

    C. $1s^2 2s^2 2p^6 3s^2 3p^1$

    D. $1s^2 2s^2 2p^6 3s^2$

GO ON TO THE NEXT PAGE

16. What is the molarity of a solution containing 0.45 moles of NaCl in 4 liters?

    A. 0.11 M NaCl

    B. 0.45 M NaCl

    C. 1.8 M NaCl

    D. 8.9 M NaCl

17. Where would you expect tap water to fall on the pH scale?

    A. Between 1 and 3

    B. Between 4 and 6

    C. Between 6 and 8

    D. Between 8 and 10

18. To the nearest whole number, what is the mass of one mole of sodium chloride?

    A. 36 g/mol

    B. 43 g/mol

    C. 58 g/mol

    D. 72 g/mol

19. What form of radiation is composed of electrons traveling at around 16,000 km/sec?

    A. Alpha radiation

    B. Beta radiation

    C. Gamma radiation

    D. Delta radiation

20. What is the correct name of $ZnSO_4$?

    A. Zinc sulfate

    B. Zinc sulfide

    C. Zinc sulfur

    D. Zinc oxide

GO ON TO THE NEXT PAGE

21. What is the oxidation state of the oxygen atom in the compound NaOH?

    A. −2

    B. −1

    C. 0

    D. +2

22. Which of these intermolecular forces would have the lowest boiling point?

    A. Dipole-dipole interaction

    B. London dispersion force

    C. Keesom interaction

    D. Hydrogen bonding

23. Concentrated HCl has a molarity of 12.0. What volume of concentrated HCl should be used to prepare 500 mL of a 3.00 M HCl solution?

    A. 75 mL

    B. 100 mL

    C. 125 mL

    D. 150 mL

24. What is the correct formula for potassium chloride?

    A. NaCl

    B. KCl

    C. KCl_2

    D. ClK

25. Which of these elements has the greatest atomic mass?

    A. Au

    B. Ba

    C. I

    D. W

**STOP. IF YOU HAVE TIME LEFT OVER,
CHECK YOUR WORK ON THIS SECTION ONLY.**

ANATOMY AND PHYSIOLOGY

| 25 items | Suggested time: 21 minutes |

1. The lateral side of the right knee would be _____.

   A. the kneecap
   B. closest to the left knee
   C. farthest from the left knee
   D. on the underside of the knee

2. In which part of the lungs do nearly all the gaseous exchanges between air and blood take place?

   A. Pleura
   B. Alveoli
   C. Bronchioles
   D. Trachea

3. How do the intercostal muscles between the ribs assist with respiration?

   A. By protecting the delicate bronchioles and alveoli
   B. By signaling a decrease in intra-alveolar pressure
   C. By enlarging and reducing the space in the thorax
   D. By maintaining a medial separation between pleurae

4. In which organ do muscles push food into the stomach via peristalsis?

   A. Mouth
   B. Small intestine
   C. Epiglottis
   D. Esophagus

5. For the average person, what is true about caloric intake?

   A. It should increase with age after age 25.
   B. It should decline with age after age 25.
   C. It should remain constant over a lifetime.
   D. It should decline and then increase with age.

| **GO ON TO THE NEXT PAGE** |

6. The corpus callosum facilitates communication between
   _____.

   A. the left and right brain
   B. the skeletal and neural systems
   C. the brain and spinal cord
   D. the thalamus and hypothalamus

7. How does the integumentary system work with the nervous system?

   A. The integumentary system removes heat from the neurons in the nervous system.
   B. The nervous system circulates nutrients outward to the integumentary system.
   C. Touch input via the integumentary system sends messages to the nervous system.
   D. Messages from the nervous system affect the color and texture of the skin.

8. When the pulmonary valve and aortic valves are open, where can blood flow?

   A. Between the two ventricles of the heart
   B. From atrium to ventricle within the heart
   C. Between the heart and the rest of the body
   D. Between the atria in the heart

9. Which might be a result of stenosis, or narrowing of a heart valve?

   A. Abdominal pain
   B. Blood clots
   C. Edema (swelling) in organs
   D. Irregular heartbeat

10. The human skull contains about how many bones?

    A. About 5
    B. About 30
    C. About 60
    D. About 210

GO ON TO THE NEXT PAGE

11. The arteries are part of the _____.

    A. nervous system

    B. endocrine system

    C. lymphatic system

    D. cardiovascular system

12. Which is a secondary defense for the body against pathogens?

    A. Tears

    B. Urine

    C. Inflammation

    D. Mucus

13. Which organ system is primarily responsible for storing minerals?

    A. The skeletal system

    B. The endocrine system

    C. The lymphatic system

    D. The cardiovascular system

14. The vena cavae drain blood from the body into the _____.

    A. right atrium

    B. right ventricle

    C. left atrium

    D. left ventricle

15. Beriberi is a disease caused by lack of _____.

    A. thiamine

    B. vitamin C

    C. niacin

    D. protein

GO ON TO THE NEXT PAGE

16. How does the endocrine system work with the reproductive system?

    A. The reproductive system transforms minerals into useful nutrients.
    B. The endocrine system determines the sex of the embryo.
    C. The reproductive system controls the growth of secondary sex organs.
    D. The endocrine system produces chemicals that regulate sexual function.

17. Which hormone controls sleep, mood, and appetite?

    A. Serotonin
    B. Oxytocin
    C. Cortisol
    D. Aldosterone

18. Which part of the brain is most posterior?

    A. Frontal lobe
    B. Occipital lobe
    C. Temporal lobe
    D. Parietal lobe

19. Which of the following is an HDL cholesterol level that might warrant regular testing?

    A. 70
    B. 60
    C. 50
    D. 40

20. How does a transverse section divide the body?

    A. Into right and left regions
    B. Into upper and lower regions
    C. Into front and back regions
    D. Between the dorsal and ventral cavities

GO ON TO THE NEXT PAGE

21. What is the function of amylase?

    A. Breaking down starch
    B. Digesting fat
    C. Breaking down protein
    D. Absorbing water

22. The spleen is part of the _____.

    A. nervous system
    B. integumentary system
    C. lymphatic system
    D. urinary system

23. Which mineral is important for the formation of red blood cells?

    A. Selenium
    B. Calcium
    C. Magnesium
    D. Copper

24. The dorsal body cavity is _____ to the ventral body cavity.

    A. medial
    B. deep
    C. posterior
    D. anterior

25. Which organ system is primarily responsible for preventing water loss?

    A. The nervous system
    B. The integumentary system
    C. The lymphatic system
    D. The urinary system

**STOP. IF YOU HAVE TIME LEFT OVER,
CHECK YOUR WORK ON THIS SECTION ONLY.**

PHYSICS

25 items | Suggested time: 50 minutes

1. A kilogram of air is compressed from 1 m³ to 0.5 m³. Which statement is true?

   A. The density is doubled.
   B. The density is halved.
   C. The mass is doubled.
   D. The mass is halved.

2. An airplane travels 500 miles northeast and then, on the return trip, travels 500 miles southwest. Which of the following is true?

   A. The displacement of the plane is 1,000 miles, and the distance traveled is 0 miles.
   B. The displacement of the plane is 1,000 miles, and the distance traveled is 1,000 miles.
   C. The displacement of the plane is 0 miles, and the distance traveled is 0 miles.
   D. The displacement of the plane is 0 miles, and the distance traveled is 1,000 miles.

3. A bicycle and a car are both traveling at a rate of 5 m/s. Which statement is true?

   A. The bicycle has more kinetic energy than the car.
   B. The bicycle has less kinetic energy than the car.
   C. Both vehicles have the same amount of kinetic energy.
   D. Only the car has kinetic energy.

4. A car, starting from rest, accelerates at 10 m/s² for 5 seconds. What is the velocity of the car after 5 seconds?

   A. 2 m/s
   B. 5 m/s
   C. 50 m/s
   D. The answer cannot be determined from the information given.

GO ON TO THE NEXT PAGE

5. A 10-kg object moving at 5 m/s has an impulse acted on it causing the velocity to change to 15 m/s. What was the impulse that was applied to the object?

    A. 10 kg·m/s

    B. 15 kg·m/s

    C. 20 kg·m/s

    D. 100 kg·m/s

6. Which substance's volume would be most affected by temperature change?

    A. Liquid nitrogen

    B. Salt crystals

    C. Hydrogen gas

    D. Iron filings

7. A box is moved by a 15 N force over a distance of 3 m. What is the amount of work that has been done?

    A. 5 W

    B. 5 N·m

    C. 45 W

    D. 45 N·m

8. A 110-volt hair dryer delivers 1,525 watts of power. How many amperes does it draw?

    A. 167,750 amperes

    B. 1,635 amperes

    C. 1,415 amperes

    D. 13.9 amperes

9. How do you determine the velocity of a wave?

    A. Multiply the frequency by the wavelength.

    B. Add the frequency and the wavelength.

    C. Subtract the wavelength from the frequency.

    D. Divide the wavelength by the frequency.

GO ON TO THE NEXT PAGE

10. A 50-kg box of iron fishing weights is balanced at the edge of a table. Peter gives it a push, and it falls 2 meters to the floor. Which of the following statements is true?

　A. Once the box hit the floor, it lost its kinetic and potential energy.

　B. The box had kinetic energy when it was balanced at the edge of the table.

　C. The box had both kinetic and potential energy after it fell.

　D. Once the box hit the floor, it still had kinetic energy.

11. When the heat of a reaction is negative, which statement is true?

　A. The products have less energy and are less stable.

　B. The products have more energy and are more stable.

　C. The products have less energy and are more stable.

　D. The products have more energy and are less stable.

12. Longitudinal waves have vibrations that move _____.

　A. at right angles to the direction of the vibrations

　B. in the direction opposite to that of the wave

　C. in the same direction as the wave

　D. in waves and troughs

13. Which of the following describes a vector quantity?

　A. 5 miles per hour due southwest

　B. 5 miles per hour

　C. 5 miles

　D. None of the above

14. Why are boats more buoyant in salt water than in fresh water?

　A. Salt increases the density of the water.

　B. Salt increases the volume of the water.

　C. Salt affects the density of the boats.

　D. Salt decreases the mass of the boats.

GO ON TO THE NEXT PAGE

15. Two objects attract each other with a gravitational force of 12 units. If you double the mass of both objects, what is the new force of attraction between the two?

    A. 3 units
    B. 6 units
    C. 24 units
    D. 48 units

16. Four 1.5 V batteries are connected in a series. What is the total voltage of the circuit?

    A. 1.5 V
    B. 3.0 V
    C. 4.5 V
    D. 6.0 V

17. The relationship between acceleration and force is expressed in _____.

    A. Newton's first law of motion
    B. Newton's second law of motion
    C. Newton's third law of motion
    D. none of Newton's laws of motion

18. A 5-cm candle is placed 20 cm away from a concave mirror with a focal length of 10 cm. What is the image distance of the candle?

    A. 20 cm
    B. 40 cm
    C. 60 cm
    D. 75 cm

19. A wave in a rope travels at 12 m/s and has a wavelength of 3.2 m. What is the frequency?

    A. 38.4 Hz
    B. 15.2 Hz
    C. 4.6 Hz
    D. 3.75 Hz

GO ON TO THE NEXT PAGE

20. Which vehicle has the greatest momentum?

    A. A 9,000-kg railroad car traveling at 3 m/s

    B. A 2,000-kg automobile traveling at 24 m/s

    C. A 1,500-kg MINI Coupe traveling at 29 m/s

    D. A 500-kg glider traveling at 89 m/s

21. How might the energy use of an appliance be expressed?

    A. Power = energy × time

    B. Time + energy = power

    C. Energy = power × time

    D. Energy/power = time

22. A force of 12 kg stretches a spring 3 cm. How far will the spring stretch given a force of 30 kg?

    A. 6 cm

    B. 7.5 cm

    C. 9 cm

    D. 10.5 cm

23. A 2,000-kg car runs around a track at 10 m/s with a centripetal acceleration of 4 m/s^2. What is the radius of the track?

    A. 1,000 m

    B. 400 m

    C. 25 m

    D. 12 m

24. Two 5-ohm resistors are placed in a series and wired into a 100-V power supply. What current flows through this circuit?

    A. 2 amp

    B. 10 amp

    C. 20 amp

    D. 50 amp

GO ON TO THE NEXT PAGE

25. An object with a charge of 4 µC is placed 1 meter from another object with a charge of 2 µC. What is the magnitude of the resulting force between the objects?

A. 0.04 N
B. 0.072 N
C. 80 N
D. 8×10^{-6} N

**STOP. IF YOU HAVE TIME LEFT OVER,
CHECK YOUR WORK ON THIS SECTION ONLY.**

ANSWER KEY

Reading Comprehension

1. A	18. B	35. B
2. B	19. A	36. B
3. A	20. B	37. D
4. C	21. C	38. C
5. C	22. D	39. D
6. D	23. B	40. A
7. C	24. D	41. B
8. D	25. A	42. C
9. B	26. D	43. B
10. A	27. B	44. D
11. A	28. A	45. C
12. D	29. D	46. D
13. A	30. C	47. B
14. C	31. D	48. C
15. A	32. A	49. B
16. D	33. C	50. A
17. C	34. C	

Vocabulary and General Knowledge

1. A	18. D	35. D
2. B	19. C	36. B
3. C	20. C	37. B
4. A	21. A	38. C
5. B	22. A	39. C
6. B	23. D	40. A
7. C	24. C	41. D
8. B	25. A	42. B
9. A	26. D	43. C
10. C	27. C	44. D
11. D	28. D	45. B
12. D	29. A	46. A
13. A	30. B	47. B
14. D	31. C	48. D
15. A	32. C	49. B
16. C	33. B	50. A
17. A	34. D	

Grammar

1. C	18. A	35. A
2. B	19. D	36. C
3. C	20. A	37. D
4. C	21. B	38. C
5. B	22. B	39. A
6. A	23. A	40. B
7. B	24. C	41. D
8. B	25. A	42. B
9. D	26. A	43. B
10. A	27. C	44. C
11. C	28. D	45. D
12. D	29. D	46. A
13. D	30. B	47. D
14. D	31. A	48. D
15. A	32. B	49. B
16. B	33. C	50. C
17. C	34. D	

Basic Math Skills

1. B	18. A	35. 1955
2. A	19. D	36. D
3. D	20. C	37. C
4. A	21. C	38. 8
5. D	22. A	39. D
6. B	23. B	40. A
7. 184	24. A	41. B
8. A	25. C	42. C
9. 2	26. C	43. C
10. B	27. 70	44. 18
11. A	28. C	45. D
12. 30	29. C	46. D
13. D	30. B	47. A
14. D	31. C	48. B
15. B	32. A	49. 2
16. B	33. B	50. D
17. 94	34. C	

Biology

1. D	10. D	19. D
2. B	11. A	20. A
3. D	12. B	21. C
4. A	13. A	22. C
5. B	14. C	23. B
6. C	15. A	24. D
7. A	16. D	25. A
8. B	17. A	
9. C	18. C	

Chemistry

1. D	10. B	19. A
2. A	11. D	20. A
3. C	12. D	21. A
4. D	13. B	22. B
5. B	14. C	23. C
6. C	15. D	24. B
7. B	16. A	25. A
8. D	17. C	
9. B	18. C	

Anatomy and Physiology

1. C	10. B	19. D
2. B	11. D	20. B
3. C	12. C	21. A
4. D	13. A	22. C
5. B	14. A	23. D
6. A	15. A	24. C
7. C	16. D	25. B
8. C	17. A	
9. D	18. B	

Physics

1. A	10. A	19. D
2. D	11. C	20. B
3. B	12. C	21. C
4. C	13. A	22. B
5. D	14. A	23. C
6. C	15. D	24. B
7. D	16. D	25. B
8. D	17. B	
9. A	18. A	

EXPLANATORY ANSWERS

Reading Comprehension

1. (A) Remember that the main idea is the most important theme, one that carries throughout the passage. If someone asked you what this passage was about, you would be most likely to answer "the role of bacteria in the development of the immune system," making A the best answer.

2. (B) Details A and C appear in paragraph 2, and detail D is in the opening sentence of paragraph 1. Detail B is never mentioned or implied.

3. (A) The author is not trying to convince you of anything, as a persuasive essay might do (choice B). The basic purpose here is to provide information on a topic.

4. (C) A summary cannot go beyond the information given in the passage, as summaries A, B, and D seem to do. Only summary C focuses on what is suggested by the passage.

5. (C) *Staphylococcus aureus* is ubiquitous in hospitals—it is found everywhere.

6. (D) Choice A is illogical, choice B is close but does not cover all of the information in the passage, and choice C is never suggested. The best overall statement about the passage is D.

7. (C) A statement of fact can be proved or checked. A statement of opinion is what someone thinks or believes. In this case, statements A, B, and D could be proved scientifically, but statement C is simply someone's belief.

8. (D) If a statement cannot be inferred by the reader, either there is not enough information to draw conclusions about it, or the passage contradicts the inference. The passage implies that MRSA is transmitted primarily by skin-to-skin contact—it is described as a "skin infection," and while using someone's razor might put you at risk, buying used clothing that has been washed is unlikely to be hazardous.

9. (B) Canola oil is a source of unsaturated fat, but it is never mentioned in the passage.

10. (A) Think about other words you know that look like the word in question. To eat foods in moderation means to eat moderate, sensible amounts of those foods.

11. (A) Each choice has something to do with the passage, but only choice A covers the breadth of the topic as it is presented.

12. (D) Although the passage gives a lot of information, the author is mainly trying to convince the reader to eat a moderate amount of unsaturated fat and to consume little or no trans fat.

13. (A) Caloric density is never mentioned. The reader can conclude that unsaturated fat is healthier than saturated fat, making A the right choice.

14. (C) Choices A and B are minor details, and choice D is never suggested. The best choice is C.

15. (A) Look at the word in context. Ordinary diets don't give enough for seniors' needs; they need extra, or supplementation.

16. (D) The passage's tone is the attitude of the author toward the material being discussed. The author sticks to the facts in a serious manner, resulting in a pragmatic, or practical, tone.

17. (C) Details A and B are found in paragraph 2, and detail D is found in the last paragraph. The author does not mention nitrates at all, and these compounds would be unlikely to be important for seniors or anyone else.

18. (B) Choice A is a stretch, choice C is even more of a stretch, and choice D is simply untrue, given the information in the final paragraph. The most logical conclusion is B.

19. (A) The word *should* is a clue that this is what someone thinks or believes. The other statements could be checked or proved.

20. (B) The paragraph discusses sleep duration—the amount of time that people sleep.

21. (C) Choices A, B, and D may be details, but choice C is the only statement that applies to every paragraph in the passage.

22. (D) Word choice can hint at the author's attitude. In this case, *frightening*, *heavy price*, and *toxic mess* all suggest strong disapproval.

23. (B) If you conform to cultural ideals, you fit in with others in your culture.

24. (D) A quick skim of the passage should reveal that choices A, B, and C are mentioned, but D is not.

25. (A) The author ends with a statement that makes a plea to the reader. He wants to persuade the reader to be a careful consumer of cosmetics.

26. (D) Choice A appears in paragraph 2; choices B and C are in paragraph 3. Choice D is never suggested.

27. (B) Patients are dying from medical errors; the author suggests that they need someone to guard against this.

28. (A) The founder suggests in his quote that even cutting-edge hospitals can be dangerous, making choice A the best conclusion.

29. (D) A fact can be proved or checked, as the location of the organization could easily be.

30. (C) Choices B and D are minor details. Choice A is major, but the passage as a whole is about Lifewings, making choice C a better response.

31. (D) The passage seems to argue against choice A. A 33 percent improvement is not a cure of all pain, making B the wrong choice. NSAIDs are one treatment, but there is no comparison of their efficacy with acupuncture, so you cannot conclude choice C. The best choice is D.

32. (A) Acupuncture may now be considered a viable option, meaning that it is practicable, or reasonable.

33. (C) The mention of the study's conclusions in the last paragraph makes the overall tone one of optimism (choice C) rather than skepticism (choice B) or concern (choice A).

34. (C) The complete list of side effects appears in paragraph 2.

35. (B) What is the passage mostly about? It's about caffeine in coffee and its link to miscarriage. Choices A and D are too broad, and choice C is not part of the essay.

36. (B) One study is not enough to reverse, or invalidate, the guidelines—but more studies might do so.

37. (D) There is no support for choices A, B, or C, but the final paragraph of the passage certainly implies that doctors will select different options (choice D).

38. (C) Choices A, B, and D could be proved, but so far, choice C cannot. It remains a matter of opinion.

39. (D) Choice A is never mentioned, choices B and C are too narrow, and choice D comes close to covering the point of the passage— that PE is being aimed at life outside of school as well as in the classroom.

40. (A) *Propagandize* (choice B) and *demand* (choice C) have more negative connotations than the context requires, and *create* (choice D) does not fit at all. To instill is to fill with something, in this case, information. *Impart* (choice A) is a reasonable synonym.

41. (B) Basketball is mentioned, but not as a low-impact sport.

42. (C) Rereading the final paragraph of the passage should prove that choice C is the only logical option here.

43. (B) Choices A and C are details from the passage. Choice D could be a main idea of a different passage; this one never deals with the cost of dementia to families. The best choice is B.

44. (D) The onset of dementia is its beginning, or commencement.

45. (C) The author is not trying to get the reader to do or believe anything (choice A); he is merely giving information (choice C).

46. (D) Referring to dementia as "heartbreaking" indicates a sympathetic tone.

47. (B) The summary must include all of the main focuses of the passage, and in this case, only choice B fulfills that objective.

48. (C) The author's attitude toward the low life expectancy of US citizens seems to be negative. The final paragraph does not offer much hope that the situation will turn around, making choice C the best answer.

49. (B) Although the longevity of Japanese women is discussed in paragraph 2, the longevity of Japanese men is not.

50. (A) Choice B may be true, but you cannot infer it from the passage. Choice C is an opinion that may or may not be the author's—there is no support for it in the text. Choice B is contradicted by the reference to Japanese women. Choice A, on the other hand, has support: Obesity is linked in the passage to heart disease and diabetes, which in turn are listed as indicators for low life expectancy.

Vocabulary and General Knowledge

1. (A) From the same root as *delete*, which means "to blot out or destroy," *deleterious* means "to injure."

2. (B) To defer to someone is to show respect.

3. (C) To peruse is to examine in detail. You can peruse a book without taking notes on it (choice D).

4. (A) The word literally translates as "before knowing." It has to do with predicting or forecasting.

5. (B) An upgrade is an improvement. Moving from serious to fair condition might be one example.

6. (B) *Concise* comes from a root that means "to cut." Other words with this root include *precise*, *excise*, and *circumcise*.

7. (C) If you are accountable, you can account for your actions.

8. (B) *Tendere* means "to stretch," as in *extend*. *Dis* means "apart," as in *distant*.

9. (A) Something that is fluid (choice C) is liquid. Something that is molten (choice B) is hot and melted. Something that is malleable (choice D) is flexible. Only choice A is a synonym for *viscous*.

10. (C) The opposite of *overt* is *covert*, or hidden (choice B).

11. (D) A toxin is any poisonous compound.

12. (D) The word is from a root that means "sharp."

13. (A) If results of tests are inconclusive, they do not imply a conclusion. The data are unsettled, or undecided.

14. (D) A boil is an inflamed, pus-filled swelling caused by local infection.

15. (A) Something that is asymmetric is not symmetrical; it is irregular, or uneven.

16. (C) *Counterfeit* literally translates as "to make in opposition." A counterfeit watch is fake.

17. (A) *Effectiveness* and *efficacy* stem from the same root; both mean "the power to produce intended results."

18. (D) The illegal operators are pretending to be licensed pharmacists.

19. (C) The large triangular muscle that raises the arm from the side is the deltoid, named for the Greek letter *delta*, which is triangular.

20. (C) Something ethereal is light and airy, like the ether, or upper regions of space.

21. (A) A lynx (choice B) is a wildcat; the pharynx (choice C) is part of the alimentary canal, and a phalanx (choice D) may be a bone in the fingers or toes.

22. (A) *Contour* means "to go around" and refers to the outline of an object.

23. (D) To be incorrigible is to be uncorrectable. It is often used to describe the behavior of rambunctious young children.

24. (C) To undergo is to go through, or experience.

25. (A) The ventral part of the body is that where the belly is located; *venter* means "belly." In humans, that part is in front.

26. (D) *Anodyne* translates to "without pain."

27. (C) Palliative care is care that lessens pain and gives comfort without actually curing.

28. (D) Although we tend to think of it as a type of material, in its adjectival form, *plastic* means "capable of being molded," or "flexible."

29. (A) To lie prone is to lie face down. Its opposite is *supine*, meaning "face up."

30. (B) Euphoria is a strong feeling of well-being or ecstasy.

31. (C) The word *gonads* may refer to either male or female sex glands—either testes or ovaries.

32. (C) A deluge is a flood, or downpour.

33. (B) If a treatment is contraindicated, it is not indicated, or inadvisable.

34. (D) Ulcers may appear on the skin or on a mucous membrane, whether external or internal.

35. (D) To permeate is to spread throughout, or to infiltrate.

36. (B) If it is detrimental, it causes damage.

37. (B) *Censure*, from the same root as *censor*, refers to the expression of extreme disapproval.

38. (C) The DTs are a product of excessive drinking of alcohol. Characteristic signs include sweating, trembling, and hallucinating.
39. (C) Essentially "post burial" (*humus* means "ground"), a posthumous donation is made from the estate of someone who has died.
40. (A) The recording of vital signs is typical of hospital rounds or checkups. It is a way to indicate the efficient functioning of the body.
41. (D) *Belli*, as in *antebellum*, means "war." Children who are bellicose exhibit warlike behavior.
42. (B) In a recall, the product in question is pulled from the shelves of retailers.
43. (C) Use the sentence context to choose the best definition.
44. (D) An audit is literally a hearing, but an audit check has nothing to do with the ears (choice C). It is an inspection, especially of financial records.
45. (B) HPV, or human papillomavirus, causes warts and lesions of the oral, genital, and anal mucous membranes.
46. (A) A volatile liquid is one that, due to its chemical instability, can easily explode, catch fire, or emit noxious gases.
47. (B) The root in *vivify* has to do with life, as in *revive* or *survival*. To vivify is to give life to, or animate.
48. (D) Truculence is fierceness and is often used to describe speech or writing.
49. (B) The best synonym for *counseling* is *advising*.
50. (A) The gingival margin is the edge of the gums.

Grammar

1. (C) A comma must appear between the introductory phrase *Having finished the exam early* and the independent clause *Rudy checked it over for errors.* No other commas are needed.
2. (B) The verbs in the sentence must be parallel.
3. (C) *Four* is an adjective that describes *boys.*
4. (C) Reading the choices aloud may help you determine which choice has a logical order of phrases and clauses. The least convoluted sentence is choice C.
5. (B) The word that means "at a previous time" is *formerly*, not *formally.*
6. (A) The correct pronoun must be a subject pronoun. Only choice A is a subject pronoun.
7. (B) The only possible pronoun that completes the sentence is a subject pronoun. It could be *she* or *he.*
8. (B) *Who's* means "who is." *Whose* means "belonging to whom."
9. (D) Substitute the choices in the blank to find the one that makes sense in context.

10. (A) The sentence is missing an end mark, which must be a period in this case.

11. (C) From the Latin word *amator*, or lover, an amateur does something for the love of it, not for money.

12. (D) Again, reading this aloud and substituting choices should help you find the one that best fits.

13. (D) She probably complimented her counselor, or one who gave her counsel, rather than her councilor, or one who serves on a council.

14. (D) *Taken* is the verb form that goes with *having*.

15. (A) Ms. Schuster is the one tapping the beat, so the modifying phrase should be as close as possible to her name.

16. (B) The subject of the sentence is *one*, so the verb should be singular.

17. (C) The notes belong to the doctor and me; they belong to us. The correct possessive pronoun is *our*.

18. (A) The role of the clinic is principal, meaning "foremost," not principle, meaning "rule."

19. (D) Placing a semicolon between the two clauses (*Dr. Levine could not answer all of our questions* and *she promised to research the topic and return with a recommendation the next day*) makes the sentence correct.

20. (A) This is a simple sentence with one independent clause.

21. (B) Only the introductory clause requires a comma to separate it from the independent clause it precedes.

22. (B) If something is situated in the middle of two other things, it is between them.

23. (A) *Played* is a past tense verb. It refers to something he did last year.

24. (C) The reflexive pronoun must correspond to the subject, *Mary Ann*. Only *herself* is appropriate in number and gender.

25. (A) If in doubt, read the sentences aloud and pick the one that is least convoluted.

26. (A) The car is not in the apartment house; the friends are. Moving the phrase *in the apartment house* to the end of the sentence would improve the logic of the sentence.

27. (C) Only the infinitive phrase works with the rest of the sentence.

28. (D) The verb form that goes with *had* is *eaten*, not *eat*.

29. (D) The action takes place tomorrow, and it takes place to Angela, not by Angela. Only choice D fits.

30. (B) Placing a comma after *freeway* separates the introductory adverbial phrase from the rest of the sentence.

31. (A) In this type of question, you must make sure that the tense of verbs remains consistent. Because *had* is past tense, the correct answer contains another past-tense verb, *spoke*.

32. (B) The boys leapt up *happily*, an adverb, not *happy*, an adjective.

33. (C) Because the pronouns follow the verb and receive the action, they must be object pronouns. That eliminates choices A and D. Grammatically, it is correct to name oneself last, making choice C the best answer.

34. (D) The wife did not collect her own belongings (choice A); she collected her husband's (choice D).

35. (A) The correct pronoun is the object of a preposition (*to*) and must therefore be an object pronoun.

36. (C) A comma is used correctly (choice B), and the sentence has an end mark (choice A). It is missing an apostrophe in *hospital's*.

37. (D) The word is related to *perceive*.

38. (C) *Everybody* is singular, so *pretends* is the correct verb. *Few* is plural, so the correct verb is *understand*.

39. (A) Notice that the first verb in the sentence is in the past tense, so it makes sense that the second verb would be, too.

40. (B) To infer is to deduce, or conclude. A person's grimace cannot do that. A grimace may, however, imply or indicate loathing.

41. (D) To be clear and correct, the phrase *with silver tires* should lie as close as possible to the word it modifies, *car*, and the phrase *parked behind the building* should clearly refer to the car with silver tires, not to the people seeing the car.

42. (B) The subject is *one*, which is singular. Therefore, the correct verb must agree with a singular subject. *Is completed* (choice D) is ungrammatical.

43. (B) A comma after *long* would separate the two independent clauses.

44. (C) The subject is *choices*, and the predicate is *put*.

45. (D) *Nurses'* is a plural possessive noun that must be replaced by a plural possessive pronoun.

46. (A) The boy must be moving *stealthily*; *stealthy* is an adjective, not an adverb.

47. (D) Who was watching the TV news? Was it the criminals, or was it the person speaking? Only choice D places the modifying phrase next to the word it modifies.

48. (D) Look for the phrase that, if moved, would improve the sentence. The danger of drugs and alcohol is not limited to the auditorium; a better sentence would be "At a presentation in the auditorium, he informed us about the dangers of drugs and alcohol."

49. (B) The word *and* indicates addition. *Or* (choice A) indicates choice, and this is not a situation in which one or the other will do. *But* (choice C) and *yet* (choice D) indicate contrast, but both actions have to do with cleaning, so no contrast is indicated.

50. (C) Choice C contains all of the information in a logical order.

Basic Math Skills

1. (B) Express $2\frac{1}{8}$ as an improper fraction: $\frac{17}{8}$. Then multiply numerators and denominators: $\frac{2}{3} \times \frac{17}{8} = \frac{34}{24}$. Finally, express this as a mixed number in lowest terms: $1\frac{10}{24} = 1\frac{5}{12}$.

2. (A) One meter is about 3.28 feet. There are 12 inches in a foot, so $65 \text{ in} \div 12 \frac{\text{in}}{\text{ft}} = 5.42$ feet. $\frac{3.28 \text{ ft}}{1 \text{ m}} = \frac{5.42 \text{ ft}}{x \text{ m}}; 5.42 \div 3.28 = 1.65$.

3. (D) Set this up as a proportion: $\frac{2}{5} = \frac{x}{145}$. You may cross-multiply to solve: $2 \times 145 = 5x$. $290 = 5x$. $x = \frac{290}{5}$, or 58.

4. (A) First, determine how much Stu spent for the cups: $\$0.25 \times 6 = \$1.50$. Then find out what he spent for the plates: $\$0.75 \times 6 = \$4.50$. Add those sums: $\$1.50 + \$4.50 = \$6.00$. Finally, subtract that total from $\$10.00$: $\$10.00 - \$6.00 = \$4.00$.

5. (D) 1.25 equals $1\frac{25}{100}$, or $1\frac{1}{4}$ in lowest terms.

6. (B) There are 3 feet in a yard, so 17 feet = 5.67 yards. If the material is only sold in whole yards, he will need to purchase 6 yards to have enough.

7. (184) First, add the cost of the supplies for one student, and then multiply that by 23 students: $5 + 2 + 1 = 8$; $8 \times 23 = 184$.

8. (A) If there are 30 breakers and 4 are off, that means that 26 are on. The ratio of on to off is 26:4, which can be reduced to 13:2.

9. (2) First, subtract 5 from both sides: $\frac{2}{x} + 5 - 5 = 6 - 5$. Now the equation is $\frac{2}{x} = 1$. Multiply both sides by x: $\frac{2}{x}(x) = 1(x)$, so $2 = x$.

10. (B) One ounce equals about 29.6 mL, so set up a proportion: $\frac{1 \text{ oz}}{29.6 \text{ mL}} = \frac{x}{60 \text{ mL}}; 60 \div 29.6 = 2.03$.

11. (A) Put the percent over 100, reduce the fraction, and then convert the improper fraction to a mixed number: $\frac{204}{100} = \frac{51}{25} = 2\frac{1}{25}$.

12. (30) The least common denominator is the least number into which both denominators divide. Finding the common multiples is the easiest way to find this number. Factors of 6 = 6, 12, 18, 24, 30, 36. Multiples of 15 = 15, 30, 45, 60, 75. The least multiple that both numbers have in common is 30.

13. (D) Military time starts with hours before noon. After noon, 1:00 P.M. is 1300, 2:00 P.M. is 1400, and so on.

14. (D) You must find the ratio that is equivalent to 6:16. 60:160 would be equivalent, making choice A incorrect. 72:192 would be equivalent, making choice B incorrect. 120:320 would be equivalent, making choice C incorrect. The answer is choice D: multiplying both sides of the original ratio by 35 gives you 210:560.

15. (B) Begin by expressing the mixed numbers as improper fractions: $3\frac{1}{2} = \frac{7}{2}$, and $1\frac{1}{10} = \frac{11}{10}$. To divide by a fraction, multiply by its reciprocal. Therefore, $\frac{7}{2} \div \frac{11}{10} = \frac{7}{2} \times \frac{10}{11}$, or $\frac{70}{22}$. Now reduce to lowest terms: $\frac{70}{22} \div \frac{2}{2} = \frac{35}{11}$. Finally, express $\frac{35}{11}$ as a mixed number: $3\frac{2}{11}$.

16. (B) First, find $\frac{1}{3}$ of \$434.79 by dividing the total by 3—\$144.93. Subtract that from \$434.79 to find what Lenore has left after putting aside her share of the rent: \$434.79 − \$144.93 = \$289.86. Now subtract the amount she spends on groceries: \$289.86 − \$75 = \$214.86.

17. (94) \$8.99 × 6 = \$53.94. \$3.99 × 10 = \$39.99. Adding the two gives you \$53.94 + \$39.99 = \$93.93. Rounding that to the nearest dollar gives you \$94. Notice that in this case (although not in every case), rounding first before you multiply gives you the correct answer: (\$9 × 6) + (\$4 × 10) = \$94.

18. (A) Solve by dividing Clara's homes by the total and expressing the resulting decimal as a percent. 244 ÷ 1,525 = 0.16, or 16%.

19. (D) Since 1 inch equals 2.54 centimeters, 12 inches (1 foot) equals 2.54 × 12, or 30.48 centimeters.

20. (C) If 1 inch is equivalent to 6 inches, 6 inches is equivalent to 36 inches, or 1 yard.

21. (C) You can eliminate choices A and B here just by rounding each added to the nearest one and estimating the answer.

22. (A) One liter is about 1.06 quarts. Convert the cups to quarts. There are 4 cups in a quart, so: $\frac{4 \text{ cups}}{1 \text{ qt}} = \frac{3 \text{ cups}}{x \text{ qt}}$; 3 ÷ 4 = 0.75. Now convert from quarts to liters: $\frac{1 \text{ liter}}{1.06 \text{ qt}} = \frac{x \text{ liters}}{0.75 \text{ qt}}$; 0.75 ÷ 1.06 = 0.71.

23. (B) First, find the lowest common denominator. $\frac{2}{15} \times \frac{4}{4} = \frac{8}{60}$. $\frac{1}{12} = \frac{5}{5} = \frac{5}{60}$. $\frac{8}{60} + \frac{5}{60} = \frac{13}{60}$.

24. (A) There are 30 women in a class of 75, so the ratio of women to total is $\frac{30}{75} = \frac{2}{5}$.

25. (C) Since this is absolute value, there will be two solutions: $x-1=3$ and $x-1=-3$. For the first, add 1 to both sides: $x-1+1=3+1$; $x=4$. Since 4 is not an answer choice, solve the second option by adding 1 to both sides: $x-1+1=-3+1$; $x=-2$.

26. (C) Don't get bogged down in the verbiage here; just do the math. A gross is 12 dozen. The farm sells 15 × 12 dozen eggs a week, or 180 dozen eggs, so 180 containers are needed.

27. (70) One kilogram is approximately 2.2 pounds. Set up a proportion: $\frac{1 \text{ kg}}{2.2 \text{ lbs}} = \frac{x}{154 \text{ lbs}}$; 154 ÷ 2.2 = 70.

28. (C) The calculation would look like this:

$$
\begin{array}{r}
121 \text{ r}1 \\
31\overline{)727} \\
\underline{6} \\
12 \\
\underline{12} \\
07 \\
\underline{6} \\
1
\end{array}
$$

29. (C) You need to multiply 15 minutes by the number of days in two weeks, 14: $15 \times 14 = 210$. 210 minutes is equal to 3 hours 30 minutes.

30. (B) Use the decimal equivalent: $0.35 \times 70 = 24.50$, or 24.5.

31. (C) Simply divide to find the decimal equivalent: $17 \div 5 = 3.4$. It should be clear from looking at the answer choices that only choice C makes sense.

32. (A) There are 16 ounces in one pound, so $\dfrac{16 \text{ oz}}{1 \text{ lb}} = \dfrac{x}{14.25 \text{ lbs}}$; $16 \times 14.25 = 228$.

33. (B) Percentages are essentially ratios where the second number is 100. Divide 13 by 60 to find a decimal equivalent: $13 \div 60 = 0.2166666$, which rounds to 22%.

34. (C) If two cost 36 cents, one costs 18 cents, and 10 cost $1.80. This should be easy enough to do in your head.

35. (1955) Reading from left to right, $M = 1{,}000$, $CM = 900$, $L = 50$, and $V = 5$, making the date 1955.

36. (D) You can do this algebraically or as a guess-and-check. Algebraically, Lulu = L, her sister = S, and their cousin = C. $L = S - 5$, and $S = C + 7$. Since $C = 15$, $S = 22$, and $L = 17$.

37. (C) Multiply the decimal by 100 to find the percent: $0.05 \times 100 = 5\%$.

38. (8) Multiply the number of each type of book by the price: $\$2 \times 7 = \$14$; $\$6 \times 3 = \$18$. Then add up the totals and subtract from $50: $\$14 + \$18 = \$32$; $\$50 - \$32 = \$8$.

39. (D) The formula is $C \times \frac{9}{5} + 32 = F$. $22 \times \frac{9}{5} + 32 = 71.6$.

40. (A) Add 6 to both sides: $\dfrac{2x}{3} - 6 + 6 = 17 + 6$; $\dfrac{2x}{3} = 23$. Multiply both sides by 3: $\dfrac{2x}{3}(3) = 23(3)$; $2x = 69$. Divide both sides by 2 to find x: $\dfrac{2x}{2} = \dfrac{69}{2}$; $x = 34.5$.

41. (B) If they replace 14 in 7 hours, they work at a rate of about 2 per hour. They can do 120 in 60 hours, or two 30-hour weeks.

42. (C) The answer will be very close to 4.5 divided by 1, so the most reasonable answer (without computation) is choice C.

43. (C) Find the least common denominator and subtract: $^8/_{20} - ^5/_{20} = ^3/_{20}$.

44. (18) If there are 20 students per teacher, divide the total number of students by 20: $360 \div 20 = 18$.

45. (D) Express each mixed number as an improper fraction: $2\frac{1}{4} - 2^3/_6$. Then find the lowest common denominator and restate those fractions: $^{126}/_{24} - ^{92}/_{24}$. Solve, and express as a mixed number in lowest terms: $^{34}/_{24} = 1^{10}/_{24} = 1^5/_{12}$.

46. (D) Put the percent over 100 and divide: $\frac{18.3}{100} = 0.183$.

47. (A) Substitute 7 for y: $2x + 1 = 7$. Subtract 1 from both sides: $2x + 1 - 1 = 7 - 1; 2x = 6$. Divide both sides by 2 to solve for x: $\frac{2x}{2} = \frac{6}{2}; x = 3$.

48. (B) One kilogram is approximately 2.2 pounds. Set up a proportion: $\frac{1 \text{ kg}}{2.2 \text{ lbs}} = \frac{68 \text{ kg}}{x \text{ lbs}}$; $68 \times 2.2 = 149.6$.

49. (2) The key here is that everyone is retaining his or her job, so you are adding to the total. You can do this by guessing and checking. Right now, there are $^5/_{25}$ male nurses, or 20% of the nursing staff. If you add just 1 more male nurse, the total will be $^6/_{26}$ male nurses, or 23% of the nursing staff. Adding another brings you to $^7/_{27}$ male nurses or just more than 25% of the nursing staff. So adding a minimum of 2 staffers would solve your diversity problem—as long as both were male.

50. (D) There are 8 ounces in a cup and 32 ounces in 4 cups.

Biology

1. (D) Protein synthesis takes place in the ribosomes.

2. (B) ATP energizes glucose so that it can be broken down, and then the glucose molecules in the cytoplasm of the cell split in half, with each half of the six-carbon glucose becoming a three-carbon substance called pyruvic acid, releasing energy in the process in the form of ATP.

3. (D) Mitosis is cell division that produces new cells with the same number of chromosomes as the original cell. Meiosis (choice A) is the type of cell division that produces cells with half of the organism's normal chromosome number.

4. (A) RNA is ribonucleic acid; its sugar is ribose. DNA is deoxyribonucleic acid; its sugar is deoxyribose.

5. (B) If the disease is carried on the dominant allele, only the *aa* combination of recessive genes represents a disease-free offspring. On a Punnett square, that would be one out of four offspring.

6. (C) If cells are placed in a very salty solution, water molecules can diffuse across the cell membrane to move from an area of greater concentration of water molecules (inside the cells) to an area with a lesser concentration of water molecules (the solution of salt water).

7. (A) Unlike many creatures, grasshoppers and other insects have a system in which blood circulates through blood vessels that open into spaces between their body organs. Carbon dioxide and oxygen are not exchanged through the blood but instead pass between the cells and the outside of the grasshopper through the tracheas and spiracles.

8. (B) Enzymes are catalysts that speed up reactions. They do this by lowering the amount of energy needed to begin the reaction.

9. (C) The pistil is the female reproductive organ in a flowering plant.

10. (D) Mutualism is the form of symbiosis through which both species receive mutual benefit.

11. (A) The taxonomic categories in order from least to most specific are: kingdom, phylum, class, order, family, genus, species.

12. (B) Carbohydrates and lipids are made up of different combinations of carbon, hydrogen, and oxygen. Proteins are made up of amino acids, which center around carbon atoms and always contain hydrogen and oxygen plus nitrogen. Nucleic acids contain carbon, hydrogen, and oxygen in their simple sugars plus nitrogen and phosphates.

13. (A) Monerans are prokaryotic, and they do not have vacuoles, centrioles, mitochondria, lysosomes, endoplasmic reticula, nuclear membranes, or Golgi apparatuses.

14. (C) During budding, a cell or cells in the parent's body produce a smaller version of the parent called a bud. All buds have the exact DNA of the parent. Yeast, hydras, and some plants use this form of asexual reproduction.

15. (A) Anaphase is the second step in mitosis. At this stage, the chromatids pull apart and move toward the centrioles at opposite sides of the cell. Once separated, they are called chromosomes. As anaphase ends, a complete set of chromosomes is at each end of the spindle.

16. (D) DNA is composed of deoxyribose, a simple sugar; nitrogen bases; and a phosphate group.

17. (A) Picture a Punnett square. Reading the chart clockwise from top left, the cross would yield one female carrier, one female hemophiliac, one male hemophiliac, and one normal male who neither carries nor manifests the disease.

18. (C) The Krebs, or citric acid cycle, is the third step in carbohydrate catabolism, the breakdown of sugar. Before it begins, glucose has been broken down via glycolysis into pyruvic acid. In the Krebs cycle, pyruvic acid breaks down into carbon dioxide, releasing two ATPs and 10 NADHs.

19. (D) The more measurements made, the more valid the data are likely to be. Using three sites rather than one allows the researcher to increase observations.

20. (A) The greatest energy content is at the base of the energy pyramid; therefore, producers > primary consumers > secondary consumers > decomposers. An herbivore would be a primary consumer; carnivores and omnivores are more likely to be secondary consumers.

21. (C) This choice reduces the possibility that one brand might emit more radiation than another; it also allows for a before-and-after measurement that is parallel for each test.

22. (C) In the carbon cycle, carbon passes from the environment through the bodies of living organisms and back into the environment. The dead bodies of organisms are broken down by bacteria and other decomposers, which produce carbon dioxide and release it into the environment.

23. (B) Basal metabolic rate refers to the number of calories that the body burns in a state of rest.

24. (D) Most bacteria are spherical (choice D), rod-shaped (choice B), or spiral-shaped (choice C).

25. (A) In hydrolysis, any class of compound is broken down into subunits through the addition of water.

Chemistry

1. (D) The ionization energy of an atom is the energy required to remove the outermost electron from the atom. This energy is needed to overcome the attraction between the positively charged protons and the negatively charged electrons.

2. (A) Phenolphthalein is a common indicator used to determine the pH of a substance. In the presence of an acid, it will be colorless. In the presence of a base, it will turn magenta.

3. (C) For a substance to decay from 56 kg to 7 kg it must undergo 3 half-lives ($56 \rightarrow 28 \rightarrow 14 \rightarrow 7$). If the half-life of the substance is 12 days, then 3 half-lives would be 36 days.

4. (D) If the elements in a covalent bond have different electronegativity values, the unequal sharing of electrons causes the bond to be polar. H_2O is the only choice with a polar covalent bond.

5. (B) This type of equation represents decomposition, the breaking down of a compound into its component parts.

6. (C) Sulfur is located on the upper right side of the periodic table. It is soft, lacks luster, and does not conduct heat or electricity well, making it a nonmetal.

7. (B) A gas with a greater mass effuses less rapidly than a gas with a lesser mass. Therefore, the gas with less mass would be smelled sooner. Since both gases are odorous, and both do effuse eventually, choices C and D are incorrect.

8. (D) White phosphorus is made by condensing phosphorus vapor. Red phosphorus is made by heating white phosphorus in a vacuum to around 250°C. Black phosphorus is less common and is made by subjecting phosphorus to extreme pressure or by crystallizing white phosphorus.

9. (B) Substances that are gases at room temperature and pressure decrease in solubility with an increase in temperature. Substances that are solids at room temperature and pressure increase in solubility with an increase in temperature.

10. (B) The compound has four carbon atoms joined by single bonds, making it a molecule of butane.

11. (D) In the original equation, there is one atom of iron (Fe) on the left side and two on the right, so the coefficient 2 is needed to balance iron. Before you limit your choices to A and C, look at the oxygen. There are two atoms of oxygen on the left and three on the right. The only way to balance this is by placing a 3 as a coefficient on the left and 2 as a coefficient on the right. That brings the atoms of iron up to four on the right, so a coefficient of 4 on the left is needed to balance.

12. (D) Reactivity has to do with the tendency of an element to lose electrons. The least reactive elements are the noble gases, and in general, reactivity increases across the periodic table from left to right. Since magnesium and barium are in the same column of the table, they are similar in reactivity.

13. (B) In a single bond, one pair of electrons are shared. In a double bond, two pairs of electrons are shared (choice D).

14. (C) Calculate the number of neutrons by subtracting the atomic number from the mass number. The mass number of carbon-12 is 12, and the atomic number for carbon is 6, so $12 - 6 = 6$.

15. (D) The electron distribution of an atom is divided into shells, which in turn contain subshells composed of the orbitals in which the electrons reside. In electron configuration, the symbols 1s, 2s, 2p, and so on, are used to designate subshells, with superscripts indicating the number of electrons in each subshell. There is a maximum number of electrons per subshell. Magnesium has atomic number 12, meaning that it has 12 protons, and in its balanced state, 12 electrons. Looking at the superscripts alone should tell you that only the superscripts in choice D add up to 12.

16. (A) You need simply to divide the number of moles by the number of liters to determine the molarity: $0.45/4 = 0.1125$, which rounds to 0.11.

17. (C) Tap water is relatively neutral and could be expected to fall in that neutral range.

18. (C) A mole of atoms consists of Avogadro's number of atoms and has a mass in grams numerically equal to the atomic weight of the element. So, one mole of salt, NaCl, has a mass in grams equal to the atomic weight of one atom of sodium plus one atom of chlorine—about $23 + 35$, or 58 g.

19. (A) Alpha particles are ejected from a radioactive substance at about 16,000 km/sec. Beta rays (choice B) are streams of electrons that travel faster, at around 130,000 km/sec.

20. (A) Zn is zinc, and SO_4 is a sulfate. ZnS would be zinc sulfide (choice B). ZnO would be zinc oxide (choice D).

21. (A) With a few rare exceptions, oxygen has an oxidation number of -2 in a compound.

22. (B) Weak intermolecular forces have a low boiling point. Strong intermolecular forces have a high boiling point.

London dispersion < dipole-dipole < H-bonding < ion-ion

London dispersion is the weakest force of those shown. (A Keesom interaction is one form of dipole-dipole interaction.)

23. (C) You can use the molarity/dilution equation to solve this.

$$M_1V_1 = M_2V_2$$

$$3 \times 500 = 12 \times x$$

$$1,500 = 12x$$

$$x = 125$$

24. (B) Potassium is K, and chlorine is Cl. Putting them together forms potassium chloride. A chloride is simply a compound of chlorine with another element.

25. (A) Gold (Au) has an atomic mass of 196.96655 amu. Barium (Ba) has an atomic mass of 137.327 amu. Iodine (I) has an atomic mass of 126.90447 amu. Tungsten (W) has an atomic mass of 183.84 amu.

Anatomy and Physiology

1. (C) Something that is lateral is toward the outer side of the body. The side of the right knee farthest from the left knee would fit this description.
2. (B) The alveoli are the tiny air sacs in the lungs where the exchange of oxygen and carbon dioxide takes place.
3. (C) The ribs themselves protect the lungs (choice A), but the intercostals are muscles that expand and contract the chest, allowing it to draw in and expel air.
4. (D) The esophagus connects the stomach and the oral cavity in the human digestive system.
5. (B) The height of calorie intake for healthy, active people is approximately their mid-20s. After that, calorie intake should decline slightly as energy needs decline.
6. (A) The corpus callosum is a broad band of nerve fibers that join the two hemispheres of the brain.
7. (C) The integumentary system includes the skin, hair, nails, and assorted glands. Receptors embedded in the skin receive information regarding heat, pain, air flow, and so on, which is transported through the nervous system to the brain.
8. (C) The two valves connect the heart to the pulmonary artery and the aorta, which carry blood from the heart to the rest of the body.
9. (D) Narrowing of the valves means that blood moves with difficulty out of the heart. Results may include chest pain, edema in the feet or ankles, and irregular heartbeat.
10. (B) At birth we have 44 separate bony structures in our skulls, but many of those fuse as we age.
11. (D) The arteries carry blood away from the heart as a key feature of the cardiovascular system.
12. (C) Tears (choice A), urine (choice B), and mucus (choice D) are all primary lines of defense, because they work to prevent infection. Inflammation (choice C) is an example of a secondary line of defense, because it kicks in once the body has been infected.
13. (A) Bone tissue stores a variety of minerals, from calcium to phosphorus, releasing them into the bloodstream as needed.
14. (A) Deoxygenated blood first enters the heart via the right atrium.

15. (A) Thiamine (B$_1$) deficiency is often found in people whose diet consists largely of polished white rice; in refining the rice, the thiamine-rich husk is removed. Beriberi may affect several systems in the body and may lead to paralysis or death.

16. (D) The hormones produced by the endocrine system are critical in sexual development and reproduction.

17. (A) Oxytocin (choice B) facilitates birth and breast-feeding. Cortisol (choice C) increases blood sugar and controls some aspects of fat breakdown. Aldosterone (choice D) controls reabsorption of ions and regulates blood pressure. Serotonin (choice A) is a neurotransmitter found in the gut that regulates appetite and sleep as well as some aspects of mood.

18. (B) The occipital lobe is farthest back in the skull, posterior to the other parts of the brain.

19. (D) HDL ("good") cholesterol levels in healthy adults range from around 40 to 120 mg/dL, with the mean being a bit over 53. Smoking, obesity, and a sedentary lifestyle may lead to lower HDL. A level of 40 would indicate the need for regular monitoring.

20. (B) A transverse section is a cross section.

21. (A) Amylase is present in saliva, where it begins to break down starch into sugar.

22. (C) The spleen uses lymphocytes and macrophages to filter out bacteria, dead tissue, and foreign matter.

23. (D) Although iron is vital for red blood formation, copper is important for proper iron metabolism. A copper deficiency can quickly lead to anemia.

24. (C) The dorsal body cavity contains the spinal column, making it posterior, or toward the back of the body, compared to the ventral body cavity, which contains the structures of the chest and abdomen.

25. (B) The integumentary system (the skin and its appendages) waterproofs the body from outside and guards against excess fluid loss from inside.

Physics

1. (A) The mass remains the same, at 1 kg. Because the volume is now halved, the density (mass/volume) is doubled.

2. (D) The plane traveled a total of 1,000 miles, but because it ended back where it started, the displacement is 0.

3. (B) Kinetic energy is the energy of an object in motion. The greater the mass of that object, the greater its kinetic energy.

4. (C) The velocity of the car is equal to the time multiplied by the acceleration.

5. (D) An impulse is a change in momentum. The 10-kg object had a change in its velocity of 10 m/s. Using the equation $\Delta p = m\Delta v$, change in momentum equals mass times change in velocity, you can see that the answer is 100 kg·m/s.

6. (C) Increasing the temperature of a substance increases its volume and decreases its density. Such changes are far more evident in gases than in liquids or solids.

7. (D) Work is the force that is applied to an object over a distance: $W = Fd$. The force is 15 N, and the distance is 3 m, giving a total amount of work equal to 45 N·m.

8. (D) Based on the equation $P = IV$, the current is P/V, or power divided by voltage. Dividing 1,525 watts by 110 volts gives you approximately 13.9 amperes.

9. (A) The velocity of a wave is determined by multiplying its frequency by its wavelength.

10. (A) The box had potential energy when it was balanced at the edge of the table—it could move toward the floor. Once the box hit the floor, it had no potential energy—and when it came to rest, it had no kinetic energy.

11. (C) Exothermic reactions are characterized by negative heat flow, because heat is lost into the environment. Exothermic reactions usually proceed from a higher-energy, less stable reactant to a lower-energy, more stable product.

12. (C) The vibrations in longitudinal waves move in the same direction as the wave.

13. (A) Only choice A has both direction and magnitude, making it a vector.

14. (A) Fresh water has a density of around 1,000 kg/m³, whereas that of salt water is around 1,030 kg/m³. The difference in density of the fluids makes objects in salt water more buoyant than those in fresh water.

15. (D) If the mass of each object is doubled, the force of attraction is quadrupled.

16. (D) Attaching batteries in a series gives you a voltage equivalent to the combined voltage of all the batteries.

17. (B) Newton's second law of motion states that the greater the force applied to an object, the greater is its acceleration.

18. (A) Look at the relationship between the object distance (d_o), the image distance (d_i), and the focal length (f). Use the equation: $1/f = 1/d_o + 1/d_i$ where $f = 10$ cm and $d_o = 20$ cm.

$$1/10 = 1/20 + 1/d_i$$

The image distance is 20 cm.

19. (D) Speed equals wavelength times frequency ($v = f\lambda$). In this problem, $12 = 3.2\lambda$, so $\lambda = 3.75$ Hz.

20. (B) Momentum is the product of velocity and mass, and the greatest product of the four presented here is 48,000 kg·m/s.

21. (C) Using this formula, energy is often measured in kilowatt-hours. For example, if you use a 100-watt light bulb 12 hours a day for 30 days, you will have used 100×360 watt-hours, or 36 kilowatt-hours.

22. (B) Force equals the extension of the spring times a constant ($F = dk$). If a force of 12 kg stretches this particular spring 3 cm, the constant is 4. Apply that same constant to the increased force: $30 = d \times 4$. The distance of the extension must be $30 \div 4$, or 7.5 cm.

23. (C) Acceleration equals the speed squared divided by the radius ($a = v^2/R$). In this case, $a = 4$ m/s^2 and $v = 10$ m/s, so the radius must be $100 \div 4$, or 25 m. The mass of the car is irrelevant to the problem.

24. (B) According to Ohm's law, current (I) equals voltage (ΔV) divided by resistance (R), or $I = \Delta V/R$. In this case, you know voltage and resistance, so $I = {}^{100}/_{10}$, or 10 amp.

25. (B) Use Coulomb's law to find the force. The equation to use is this:

$$F_{\text{elect}} = \frac{k \times Q_1 \times Q_2}{d^2}$$

Remember that 1 coulomb = 10^6 microcoulombs. Q_1 this case equals 4×10^{-6} C, Q_2 equals 2×10^{-6} C, and d, distance, = 1 m. Now, you must recall Coulomb's constant, $k = (9.0 \times 10^9$ N·m^2/C^2). Once more, it's all about computation:

$$\frac{9.0 \times 10^9 \, \text{N·m}^2 \times (4 \times 10^{-6} \, \text{C}) \times (2 \times 10^{-6} \, \text{C})}{(1 \, \text{m})^2} = \frac{72 \times 10^{-3}}{1} = 0.072 \, \text{N}$$

CHAPTER 5

A2 Practice Test 3

READING COMPREHENSION

| 50 items | Suggested time: 55 minutes |

Boys Will Be Boys

One of the most common stereotypes surrounding young teenage boys is that they are hostile, belligerent, and generally display "attitude." Some considered this just a phase in the maturing process, some thought it was a reflection of poor parenting skills, and others placed blame on everything from violent video games to too much television.

A recent study by a team of Australian and American researchers may prove all of those theories wrong. These researchers say that boys' aggressive behaviors may actually be due to overly large amygdalae in the boys' brains.

The amygdala is a part of the brain found deep within the medial temporal lobes. It is intricately involved in emotional responses such as fear and anger. As the researchers reported in an article for the *Proceedings of the National Academy of Science*, boys may show no ability to control their emotions because they literally do not have the brain development to do so until their early twenties.

| GO ON TO THE NEXT PAGE |

The study required 137 twelve-year-old boys and their parents to sit down and discuss emotionally sensitive issues such as homework, bedtime, and hours spent on the Internet. Afterward, the boys' brains were scanned. The boys who had the largest amygdalae behaved more aggressively than boys who had smaller ones. They also appeared to have smaller-than-usual prefrontal cortexes, the region of the brain that is involved with regulating emotions.

The researchers concluded that those boys who had less brain development—less development of critical connections among parts of the brain—had a much stronger tendency to be negative and even hostile when they interacted with their parents. Just do not tell the teenage boys—it gives them a built-in excuse!

1. What is the main idea of the passage?

   A. How best to discipline unruly young people
   B. Why scientists think that the amygdala affects emotions
   C. How behavior may be linked to brain development
   D. Why parents and teenage boys tend to have disagreements

2. Which of the following is *not* listed as a detail in the passage?

   A. The location of the amygdala
   B. The number of boys in the study
   C. The size of the boys' amygdalae
   D. The homeland of the researchers

3. What is the author's primary purpose in writing this essay?

   A. To inform
   B. To persuade
   C. To entertain
   D. To analyze

GO ON TO THE NEXT PAGE

4. Choose the best summary of the passage.

   A. By looking at teenage boys' reactions to violent videos, researchers were able to establish that brain development is related to aggressive behavior. The boys who behaved most aggressively had the least developed prefrontal cortexes.

   B. Researchers studying aggressive responses in young boys determined that the amygdalae of aggressive boys were larger than those in other boys. Their lack of brain development may inhibit them from controlling their emotions.

   C. Boys in Australia are known to be less aggressive than boys in the United States, and researchers suspect that this is because of an excess of violent video games and television. Now it appears that a little-understood part of the brain may be to blame.

   D. While studying the effect of certain aggressive behaviors on young boys, researchers on two continents accidentally located the part of the brain that controls aggressive response and regulates emotions. The next step is to study this in girls as well.

Using Light to Heal

Phototherapy, commonly referred to as light therapy, has been an established form of medicine for more than a century. In recent years it has become closely associated with seasonal affective disorder, of which it is an effective and well-known treatment, but it is also used to treat a broad range of medical issues, including acne, psoriasis, and eczema.

The most common form of light therapy involves a patient sitting in front of a medically designed light box for a prescribed amount of time every morning. The light is positioned at an exact distance from the patient's eyes so that it strikes both the skin and the retina. The light box mimics the effects of natural sunlight, but the UV rays are filtered to ensure there is no damage to the patient's skin or eyes. Phototherapy is thought to be a safe method of reducing the amount of bacteria on the skin, reducing inflammatory responses, and affecting the chemicals in the brain associated with mood.

GO ON TO THE NEXT PAGE

One of the most recent technologies to be associated with phototherapy is the phototherapy blanket. In the late 1960s it was discovered that phototherapy can be used to treat jaundice in newborn babies. Neonatal jaundice, a yellowing of the skin in newborn infants due to excess bilirubin levels in the blood, is usually harmless but can cause brain damage if left untreated. Newborns are given a phototherapy blanket, a small pad with flexible LED light panels sewn into the fabric, to sleep with until their livers are able to process the excess bilirubin.

The many benefits of phototherapy make it a valuable resource for addressing a variety of ailments. Emerging innovations in LED and photo technologies ensure that many more practical applications will be developed for this particular form of treatment in the years to come.

5. What is the meaning of the word *established* as used in the first paragraph?

   A. Created
   B. Ascertained
   C. Founded
   D. Reputable

6. What is the main idea of the passage?

   A. Phototherapy has been an established form of medicine for more than a century.
   B. Phototherapy is a safe method of reducing the amount of bacteria on a person's skin.
   C. The many benefits of phototherapy make it a valuable resource for addressing a variety of ailments.
   D. Emerging innovations in LED and photo technologies ensure that many more practical applications will be developed for phototherapy in the years to come.

7. Which of the following statements is a fact?

   A. Nurses should watch for jaundice in newborns.
   B. Untreated jaundice may cause brain damage.
   C. Phototherapy blankets are a valuable invention.
   D. Avoid neonatal units that lack phototherapy.

GO ON TO THE NEXT PAGE

8. Which statement would *not* be inferred by the reader?

    A. Some forms of phototherapy have been around for decades.

    B. New applications of phototherapy continue to be developed.

    C. Phototherapy is most often used to treat skin problems.

    D. Ultraviolet rays can cause damage to eyes and skin.

Risks of Spanking

Put a dozen parents together in a room, and you will most likely have a dozen different theories of parenting. One of the most debated issues in raising kids is how to discipline them, especially when it comes to the question of to spank or not to spank. Some moms and dads are sure that it is an integral part of showing their kids what is right and wrong. Others are equally sure that spanking is a cruel act of violence against kids. Which is it?

According to a new study reported at the American Psychological Association Summit Conference on Violence and Abuse in Relationships, spanking or other forms of corporal punishment apparently increase the risk of future sexual problems such as violent or coercive sex with partners. "The more children are spanked, the more aggressive they are and the more likely they are to engage in delinquent or at-risk behaviors," says Elizabeth Gershoff from the University of Michigan's School of Social Work. "Kids may learn that sometimes there's pain and fear involved in loving relationships."

Naturally, there are those who disagree as well. Some scientists believe that spanking two- to six-year-old children can be very helpful as long as parents are not angry or out of control emotionally. Human development researcher Robert Larzelere adds that parents simply must be able to differentiate between appropriate and inappropriate use.

Although opinion on spanking remains divided, research continues on this contentious issue. In the meantime, however, the American Academy of Pediatrics advises parents to use other methods of discipline.

GO ON TO THE NEXT PAGE

9. Which is *not* mentioned as a possible result of being spanked in childhood?

    A. Aggression
    B. Coercive sex
    C. Delinquency
    D. Incontinence

10. What does the word *integral* mean as used in the first paragraph of the passage?

    A. Central
    B. Initial
    C. Trifling
    D. Irrelevant

11. Choose the best summary of the passage.

    A. Although some parents believe firmly in spanking, others disagree. Researchers continue to study both the perpetrators and the recipients of regular spankings, but they have found little to corroborate either side of the argument.
    B. Is spanking a cruel act of violence, or is it a necessary form of discipline? A nationwide study reviewed the use of spanking in different cultures and determined that violent aggressors were frequently those who had been spanked in their youth.
    C. A new study on spanking indicates that being a recipient of multiple spankings can result in sexual problems later in life as well as other troublesome behaviors. Nevertheless, there remains no solid agreement on whether spanking is always bad.
    D. Whether or not you choose to use spanking as a form of discipline in your household, you should be aware of the negative effects it has on certain children later in life, and you should use it sparingly and with control.

12. What is the author's primary purpose in writing this essay?

    A. To reflect
    B. To persuade
    C. To inform
    D. To entertain

GO ON TO THE NEXT PAGE

13. Which statement would *not* be inferred by the reader?

    A. Most criminals were victims of childhood abuse.

    B. Aggression may have roots in childhood discipline.

    C. Parents disagree over the use of spanking.

    D. Researchers disagree over the value of spanking.

Forty Winks

When most people think about taking a nap, they typically envision being down for the count for at least an hour or two. A German study, however, has shown that if you really want to refresh your brain, a six-minute catnap will do it. Not only will you feel better afterward, but your ability to learn and remember will have improved as well.

As described in a recent article in the *Journal of Sleep Research*, students at the University of Dusseldorf participated in experiments in which they had to memorize a list of words and then either take a nap or play a video game. The ones who napped scored consistently higher than those who stayed awake.

The study may help scientists learn more about what happens when people go to sleep. They already know that the brain undergoes a number of significant changes in the process. "There are dramatic shifts in brain chemistry and electrophysiology," said Dr. Matthew Tucker, researcher at Harvard University School of Medicine and the Center for Sleep and Cognition. "For example, we know that levels of the transmitter acetylcholine go down. And we think that when acetylcholine gets to a low point, it should have an enhancing effect on memory."

Experts believe that sleeping is the brain's chance to decide which details and memories from the day need to be placed in permanent storage and which ones need to be thrown out. It has to do this because there is only so much room in the brain for information.

Of course, those catnaps may be wonderful, but they can never replace the value of a solid eight hours of sleep. As Dr. Olaf Lahl, the study's lead author, remarks, "A regular sleep schedule still plays an important role in overall well-being and health."

GO ON TO THE NEXT PAGE

14. What is the main idea of the passage?

 A. Everyone has to have eight hours of sleep each night.
 B. Brief naps are enough to help energize most people.
 C. There is a limited amount of room in the brain for storage.
 D. Memorizing lists of words is more difficult than you'd think.

15. What is the meaning of the word *shifts* as used in the third paragraph?

 A. Alterations
 B. Stints
 C. Removals
 D. Transfers

16. Identify the overall tone of the essay.

 A. Impersonal
 B. Instructive
 C. Disgusted
 D. Disbelieving

17. Sleeping apparently helps with everything EXCEPT _____.

 A. fatigue
 B. memory
 C. learning
 D. appetite

Get Off the Couch!

It sounds contradictory, but here is some new advice for people who are feeling unusually tired: get out and get some exercise. Studies have shown that regular, low-impact workouts such as short strolls or brief bike rides can help increase overall energy levels by 20 percent and decrease fatigue levels by 65 percent. In other words, if you are feeling tired, the best way to feel more energetic is to get some exercise.

GO ON TO THE NEXT PAGE

This advice is based on a study done by the University of Georgia's Exercise Pathology Lab. Three dozen people who did not get any kind of regular exercise yet consistently felt exhausted were divided into three groups. One group did not exercise at all. A second group worked out intensively on an exercise bike three times a week. The third group also worked out but at a slower pace. Of the two groups that exercised, both reported a 20 percent increase in energy levels. However, the group that exercised at a more leisurely pace stated that they experienced far less fatigue than the high-intensity group.

This was not the first study to point out a link between regular exercise and energy levels. The same team that conducted it also published one several years ago that stated that low-impact exercise can also help reduce fatigue in patients with serious health conditions such as heart disease and cancer. Clearly, it is time to get off the couch and onto the track.

18. Which statement could be inferred from the passage?

    A. The Georgia lab had done a previous study on the connection between exercise and energy.

    B. Exercise regimes are not recommended for patients with serious health problems.

    C. An increase in energy levels always corresponds directly to a reduction in fatigue.

    D. There were fewer than 10 participants in each group in the Georgia study.

19. Which of the following statements is an opinion?

    A. The laboratory in Georgia studied 36 subjects.

    B. One group worked out on an exercise bike.

    C. Low-impact exercise can increase energy levels.

    D. Fatigued people need to get out and exercise.

20. The word *track* as used in the last paragraph of the passage can best be defined as _____.

    A. keep a record of

    B. a new attitude

    C. follow carefully

    D. a paved, circular path

GO ON TO THE NEXT PAGE

21. What is the main idea of the passage?

    A. Low-impact exercise is always better for people than intensive exercise.
    B. The best way to address fatigue is to get out and exercise hard every single day.
    C. If people feel tired, they can best improve their energy levels by regular exercise.
    D. Low-impact exercise helps people with serious conditions such as heart disease and cancer.

Obsession Plus Addiction

It is hard to imagine how the eating disorders anorexia and bulimia could be any worse than they already are, but somehow people have found a way. Known unofficially as *drunkorexia*, this condition is a blend of self-imposed starvation or binging and purging mixed with alcohol abuse. Anorexics may use alcohol either to soothe their conscience for eating something they feel they should not, or as their only sustenance. Bulimics binge on alcohol for emotional reasons and then purge by vomiting it back up.

Our current culture's obsession with thinness, coupled with widespread acceptance of drug and alcohol abuse, have made this combination particularly attractive. Dr. Doug Bunnell, former president of the National Eating Disorders Association, said, "Binge drinking is almost cool and hip, and losing weight and being thin is a cultural imperative for young women in America. Mixing both is not surprising, and it has reached a tipping point in terms of public awareness."

Some experts are beginning to explore the possible psychological and neurological links between eating disorders and substance abuse. Does eating or binging somehow trigger the same pleasure centers as drugs or alcohol? Another avenue being explored is what to do if a person has both conditions.

GO ON TO THE NEXT PAGE

Treatment for addiction is abstinence, but no one can abstain completely from food. As Dr. Kevin Wandler, vice president for medical services at an eating disorders center, phrases it, "Eating normally would be an effective behavior, but it's easier to give up alcohol and drugs because you never need them again. If your drug is food, that's a challenge."

22. Identify the overall tone of the essay.

    A. Dismayed

    B. Fascinated

    C. Reassured

    D. Suspicious

23. What is the meaning of the word *abstain* as used in the last paragraph?

    A. Dishonor

    B. Go without

    C. Connect to

    D. Liberate

24. Which of the following is *not* listed as a detail in the passage?

    A. Anorexics' use of alcohol as sustenance

    B. Bulimics' use of alcohol for emotional reasons

    C. Cultural reasons for drunkorexia

    D. Medical cures for drunkorexia

25. What is the author's primary purpose in writing this essay?

    A. To inform

    B. To persuade

    C. To entertain

    D. To analyze

GO ON TO THE NEXT PAGE

Sleep Loss

The Centers for Disease Control and Prevention (CDC) is always busy monitoring health issues and sending out regular warnings to make sure people know of any impending threats. One of the most recent warnings, however, caught Americans by surprise. The CDC announced that one of today's most underrecognized public health problems is sleep loss. It is estimated that between 50 and 70 million Americans suffer from this problem.

Adequate sleep is essential to good mental and physical health. If you do not get enough sleep on a regular basis, you run an increased risk of obesity, diabetes, high blood pressure, stroke, cardiovascular disease, depression, cigarette smoking, and excessive drinking. Those are not minor health issues!

To find out how many Americans are not getting enough sleep, the CDC surveyed almost 20,000 adults in four states. Ten percent of the people studied reported not getting enough sleep every single day of the previous month, and 38 percent reported not getting enough in seven or more days in the previous month.

How much sleep is enough sleep? According to the National Sleep Foundation, adults need 7 to 9 hours each night, whereas children under 12 need 9 to 11 hours and teenagers need between 8½ and 9½ hours. Unfortunately, instead of sleeping, many people stay up late at night to surf the Internet or watch television.

Along with the health risks that chronic sleep loss can bring, experts also believe it is responsible for thousands of people who die on the road each year from accidents caused by sleepy drivers. There is no doubt that spending less time with eyes closed can make your days longer, your health worse, and your driving riskier.

26. All of the following are mentioned in the passage as potential risks from inadequate sleep EXCEPT _____.

     A. cancer
     B. obesity
     C. diabetes
     D. depression

GO ON TO THE NEXT PAGE

27. What does the word *surf* mean as used in the fourth paragraph?

    A. Spend time swimming in the ocean

    B. Look at different websites

    C. Watch late-night television

    D. Complete online assignments

28. Which statement would *not* be inferred by the reader?

    A. Children need more sleep than adults do.

    B. The CDC study was not nationwide.

    C. Most auto accidents are caused by tired drivers.

    D. Sleep loss can have dramatic effects on health.

29. Which of the following statements is an opinion?

    A. Lack of sleep correlates with obesity and diabetes.

    B. The CDC surveyed several thousand people.

    C. Many people stay up late to watch TV.

    D. Driving when tired is irresponsible behavior.

30. The main idea of the passage is _____.

    A. the CDC keeps an eye out for new potentially threatening health issues

    B. children require several more hours of sleep per night than adults do

    C. more people are staying up at night to surf the Internet or watch television

    D. lack of adequate sleep is becoming a major national health problem

GO ON TO THE NEXT PAGE

Eat Your Vegetables

By studying the role diet might have in the prevention of cancer, recent studies have also noted that a vegetarian, or meatless, diet can help improve a person's overall health. A true vegetarian diet consists of a variety of grains, fruits, vegetables, nuts, and pulses—edible seeds from legumes such as peas, beans, and lentils. A modified vegetarian diet, known as lacto-ovo vegetarian, may include dairy products and eggs. A vegan diet excludes any food with animal origins, including butter, eggs, and honey.

When properly planned, a true vegetarian diet can provide a person with all essential nutrients, protein, and carbohydrates. In one study, researchers at Oxford University noted that overall, a vegetarian diet is lower in saturated fats and higher in fiber than other diets. The study noted that people who followed a vegetarian diet were generally found to have lower cholesterol and lower BMI (a measure of body fat based on a person's weight and height) and to be at a lower risk for certain types of heart disease. From the evidence presented, researchers suggested that the adoption of a vegetarian diet could prevent more than 30,000 deaths a year that are attributed to heart disease.

Other available information indicates that vegetarians live, on average, seven years longer than meat eaters do. Throughout the world, breast, colon, and prostate cancers are more common among people who have a high-fat, high-meat, low-fiber diet. Former Surgeon General C. Everett Coop has said that diet is a factor in 70 percent of all people who die from disease in the United States. On the whole, vegetarians are less likely to be afflicted with chronic diseases than those who make meat a centerpiece of their diet.

31. Which statement would *not* be inferred by the reader?

     A. Removing meat from the diet may lower risk of heart disease.

     B. High-fat diets correlate to certain kinds of cancers.

     C. People on a vegan diet may eat yogurt and cheese.

     D. Fiber is more prevalent in vegetables than in meat.

GO ON TO THE NEXT PAGE

32. What is the meaning of the word *pulses* as it appears in the first paragraph?

    A. The regular throbbing of the arteries caused by successive contractions of the heart

    B. The general attitude of the public or a specific population toward health concerns

    C. The edible seeds produced by legumes such as peas, beans, or lentils

    D. Any type of food with animal origins such as butter, honey, or eggs

33. What is the author's attitude toward vegetarianism?

    A. Scoffing

    B. Positive

    C. Cautious

    D. Uninterested

34. A vegetarian diet is said to lower all of the following EXCEPT
_____.

    A. the need for protein

    B. the percentage of body fat

    C. the risk of heart disease

    D. cholesterol

. . . And I Can't Get Up!

Without a doubt, one of the biggest risks to older adults today is falling. It is also one of the most common accidents that people age 65 and older experience. Some just receive a few bumps and bruises, while others are hurt so badly that they cannot ever fully recover.

GO ON TO THE NEXT PAGE

US health officials surveyed thousands of elderly people and found that approximately one in six of them had fallen in the past three months. A third of these people sustained considerable injuries, including the most dreaded break of all, a hip fracture. Approximately 16,000 people even died from the injuries they suffered, whereas even more were left completely disabled. Centers for Disease Control and Prevention (CDC) epidemiologist Judy Stevens stated, "It's a tremendous public health problem because so many older adults are affected."

It only takes one fall to completely steal an older person's self-confidence. According to a CDC report, "Even when those injuries are minor, they can seriously affect older adults' quality of life by inducing a fear of falling, which can lead to self-imposed activity restrictions, social isolation, and depression."

Along with an admonition to move slowly and carefully, the CDC also recommends that older adults get enough gentle exercise or physical therapy to help strengthen their muscles and improve their balance. This will not only reduce the number of falls but also give a real boost to older adults' self-esteem.

35. What is the main idea of the passage?

    A. Most falls experienced by older adults are either disabling or fatal.
    B. Falling is one of the biggest health risks for older people.
    C. Elderly people's self-confidence is threatened by falling.
    D. The CDC claims that regular exercise will prevent all falls.

36. What is the meaning of the word *admonition* as used in the last paragraph?

    A. Permission
    B. Prescription
    C. Caution
    D. Verdict

37. Which statement would *not* be inferred by the reader?

    A. Falls can result in permanent disability.
    B. One-third of all falls involve hip fractures.
    C. Physical therapy can reduce the risk of falling.
    D. Some elderly people die from falling.

GO ON TO THE NEXT PAGE

38. Which of the following statements is an opinion?

    A. Elderly people fall frequently.

    B. Elderly people may restrict activities.

    C. Elderly people can improve their balance.

    D. Elderly people should not live alone.

Bone Density Testing

Almost everyone knows, thanks to everything from newspaper articles to endless television commercials, that bone density is a major health concern for women. Osteoporosis has become a familiar term, and more and more women are booking bone density tests to make sure all is well underneath the skin.

In all the hype, however, there are certain people who are being overlooked: men. It appears that older men need routine checks for bone thinning as well. A new computerized tool sponsored by the World Health Organization is being used to identify the people most at risk for experiencing a broken bone. One of its findings is that men older than 70 years of age should have a bone mineral density x-ray test on a regular basis.

This tool, called FRAX, calculates the risk of a person experiencing a hip, wrist, shoulder, or spine fracture within the next decade. Those tested were age 40 or older and either had osteoporosis or low bone mass. FRAX takes many different elements into consideration when figuring a person's risk level. It factors in diet, exercise, and exposure to sunlight, for example. It also looks at where people live, what genetic factors might be involved, as well as lifestyle factors such as smoking, heavy alcohol consumption, and the use of steroids.

The National Osteoporosis Foundation has used the FRAX predictions to create updated guidelines. Their new recommendations not only include bone density tests for men but also a stronger emphasis on the importance of weight-bearing and muscle-strengthening exercises and an increased amount of vitamin D supplementation.

GO ON TO THE NEXT PAGE

39. What is the main idea of the passage?

   A. Osteoporosis is a terrible disease for women to have.

   B. The risk of osteoporosis is greater than it was decades ago.

   C. The World Health Organization is concerned about osteoporosis.

   D. New technology shows that men are also at risk from osteoporosis.

40. What is the meaning of the word *booking* as used in the first paragraph?

   A. Scheduling

   B. Contracting

   C. Traveling

   D. Charging

41. FRAX takes into account all of the following factors EXCEPT _____.

   A. lifestyle choices

   B. exposure to toxins

   C. genetic heritage

   D. exposure to sunlight

42. What conclusion can you draw from the first sentence of the passage?

   A. Osteoporosis is more common than anyone previously imagined.

   B. The media give a lot of overall coverage to osteoporosis.

   C. Only women are at high risk for developing bone thinning.

   D. Thinning bones is not considered a serious medical problem.

GO ON TO THE NEXT PAGE

Singing the Blues

Almost anyone who lives in a place where the winter months are mostly dark and rainy or snowy knows what it is like to yearn longingly for "just a few rays." For some people, however, this feeling is much more than a simple longing; it is a physical and emotional need. These people suffer from seasonal affective disorder (SAD).

Although in the past the experience has been put down to nothing more than "winter blues," more and more physicians are recognizing the fact that for some, it is much more than a mood swing. Those with SAD not only get depressed, they struggle with lethargy and chronic fatigue, often to the point of impairing their daily lives. Other symptoms include anxiety, social withdrawal, appetite changes, weight gain, and insomnia.

Although more women than men are diagnosed with SAD, men seem to have the most severe symptoms. Those who live in the north and those with a family history of SAD are at highest overall risk.

Currently SAD is considered a subtype of bipolar disorder and/or depression, and physicians rely on thorough psychological and physical examinations to determine if a patient actually has the condition. If left untreated, SAD can actually lead to complications such as substance abuse or even suicidal thoughts. Treatment focuses primarily on light therapy but may be supplemented with medications and psychotherapy.

43. What is the main idea of the passage?

    A. Everyone should move to the Sunshine State.
    B. The "winter blues" are exaggerated.
    C. Sadness may sometimes be seasonal.
    D. Men get the worst SAD symptoms.

44. The word *lethargy* as used in the second paragraph of the passage can best be defined as _____.

    A. sluggishness
    B. irritability
    C. energy
    D. starvation

GO ON TO THE NEXT PAGE

45. What is the author's primary purpose in writing this essay?

    A. To entertain
    B. To inform
    C. To reflect
    D. To persuade

46. Identify the overall tone of the essay.

    A. Sympathetic
    B. Lighthearted
    C. Irritated
    D. Offended

47. Choose the best summary of the passage.

    A. Sufferers of SAD know that it is more than just longing for light, but doctors have been slow to recognize that it is a real syndrome with serious consequences. Doctors whose patients gain weight or have trouble sleeping in winter might wish to test for SAD.
    B. SAD is a series of symptoms rather than a disorder in its own right. It affects mostly women during the winter months. Treatments for SAD include light therapy, and complications may include suicidal thoughts.
    C. SAD is a physical and emotional need for light that can have ill effects on health. It affects northern dwellers and is considered a type of depression or bipolar disorder. Light therapy, psychotherapy, and medication may help.
    D. More women than men have SAD, but men have worse symptoms, which may include anxiety, weight gain, and insomnia. Physicians are beginning to recognize that this phenomenon is more than just a mood swing and are treating it energetically.

GO ON TO THE NEXT PAGE

Ranking Hospitals

You probably know that *U.S. News & World Report* publishes an annual ranking of colleges and universities. Since 1990, the magazine has also published an annual list of the best hospitals in the United States. Unfortunately, we cannot always choose what hospital to go to the way we choose colleges—nearly all of us are forced to visit the hospital that is closest to where we live. However, the list is interesting in the criteria it uses to rate hospitals, and the revelations about hospitals' specialties may be important for those of us with illnesses that require specialized care.

The magazine's rankings look first and foremost at outcomes. Survival rate is important. So, too, are safety, numbers of nurses, modern technology, and reputation.

The magazine also looks at 16 specialties, including cancer, cardiology, diabetes, geriatrics, and urology. For 12 of the specialties, they use data to rate hospitals. In four specialties—psychiatry, rehabilitation, rheumatology, and ophthalmology—they rely on a doctor survey and grade hospitals based on their reputations. Your acceptance of these scores will depend, in large part, on your belief in the abilities of doctors to stay up-to-date and assess their colleagues fairly.

The results this year are not unexpected. In the top five are the Mayo Clinic, Cleveland Clinic, Mass General, Johns Hopkins, and UCLA. Still, it may be comforting to peruse the list and realize that a hospital in a city nearby ranks high in a procedure you or a loved one needs or that several hospitals in your region get good grades for survival and overall performance. We Americans love to evaluate everything, from restaurants to reality show contestants. Why not hospitals?

48. What is the overall tone of the essay?

    A. Enthusiastic

    B. Skeptical

    C. Anxious

    D. Gratified

49. Which of the following is *not* listed as a detail in the passage?

    A. *U.S. News & World Report* used surveys for some scores.

    B. Hospitals in Ohio and California made the top five.

    C. The magazine also publishes rankings of colleges.

    D. Orthopedics was one of the specialties considered.

GO ON TO THE NEXT PAGE

50. A reader might infer from this passage that _____.

    A. the Mayo Clinic is well known as a great hospital

    B. psychiatry is not a specialty at most US hospitals

    C. staffing is not a key factor in hospital success

    D. geriatrics is rapidly becoming a critical specialty

STOP. IF YOU HAVE TIME LEFT OVER, CHECK YOUR WORK ON THIS SECTION ONLY.

VOCABULARY AND GENERAL KNOWLEDGE

| 50 items | Suggested time: 45 minutes |

1. Select the meaning of the underlined word in the following sentence.

   The steady breeze caused dry leaves to <u>waft</u> over the creek.

   A. Sink
   B. Dive
   C. Wave
   D. Float

2. What is another word for *contemptuous*?

   A. Sympathetic
   B. Exhausted
   C. Scornful
   D. Insensitive

3. What is the meaning of *ostracize*?

   A. Snub
   B. Hide from
   C. Condescend to
   D. Hire

4. Select the meaning of the underlined word in the following sentence.

   The hospital accepts a certain quota of <u>indigent</u> patients.

   A. Impoverished
   B. Resentful
   C. Apathetic
   D. Uninjured

5. A nit is a kind of _____.

   A. abscess
   B. parasite
   C. bandage
   D. infection

GO ON TO THE NEXT PAGE

6. *Hypothetical* is best defined as being _____.

   A. rigorous
   B. short-term
   C. assumed
   D. convinced

7. Select the meaning of the underlined word in the following sentence.

   Please <u>swathe</u> the baby and take her to the nursery.

   A. Nurse
   B. Cleanse
   C. Change
   D. Wrap

8. In medicine, to be resistant is to be _____.

   A. unwilling
   B. unaffected by
   C. opposed to
   D. accepting of

9. Something that is systematic is organized and planned. Another word for this might be _____.

   A. involuntary
   B. universal
   C. formulaic
   D. manual

10. A synthetic drug is _____.

    A. man-made
    B. phony
    C. atypical
    D. futile

GO ON TO THE NEXT PAGE

11. What is another word for *antidote*?

    A. Purity
    B. Habitat
    C. Remedy
    D. Venom

12. Select the meaning of the underlined word in the following sentence.

    Surgery is often a <u>sanguinary</u> procedure.

    A. Hopeful or cheerful
    B. Involving bloodshed
    C. Difficult and protracted
    D. Tricky and sensitive

13. Select the meaning of the underlined word in the following sentence.

    Older patients with dementia may show signs of <u>puerilism</u>.

    A. Congeniality
    B. Depression
    C. Irritability
    D. Childishness

14. Which word refers to the surgical removal of an organ's contents?

    A. Vivisection
    B. Amputation
    C. Evisceration
    D. Augmentation

15. What is another word for *flux*?

    A. Quantity
    B. Discharge
    C. Inflation
    D. Strength

GO ON TO THE NEXT PAGE

16. What is the meaning of *regulations*?

   A. Adjustments
   B. Supervisors
   C. Rules and laws
   D. Government officials

17. What is the best description for *assembled product* in the following sentence?

> The provisions apply to any "electronic product," which is defined as any manufactured or assembled product (or component, part, or accessory of such product) that, when in operation, (i) contains or acts as part of an electronic circuit and (ii) emits electronic product radiation.

   A. A product that is collected
   B. A product that is legislated
   C. A product that is agreed upon
   D. A product that is put together

18. What is the best description of the verb *emit*?

   A. To discharge
   B. To exclude
   C. To dismiss
   D. To moderate

19. One cranial bone is the _____.

   A. partial
   B. parietal
   C. pariah
   D. parhelion

GO ON TO THE NEXT PAGE

20. Select the meaning of the underlined word in the following sentence.

This vaccine must only be used <u>intramuscularly</u> and as a single-dose vial.

A. Between muscles
B. Into muscles
C. Without muscles
D. On top of muscles

21. The ankle bone may be called the _____.

A. talus
B. talon
C. fascia
D. fascine

22. Select the meaning of the underlined word in the following sentence.

The professor's lecture seemed to be a bit <u>derivative</u>.

A. Unoriginal
B. Monotonous
C. Condescending
D. Long-winded

23. What is the meaning of *histrionics*?

A. Accomplishments
B. Daring acts
C. Examinations
D. Emotional behavior

24. Select the meaning of the underlined word in the following sentence.

Did the interns <u>contravene</u> the doctor's orders?

A. Comply with
B. Misjudge
C. Comprehend
D. Disregard

GO ON TO THE NEXT PAGE

25. *Caudal* refers to which part of the human torso?

    A. Top
    B. Bottom
    C. Front
    D. Back

26. What is the best description for the term *aseptic*?

    A. Combined
    B. Purified
    C. Sedating
    D. Tainted

27. Select the meaning of the underlined word in the following sentence.

    Ten patients will receive the experimental drug while 10 take a placebo.

    A. Fallback
    B. Substitute
    C. Control
    D. Curative

28. What does *simulated* mean?

    A. Imitated
    B. Dampened
    C. Motivated
    D. Recapped

29. Select the meaning of the underlined word in the following sentence.

    Did that dosage appear to ameliorate the tenderness?

    A. Cause
    B. Improve
    C. Reveal
    D. Restore

GO ON TO THE NEXT PAGE

30. What is the best description for the term *doleful*?

    A. Unwell

    B. Deprived

    C. Conceited

    D. Downcast

31. Another word for the collarbone might be the _____.

    A. cloaca

    B. cannula

    C. clavicle

    D. clavier

32. What is another word for *unruffled*?

    A. Concerned

    B. Wholesome

    C. Tedious

    D. Composed

33. Select the meaning of the underlined word in the following sentence.

    Occasionally, this medicine causes an <u>adverse</u> reaction.

    A. Unfavorable

    B. Contrary

    C. Noticeable

    D. Startling

34. The *C* in *C-section* stands for _____.

    A. Carthusian

    B. Caesarean

    C. Cartesian

    D. Caedmon

GO ON TO THE NEXT PAGE

35. Select the meaning of the underlined word in the following sentence.

Contusions or scratches may be treated on-site.

A. Breaks
B. Disorientation
C. Bruises
D. Abrasions

36. A condition that is chronic is _____.

A. harmless
B. critical
C. contagious
D. recurring

37. To alleviate a symptom is to _____.

A. relieve it
B. diagnose it
C. suffer from it
D. manage it

38. If you give a patient medication BID, you give it _____.

A. as needed
B. every two hours
C. twice daily
D. with food

39. Select the meaning of the underlined word in the following sentence.

Many interesting discoveries were made at the inquest.

A. Tryout
B. Intake
C. Checkup
D. Autopsy

GO ON TO THE NEXT PAGE

40. A mass of tissue formed in the ovary is known as the _____.

    A. corpus delicti

    B. corpus luteum

    C. corpus striatum

    D. corpus callosum

41. Select the meaning of the underlined word in the following sentence.

    Julia and her <u>coterie</u> are often out at local clubs until the wee hours.

    A. A close group of friends

    B. An extended family

    C. An engaged person

    D. A manager or director

42. What is the meaning of *verified*?

    A. Belittled

    B. Confirmed

    C. Anecdotal

    D. Implicit

43. If a pharmacy is in compliance, it _____.

    A. shows flexibility

    B. receives criticism

    C. meets requirements

    D. has been disciplined

44. What is the best description for the abbreviation *CDC*?

    A. An online social network

    B. A test for postgraduate students

    C. A well-known pharmaceutical

    D. A public health association

GO ON TO THE NEXT PAGE

45. The abbreviation PDR refers to a _____.

    A. book

    B. procedure

    C. drug

    D. muscle group

46. Select the meaning of the underlined word in the following sentence.

    The accident left her with a painful <u>laceration</u>.

    A. Gait

    B. Cut

    C. Headache

    D. Welt

47. A hemostat would be used to limit _____.

    A. pain

    B. bleeding

    C. fever

    D. coughing

48. An enervated patient is _____.

    A. anxious

    B. immature

    C. tired

    D. frightened

49. If a lump under the skin is palpable, what is true?

    A. It is malignant.

    B. It has burst.

    C. It is warm.

    D. It can be felt.

GO ON TO THE NEXT PAGE

50. Select the meaning of the underlined word in the following sentence.

Apply a thin film of cream to the <u>affected</u> area once or twice a day depending on the acuteness of the condition.

A. Involved
B. Diseased
C. Assumed
D. Perceived

> **STOP. IF YOU HAVE TIME LEFT OVER,
> CHECK YOUR WORK ON THIS SECTION ONLY.**

GRAMMAR

50 items	Suggested time: 45 minutes

1. Which sentence is written correctly?

    A. Maria has an unusual background, she started off as a student of geology.

    B. Maria has an unusual background; she started off as a student of geology.

    C. Maria has an unusual background she started off as a student of geology.

    D. Maria has an unusual background: she started off as a student of geology.

2. Select the phrase that will make the following sentence grammatically correct.

    Until the semester ends, Lily _____.

    A. is not traveling far from town

    B. has not traveled far from town

    C. will not have traveled far from town

    D. will not travel far from town

3. Which word is *not* spelled correctly in the context of the following sentence?

    The ingenuous foxes managed to lever open one side of the coop.

    A. ingenuous

    B. foxes

    C. lever

    D. coop

GO ON TO THE NEXT PAGE

4. Which sentence is grammatically correct?

A. When the word was unfamiliar, Bonita grabbed the dictionary and looked up the word in her textbook.

B. Bonita looked up the unfamiliar word from her textbook, having grabbed the dictionary.

C. Bonita looked up the word in the dictionary, which was unfamiliar in her textbook.

D. Grabbing the dictionary, Bonita looked up the unfamiliar word from her textbook.

5. Which word is used incorrectly in the following sentence?

Her mentor's advice was bound to effect her final decision.

A. mentor's
B. advice
C. effect
D. decision

6. Select the correct word for the blank in the following sentence.

Without _____, I never would have finished my degree.

A. she
B. he
C. them
D. hers

7. What word is best to fill in the blank in the following sentence?

Jenny loaned Luis 50 dollars, and he repaid _____ within the month.

A. her
B. she
C. him
D. its

GO ON TO THE NEXT PAGE

8. Which word is used incorrectly in the following sentence?

She is already an adjunct at a college in Raleigh, the capitol of North Carolina.

A. already
B. adjunct
C. college
D. capitol

9. Which of the following words fits best in the following sentence?

_____ having finished her coursework, Lorene expects to spend another year on campus.

A. Despite
B. Although
C. Thus
D. However

10. What punctuation is needed in the following sentence to make it correct?

Please order these supplies stethoscopes, notepads, and thermometers.

A. Period
B. Question mark
C. Semicolon
D. Colon

11. Which of the following is a compound sentence?

A. Landon rode his bicycle down the road while William walked beside him.
B. The teacher said Molly passed the exam because she had studied for it.
C. Anna Belle loved going to Captiva Island in Florida; it was her favorite vacation spot.
D. Jenna wanted to stop for a break and then continue her walk.

GO ON TO THE NEXT PAGE

12. Select the word or phrase that makes the following sentence grammatically correct.

    I was extremely surprised _____ of her dismissal from the staff.

    A. learning
    B. to learn
    C. of learning
    D. have learned

13. Select the word in the following sentence that is *not* used correctly.

    Try not to loose patience or suffer a drop in morale.

    A. loose
    B. patience
    C. suffer
    D. morale

14. Select the word that makes the following sentence grammatically correct.

    The girls have apparently _____ curfew at least twice this week.

    A. broke
    B. break
    C. breaking
    D. broken

15. Which sentence is grammatically correct?

    A. With the black mustache, the actor had the largest role.
    B. The actor had the largest role with the black mustache.
    C. Having the largest role, the actor had a black mustache.
    D. The actor with the black mustache had the largest role.

GO ON TO THE NEXT PAGE

16. Select the word that makes the following sentence grammatically correct.

   The flock huddle against the wind that ruffles _____ feathers.

   A. its
   B. their
   C. it's
   D. they're

17. What word is best to substitute for the underlined words in the following sentence?

   <u>The staff sergeant and I</u> reviewed the enlisted men's records.

   A. Us
   B. We
   C. They
   D. He

18. In the sentence below, what part of speech is *delightful*?

   Nothing can be more delightful than a late-night swim in the reservoir.

   A. Noun
   B. Verb
   C. Adjective
   D. Adverb

19. What punctuation is needed in the following sentence to make it correct?

   Although we had met earlier the busy doctor could not recall my name.

   A. Period
   B. Question mark
   C. Comma
   D. Semicolon

GO ON TO THE NEXT PAGE

20. Which of the following is spelled correctly?

   A. Labertory
   B. Laberatory
   C. Labratory
   D. Laboratory

21. Which sentence is written correctly?

   A. Bao Lin has an excellent memory for faces; she recognized the patient at once.
   B. Bao Lin has an excellent memory for faces, she recognized the patient at once.
   C. Bao Lin has an excellent memory, for faces; she recognized the patient at once.
   D. Bao Lin has an excellent memory (for faces) she recognized the patient at once.

22. Select the word that makes the following sentence grammatically correct.

   She is very caring; _____, she needs more training before she is ready to work in the hospital.

   A. also
   B. nevertheless
   C. hitherto
   D. otherwise

23. Which word is *not* spelled correctly in the context of the following sentence?

   To succeed in this position, it is necessary to menage people well.

   A. succeed
   B. position
   C. necessary
   D. menage

GO ON TO THE NEXT PAGE

24. Select the word that makes the following sentence grammatically correct.

    The centrifuge cannot run by _____; it requires constant attention.

    A. oneself
    B. itself
    C. herself
    D. themselves

25. Which sentence is the clearest?

    A. A vegetable garden was planted by the family behind their house.
    B. The family planted a vegetable garden behind their house.
    C. The family behind their house planted a vegetable garden.
    D. A vegetable garden behind their house was planted by the family.

26. Select the phrase or clause that is misplaced in the following sentence.

    With torn pages, I returned the book I'd just bought to the store.

    A. With torn pages
    B. I returned the book
    C. I'd just bought
    D. to the store

27. Select the word or phrase that makes the following sentence grammatically correct.

    Two students _____ the machine while the third oversaw their work.

    A. operate
    B. operating
    C. were operating
    D. has been operating

GO ON TO THE NEXT PAGE

28. Select the phrase in the following sentence that is *not* used correctly.

    Having complete the coursework that was required, Jorge now prepared for exam week.

    A. Having complete
    B. was required
    C. now prepared
    D. prepared for

29. Select the phrase that makes the following sentence grammatically correct.

    I hope that my parents _____ if I am able to graduate early.

    A. are delighted
    B. were delighted
    C. will be delighted
    D. will have been delighted

30. What punctuation is needed in the following sentence to make it correct?

    Were you able to make sense out of the material in the third chapter

    A. Period
    B. Comma
    C. Question mark
    D. Semicolon

31. Select the phrase that will make the following sentence grammatically correct.

    Over the next few months, we _____.

    A. listen and learn
    B. listening and learning
    C. had listened and learned
    D. will listen and learn

32. Which word is used incorrectly in the following sentence?

    Jeremiah seemed enthusiastically when we reported on our astonishing success.

    A. seemed
    B. enthusiastically
    C. astonishing
    D. success

33. Select the sentence that is grammatically correct.

    A. Kindly hand the keys over to him and me.
    B. Kindly hand the keys over to him and I.
    C. Kindly hand the keys over to me and him.
    D. Kindly hand the keys over to he and I.

34. What word is best to substitute for the underlined words in the following sentence?

    Could Kendra manage to carry both Kendra's books and yours?

    A. her
    B. his
    C. she's
    D. hers

35. Which sentence is grammatically correct?

    A. Dr. Lucas showed Jeb and they how to run the spectrometer.
    B. Dr. Lucas showed Jeb and their how to run the spectrometer.
    C. Dr. Lucas showed Jeb and theirs how to run the spectrometer.
    D. Dr. Lucas showed Jeb and them how to run the spectrometer.

GO ON TO THE NEXT PAGE

36. What punctuation is needed in the following sentence to make it correct?

> Do not be afraid to ask questions in his class he is very approachable and explains things well.

A. Hyphen
B. Comma
C. Apostrophe
D. Semicolon

37. Which of the following is a dependent clause?

A. After Marisa walked to the store
B. John wanted to play a game
C. Nick had been dancing with Kalee all evening
D. Since Sergio loves animals, he adopted a dog

38. Which word is used incorrectly in the following sentence?

> Many pass through those doors, but only a few deserves their degrees.

A. pass
B. through
C. deserves
D. degree

39. Which of the following words or phrases fits best in the following sentence?

> If you ever _____ at County Medical, you would know how grueling a shift there can be.

A. work
B. are working
C. had worked
D. working

GO ON TO THE NEXT PAGE

40. In the sentence below, what part of speech is *complements*?

> I like the way the bride's green stationery complements her elegant wedding decor.

A. Adjective
B. Adverb
C. Verb
D. Noun

41. Which sentence is grammatically correct?

A. Lying on the sidewalk, Jon found a silver woman's ring.
B. Jon found a silver woman's ring lying on the sidewalk.
C. Jon found a woman's silver ring lying on the sidewalk.
D. Lying on the sidewalk, Jon found a woman's silver ring.

42. Select the word that makes the following sentence grammatically correct.

> The committee finished _____ report in time for the annual review.

A. its
B. their
C. it's
D. they're

43. What punctuation is needed in the following sentence to make it correct?

> Courtney ran around the track and her roommates kept track of her time.

A. Period
B. Comma
C. Colon
D. Apostrophe

GO ON TO THE NEXT PAGE

44. Which of the following is spelled correctly?

    A. Insessant

    B. Incesant

    C. Incessent

    D. Incessant

45. What word is best to substitute for the underlined words in the following sentence?

       The coats hanging on the hooks are <u>the patients'</u>.

    A. his

    B. their

    C. them

    D. theirs

46. Which word is used incorrectly in the following sentence?

       Please give the folder to whoever replies to your page.

    A. give

    B. envelope

    C. whoever

    D. replies

47. Which sentence is the clearest?

    A. The car with the broken axle is now on blocks in his yard.

    B. The car is now on blocks with the broken axle in his yard.

    C. In his yard the car is now on blocks with the broken axle.

    D. With the broken axle the car is now in his yard on blocks.

48. Select the phrase or clause that is misplaced in the following sentence.

       I noticed a number of workers from my car window who were repairing the road alongside the mall.

    A. of workers

    B. from my car window

    C. who were repairing the road

    D. alongside the mall

GO ON TO THE NEXT PAGE

49. Select the word that will make the following sentence grammatically correct.

The patients are resting comfortably; _____, bed checks should still be done every half hour.

A. despite
B. however
C. otherwise
D. afterward

50. Which sentence is grammatically correct?

A. Having cancelled her flight and driven home, Jessica typed an angry letter to the airline.
B. After her flight was cancelled, Jessica drove home and typed an angry letter to the airline.
C. When Jessica's flight was cancelled and she drove home, she typed to the airline an angry letter.
D. Jessica typed an angry letter to the airline, driving home after her flight was cancelled.

**STOP. IF YOU HAVE TIME LEFT OVER,
CHECK YOUR WORK ON THIS SECTION ONLY.**

BASIC MATH SKILLS

50 items | Suggested time: 45 minutes

1. Multiply and simplify: $2\frac{3}{5} \times 1\frac{1}{8} =$

   A. $2\frac{37}{40}$
   B. $2\frac{5}{8}$
   C. $2\frac{3}{40}$
   D. $3\frac{1}{20}$

2. In Downsville, a bus token cost 25¢ in 1990. This year, a bus token cost 75¢. What is the percent of increase in the cost of the token?

   A. 50%
   B. 75%
   C. 200%
   D. 300%

3. Amee is baking a batch of muffins that calls for a ratio of $2\frac{1}{2}$ cups of flour and $\frac{1}{2}$ cup of sugar. If she only wants to make half a batch of muffins, how much flour does she need?

   A. 3 cups
   B. $1\frac{1}{4}$ cups
   C. $\frac{3}{4}$ cup
   D. $\frac{1}{4}$ cup

4. Takuo bought snacks from the vending machine. He paid $1.35 for cookies and got change from his $5. Then he paid another $1.75 for a bag of chips. How much money did he have left?

   A. $1.50
   B. $1.70
   C. $1.90
   D. $2.10

5. Express $\frac{4}{5}$ as a percent.

   A. 20%
   B. 40%
   C. 50%
   D. 80%

GO ON TO THE NEXT PAGE

6. How many kilometers are there in 12 miles?

   A. 7.5 kilometers
   B. 13.2 kilometers
   C. 19.2 kilometers
   D. 22 kilometers

7. Lori is buying fabric for a curtain. She needs a length of 108 inches. The fabric is sold by the yard. How many yards will she need to purchase? (Enter numeric value only.) _____

8. Ryan wants to share his candies with all the students in his class. He has 4 bags with 36 candies each. If there are 16 students in the class, including Ryan, how many candies will each student get?

   A. 4
   B. 9
   C. 18
   D. 64

9. Multiply: $0.22 \times 0.75 =$

   A. 0.00165
   B. 0.0165
   C. 0.165
   D. 1.65

10. Approximately how many tons is 2,267.5 kilograms?

   A. 1.3 tons
   B. 2.5 tons
   C. 22.7 tons
   D. 25.0 tons

11. Vicki went to a garage sale and bought a chair for $12, a table for $19, a painting for $8, and six decorative vases for $2 each. If she paid with three $20 bills, how much change did she receive?

   A. $9
   B. $11
   C. $15
   D. $19

GO ON TO THE NEXT PAGE

12. Express 2.68 as an improper fraction.

    A. $^{68}\!/_{25}$

    B. $^{67}\!/_{25}$

    C. $^{34}\!/_{25}$

    D. $^{17}\!/_{25}$

13. If $\dfrac{x}{14} = y + 4$, what is the value of x when $y = 7$?

    A. 11

    B. 14

    C. 25

    D. 154

14. At Teeburg Community College, the ratio of teachers to students is 1:12. Which could be the actual student and teacher population at Teeburg?

    A. 24 teachers, 312 students

    B. 85 teachers, 1,020 students

    C. 89 teachers, 979 students

    D. 92 teachers, 1,288 students

15. Divide and simplify: $4\frac{5}{8} \div 1\frac{1}{2} =$

    A. $4\frac{1}{24}$

    B. $3\frac{23}{24}$

    C. $3\frac{1}{12}$

    D. $3\frac{1}{16}$

16. If Bruce's gas tank holds 52 liters, about how many gallons is that?

    A. 13.7 gallons

    B. 23.6 gallons

    C. 37.9 gallons

    D. 49.1 gallons

17. David will earn \$15 per hour at his new job. If he works 40 hours per week, what is his total yearly salary? (Enter numeric value only.) _____

GO ON TO THE NEXT PAGE

18. Express 21.5% as a decimal.

    A. 215.0

    B. 21.5

    C. 2.15

    D. 0.215

19. How many liters are there in 500 milliliters?

    A. 0.5 liters

    B. 5 liters

    C. 50 liters

    D. 500,000 liters

20. A plan for a shed is drawn on a 1:10 scale. If the roof of the real shed measures 4 feet by 5 feet, what were the measurements on the plan?

    A. 80 inches by 100 inches

    B. 40 inches by 50 inches

    C. 4.8 inches by 6 inches

    D. 4 inches by 5 inches

21. Subtract: $43.21 - 1.234 =$

    A. 41.976

    B. 41.067

    C. 30.87

    D. 30.717

GO ON TO THE NEXT PAGE

22. Solve the system of equations for x:

$x + y = 11$
$3x - y = 9$

    A. 2
    B. 5
    C. 6
    D. 20

23. Add and simplify: $5\frac{2}{3} + \frac{6}{7} =$

    A. $6\frac{1}{21}$
    B. $6\frac{1}{7}$
    C. $6\frac{3}{14}$
    D. $6\frac{11}{21}$

24. How many grams are there in 14 kilograms? (Enter numeric value only.) _____

25. Convert this military time to regular time: 2120 hours.

    A. 9:20 A.M.
    B. 9:20 P.M.
    C. 2:12 A.M.
    D. 2:12 P.M.

26. Olivia's Bakery gives out one extra cupcake for each dozen sold, to make a "baker's dozen" of 13 in all. How many extra cupcakes does the bakery add to a special order of 180 cupcakes?

    A. 12
    B. 13
    C. 14
    D. 15

GO ON TO THE NEXT PAGE

27. What is 110% of 40?

    A. 44

    B. 50

    C. 55

    D. 60

28. Divide: $92 \div 11 =$

    A. 8 r3

    B. 8 r4

    C. 8 r7

    D. 9 r1

29. Stanton runs 2 miles twice a week and 3 miles once a week. If he runs every week, how many miles does he run in a year?

    A. 185 miles

    B. 260 miles

    C. 330 miles

    D. 364 miles

30. Hayleigh wants to buy drinks for her baseball team. There are 14 people on the team, and drinks at the concession stand are $1.50 each. Which of the following equations could be used to find the total amount of money Hayleigh will need?

    A. $14 + 1.5 = x$

    B. $14 \times 1.5 = x$

    C. $14 \div 1.5 = x$

    D. $x \times 1.5 = 14$

31. Express $^{12}\!/_{30}$ as a decimal.

    A. 0.004

    B. 0.04

    C. 0.4

    D. 4

32. How many kilograms are there in 11 pounds?

    A. 5 kilograms

    B. 5.5 kilograms

    C. 22.2 kilograms

    D. 24.2 kilograms

GO ON TO THE NEXT PAGE

33. What percent is 0.502?

    A. 0.502%

    B. 5.02%

    C. 5.2%

    D. 50.2%

34. At Cosmic Comix, Svante can buy three comic books for $9.99. How many can he buy for $50?

    A. 12

    B. 15

    C. 18

    D. 21

35. Write the date 1776 in Roman numerals.

    A. MDCCLXXVI

    B. MDDLXXI

    C. MCCDLXVI

    D. MCMLXXVI

36. In his stamp collection, Bruno has 15 more stamps from Europe than from Africa, and 18 more stamps from Asia than from Africa. If he has 27 stamps from Europe, how many Asian stamps does he have?

    A. 12

    B. 22

    C. 30

    D. 40

37. Rhonda is making shortbread cookies. The recipe says to use four parts flour, two parts butter, and one part sugar. Rhonda has plenty of flour and sugar, but only one cup of butter. If she uses the entire cup of butter, how much flour will she need? (Enter numeric value only.) _____

GO ON TO THE NEXT PAGE

38. Multiply: $0.88 \times 2.1 =$

  A. 0.01848
  B. 0.1848
  C. 1.848
  D. 18.48

39. If the outside temperature is currently 15 degrees on the Celsius scale, what is the approximate temperature on the Fahrenheit scale?

  A. 59°F
  B. 61°F
  C. 63.5°F
  D. 65.2°F

40. A landscaping plan is drawn on a 1:50 scale. If a deck in the plan measures 12 cm by 10 cm, how large is the deck in real life?

  A. 12 m by 10 m
  B. 6 m by 5 m
  C. 5 m by 2 m
  D. 4 m by 3 m

41. Rebecca is able to paint 12 pickets on her picket fence in an hour. Her fence is 72 feet long, with 2 pickets per foot. How many hours will it take her to paint the fence? (Enter numeric value only.)

_____

42. Divide: $14.152 \div 12.2 =$

  A. 0.0116
  B. 0.116
  C. 1.16
  D. 11.6

GO ON TO THE NEXT PAGE

43. Subtract and simplify: $\frac{7}{4} - \frac{1}{12} =$

    A. $\frac{1}{2}$

    B. $1\frac{3}{8}$

    C. $1\frac{1}{4}$

    D. $1\frac{2}{3}$

44. Approximately how many liters is 460 ounces?

    A. 13.56 liters

    B. 14.38 liters

    C. 30.19 liters

    D. 32.00 liters

45. Subtract and simplify: $2\frac{11}{12} - \frac{3}{16} =$

    A. $1\frac{7}{8}$

    B. $2\frac{1}{8}$

    C. $2\frac{5}{6}$

    D. $2\frac{35}{48}$

46. Express 85% as a fraction in lowest terms.

    A. $\frac{17}{20}$

    B. $\frac{5}{6}$

    C. $\frac{13}{15}$

    D. $\frac{9}{10}$

47. Simplify this expression: $(4x+7)(x-3)$.

    A. $5x+4$

    B. $4x^2+4$

    C. $4x^2-5x+21$

    D. $4x^2-5x-21$

48. Carlotta earned 2% on her savings of $1,050. How much did she have then?

    A. $1,052

    B. $1,060

    C. $1,071

    D. $1,075

GO ON TO THE NEXT PAGE

49. Of the 300 patients receiving a placebo, 60% showed improvement in their symptoms. How many patients showed no improvement? (Enter numeric value only.)

_____

50. How many meters are in 17 feet?

    A. 3.28 meters
    B. 5.18 meters
    C. 51.00 meters
    D. 55.76 meters

**STOP. IF YOU HAVE TIME LEFT OVER,
CHECK YOUR WORK ON THIS SECTION ONLY.**

BIOLOGY

25 items | Suggested time: 21 minutes

1. Which organelle provides storage space for the cell?

   A. Mitochondrion
   B. Vacuole
   C. Cell membrane
   D. Ribosome

2. Which is a byproduct of fermentation in muscle cells?

   A. Ethanol
   B. Pyruvic acid
   C. Lactic acid
   D. Oxygen

3. In which phase of mitosis do new nuclear membranes form around sets of chromosomes?

   A. Prophase
   B. Anaphase
   C. Telophase
   D. Interphase

4. Which names a final step in protein synthesis?

   A. DNA unzips.
   B. Amino acids bond.
   C. Transfer RNA bonds to messenger RNA.
   D. Messenger RNA moves to ribosomes.

5. Polydactylism, the presentation of extra digits on hands or feet, is carried on the dominant allele. In the case of two parents with polydactylism, what percentage of their offspring is predicted to manifest the anomaly?

   A. 25%
   B. 50%
   C. 75%
   D. 100%

| **GO ON TO THE NEXT PAGE** |

6. Foods with a high salt content do not have to be refrigerated. What natural process prevents these foods from spoiling?

   A. Osmosis
   B. Diffusion
   C. Active transport
   D. Passive transport

7. What is necessary for active transport through a membrane to take place?

   A. Glucose
   B. Oxygen
   C. Sodium
   D. ATP

8. Which is true of enzymes?

   A. They are made from lipids.
   B. They are made from proteins.
   C. They form double chains of DNA.
   D. They bind with catalysts.

9. Which is an example of a gymnosperm?

   A. Red cedar
   B. Japanese cherry
   C. Flowering dogwood
   D. American chestnut

10. _____ is a symbiotic relationship in which one organism benefits and the other is not affected.

    A. Mutualism
    B. Parasitism
    C. Commensalism
    D. Competition

GO ON TO THE NEXT PAGE

11. Dogs are part of a larger animal group, the Carnivora. What classification is this?

    A. Kingdom

    B. Class

    C. Order

    D. Genus

12. What are saturated fats saturated with?

    A. Hydrogen atoms

    B. Carbon atoms

    C. Oxygen atoms

    D. Nitrogen atoms

13. Which is found in animal cells but not in plant cells?

    A. Centriole

    B. Cytoplasm

    C. Vacuole

    D. Golgi apparatus

14. Ocean waves may tear sponges into pieces, each of which may grow into a new sponge. What is this form of reproduction called?

    A. Budding

    B. Vegetative propagation

    C. Binary fission

    D. Fragmentation

15. How many pairs of homologous chromosomes do humans have?

    A. 13

    B. 23

    C. 26

    D. 46

16. What happens to messenger RNA as it reaches the cytoplasm?

    A. It attaches to a ribosome.

    B. It unzips, exposing nitrogen bases.

    C. It pairs with the DNA bases.

    D. It pulls free of the DNA strand.

GO ON TO THE NEXT PAGE

17. Hemophilia is a sex-linked trait carried on the X chromosome. In an example of a male with hemophilia and a female carrier, what percentage of the offspring is predicted to be carriers only?

    A. 0%
    B. 25%
    C. 50%
    D. 100%

18. Which is *not* one of the raw materials needed for cellular respiration?

    A. ADP
    B. Phosphate
    C. Water
    D. Glucose

19. Patient A, who weighs 68 kilograms, steps onto a scale 20 times. The scale consistently weighs Patient A as 75 kilograms. What is true of the measurement?

    A. It is valid, but not reliable.
    B. It is neither reliable nor valid.
    C. It is both valid and reliable.
    D. It is reliable, but not valid.

20. Which of the following organs manufactures digestive enzymes?

    A. Kidneys
    B. Liver
    C. Spleen
    D. Pancreas

GO ON TO THE NEXT PAGE

21. How should a researcher test the hypothesis that practicing yoga reduces blood pressure?

   A. Record the blood pressure of one male and one female participant before and after participating in a yoga class.

   B. Divide 30 female participants into two groups with similar average blood pressure; test each participant's blood pressure after having her participate in a yoga class.

   C. Divide 30 female participants into two groups with similar average blood pressure, have one group watch television for an hour while the other takes a yoga class, and record each participant's blood pressure after the hour. Repeat daily for two weeks.

   D. Start with 15 men and 15 women, have the men watch television for an hour while the women take a yoga class, and record each participant's blood pressure after the hour. Reverse, having the men take a yoga class while the women watch television.

22. How do green plants use nitrates in the nitrogen cycle?

   A. To synthesize proteins

   B. To store food

   C. To decompose ammonia

   D. To break down nitrites

23. Which of the following is an example of osmosis?

   A. Minerals and water travel from a plant's roots to its stem.

   B. The leaves of a plant absorb solar energy.

   C. The leaves of a plant produce oxygen.

   D. Plant roots absorb water from the soil.

24. Which might be described as a core of nucleic acid surrounded by a protein coat?

   A. RNA

   B. Virus

   C. Blue-green alga

   D. Saprophyte

GO ON TO THE NEXT PAGE

25. In contrast with triglycerides, phospholipids are lacking one of which of the following components?

A. Monosaccharide
B. Glycerol
C. Phosphates
D. Fatty acid

**STOP. IF YOU HAVE TIME LEFT OVER,
CHECK YOUR WORK ON THIS SECTION ONLY.**

CHEMISTRY

25 items | Suggested time: 21 minutes

1. Aluminum (Al) has 13 protons in its nucleus. What is the number of electrons in an Al^{3+} ion?

   A. 16
   B. 13
   C. 10
   D. 3

2. Blood with a pH of 1.3 indicates what about the blood sample?

   A. It is strongly acidic.
   B. It is strongly basic.
   C. It is weakly acidic.
   D. It is weakly basic.

3. A radioactive isotope has a half-life of 20 years. How many grams of a 6-gram sample will remain after 40 years?

   A. 8
   B. 6
   C. 3
   D. 1.5

4. Which compound has a nonpolar bond in which the electrons are shared equally?

   A. H_2O
   B. NH_3
   C. Cl_2
   D. CH_4

5. Name the reaction shown.

   $$8Fe + S_8 \rightarrow 8FeS$$

   A. Single displacement
   B. Double displacement
   C. Synthesis
   D. Acid-base

GO ON TO THE NEXT PAGE

6. In the solid state, you would expect a nonmetal to be _____.

   A. brittle

   B. lustrous

   C. malleable

   D. conductive

7. The molar mass of some gases is as follows: carbon monoxide—28.00 g/mol; helium—4.00 g/mol; nitrogen—14.01 g/mol; and oxygen—16.00 g/mol. Which would you expect to diffuse most rapidly?

   A. Carbon monoxide

   B. Helium

   C. Nitrogen

   D. Oxygen

8. Which is a triatomic allotrope of oxygen?

   A. Acidic oxide

   B. Water

   C. Ozone

   D. Carbon dioxide

9. Which substance shows a decrease in solubility in water with an increase in temperature?

   A. NaCl

   B. O_2

   C. KI

   D. $CaCl_2$

10. What is the product of combustion of a hydrocarbon in excess oxygen?

   A. Chlorine and bromine

   B. Naphthalene

   C. Carbon dioxide and water

   D. Carbonium ions

GO ON TO THE NEXT PAGE

11. Balance this equation: $Zn + HCl \rightarrow ZnCl_2 + H_2$.

    A. $Zn + 2HCl \rightarrow ZnCl_2 + H_2$
    B. $Zn + HCl \rightarrow 2ZnCl_2 + H_2$
    C. $2Zn + HCl \rightarrow 2ZnCl_2 + H_2$
    D. $Zn + 4HCl \rightarrow ZnCl_2 + H_2$

12. On the periodic table, where are atoms with the largest atomic radius located?

    A. At the top of their group
    B. In the middle of their group
    C. At the bottom of their group
    D. Along the right-hand side

13. Which of the following compounds is ionic?

    A. NaCl
    B. H_2O
    C. HCl
    D. NH_4

14. How many electrons are in a neutral atom of neon?

    A. 9
    B. 10
    C. 11
    D. 12

15. What is the correct electron configuration for carbon?

    A. $1s^2 2s^2 2p^1$
    B. $1s^2 2s^2 2p^2$
    C. $1s^2 2s^2 2p^3$
    D. $1s^2 2s^2 2p^6 3s^1$

16. A chemist takes 100 mL of a 0.40 mL NaCl solution. She then dilutes it to 1 L. What is the concentration (molarity) of the new solution?

    A. 0.04 M NaCl
    B. 0.25 M NaCl
    C. 0.40 M NaCl
    D. 2.5 M NaCl

GO ON TO THE NEXT PAGE

17. A drop of one of these substances rapidly turns litmus dye from blue to red. What substance is it?

   A. Milk
   B. Sea water
   C. Ammonia
   D. Lemon juice

18. To the nearest whole number, what is the mass of one mole of hydrogen chloride?

   A. 74 g/mol
   B. 71 g/mol
   C. 38 g/mol
   D. 36 g/mol

19. What is the charge of a gamma ray?

   A. −1
   B. +1
   C. +2
   D. No charge

20. What is the correct name of MgO?

   A. Manganese oxide
   B. Magnesium oxide
   C. Magnesium oxate
   D. Magnesium hydroxide

21. What is the oxidation state of the nitrogen atom in the compound NH_3?

   A. −3
   B. −1
   C. +1
   D. +3

GO ON TO THE NEXT PAGE

22. Which of these intermolecular forces might represent attraction between atoms of a noble gas?

    A. Dipole-dipole interaction
    B. Keesom interaction
    C. London dispersion force
    D. Hydrogen bonding

23. If 58.5 g of NaCl (1 mole of NaCl) are dissolved in enough water to make 0.500 L of solution, what is the molarity of the solution?

    A. 1.0 M
    B. 2.0 M
    C. 11.7 M
    D. The answer cannot be determined from the information given.

24. What is the correct formula for sodium nitrate?

    A. Na_2NO
    B. Na_3NO
    C. $NaNO_2$
    D. $NaNO_3$

25. Why does fluorine have a higher ionization energy than oxygen?

    A. Fluorine has a smaller number of neutrons.
    B. Fluorine has a larger number of neutrons.
    C. Fluorine has a smaller nuclear charge.
    D. Fluorine has a larger nuclear charge.

**STOP. IF YOU HAVE TIME LEFT OVER,
CHECK YOUR WORK ON THIS SECTION ONLY.**

ANATOMY AND PHYSIOLOGY

25 items | Suggested time: 21 minutes

1. Which is an anterior feature of the human head?

    A. The nose
    B. The ears
    C. The occipital lobe
    D. The temporal lobe

2. What is the primary hormone secreted by the thyroid?

    A. Oxytocin
    B. TSH
    C. Adrenaline
    D. T4

3. Enlargement of the thyroid, commonly known as a goiter, might be expected to affect _____.

    A. swallowing
    B. insulin levels
    C. sleep
    D. digestion

4. Which kinds of muscles are involved in peristalsis?

    A. Smooth muscles
    B. Cardiac muscles
    C. Skeletal muscles
    D. Epaxial muscles

5. Why might certain young people be underweight?

    A. They are growing in height faster than they are gaining weight.
    B. They eat little protein and too much fat and sugar.
    C. They eat several meals a day and fail to exercise enough.
    D. They seldom eat a meal that contains foods from all food groups.

GO ON TO THE NEXT PAGE

6. What might an injury to the parietal lobe affect?

  A. Breathing
  B. Attention
  C. Perception
  D. Memory

7. How does the digestive system work with the urinary system?

  A. The digestive system controls the function of the ureter.
  B. The urinary system removes toxins from the products of digestion.
  C. The digestive system manufactures hormones that influence urination.
  D. The urinary system eliminates some waste products of digestion.

8. Which gland is located superior to the kidney?

  A. Pituitary
  B. Adrenal
  C. Hypothalamus
  D. Pancreas

9. To what two systems might the urethra belong?

  A. Reproductive and endocrine
  B. Urinary and reproductive
  C. Endocrine and urinary
  D. Digestive and cardiovascular

10. The axial skeletal system contains all of these EXCEPT
  _____ .

  A. the skull
  B. the ribs
  C. the breastbone
  D. the radius

GO ON TO THE NEXT PAGE

11. The gallbladder is part of the _____.

    A. endocrine system

    B. urinary system

    C. digestive system

    D. nervous system

12. Which is *not* an example of a nonspecific immune response?

    A. Inflammation

    B. Vasodilation

    C. Releases of histamine

    D. Production of antibodies

13. Which organ system is primarily responsible for regulating electrolytes?

    A. The endocrine system

    B. The urinary system

    C. The lymphatic system

    D. The nervous system

14. What is the function of the coronary artery?

    A. It carries oxygenated blood to the heart.

    B. It carries deoxygenated blood to the lungs.

    C. It supplies blood to the heart muscle.

    D. It distributes blood to the body.

15. What condition might result from lack of vitamin C?

    A. Kwashiorkor

    B. Pellagra

    C. Rickets

    D. Scurvy

GO ON TO THE NEXT PAGE

16. How does the muscular system work with the skeletal system?

   A. Muscles attached to tendons contract to bend the skeleton at the joints.

   B. The hard bones of the skeleton protect the voluntary muscles of the limbs.

   C. The cardiac muscles produce calcium that is needed for sturdy bones.

   D. Smooth muscles on internal organs leach excess minerals from the bones.

17. Which is *not* produced by the pituitary gland?

   A. FSH

   B. TRH

   C. LH

   D. ADH

18. The ribs are _____ to the lungs in the human body.

   A. medial

   B. superior

   C. anterior

   D. deep

19. What is the normal pH of human arterial blood?

   A. 6.8

   B. 7.4

   C. 7.9

   D. 8.2

20. Which cut is considered a cross section?

   A. A sagittal or frontal section

   B. A cut along the coronal plane

   C. A cut through the transverse plane

   D. A cut along the median plane

GO ON TO THE NEXT PAGE

21. Which enzyme functions to break down a specific sugar?

    A. Catalase
    B. Lipase
    C. Protease
    D. Lactase

22. The hypothalamus is part of the _____.

    A. cardiovascular system
    B. endocrine system
    C. respiratory system
    D. lymphatic system

23. Which mineral helps maintain fluid balance in the body?

    A. Potassium
    B. Cobalt
    C. Chromium
    D. Sulfur

24. The skull is _____ to the spinal cord.

    A. anterior
    B. posterior
    C. lateral
    D. superior

25. Which organ system is primarily responsible for integrating voluntary movements?

    A. Cardiovascular system
    B. Digestive system
    C. Nervous system
    D. Respiratory system

STOP. IF YOU HAVE TIME LEFT OVER,
CHECK YOUR WORK ON THIS SECTION ONLY.

PHYSICS

| 25 items | Suggested time: 50 minutes |

1. Which one has the lowest density?

   A. Water
   B. Cork
   C. Aluminum
   D. Steel

2. Marilyn is driving to a wedding. She drives 4 miles south before realizing that she left the gift at home. She makes a U-turn, returns home to pick up the gift, and sets out again driving south. This time, she drives 1 mile out of her way to pick up a friend. From there, they continue 5 miles more to the wedding. Which of these statements is true about Marilyn's trip?

   A. The displacement of her trip is 6 miles, and the distance traveled is 6 miles.
   B. The displacement of her trip is 14 miles, and the distance traveled is 14 miles.
   C. The displacement of her trip is 8 miles, and the distance traveled is 14 miles.
   D. The displacement of her trip is 6 miles, and the distance traveled is 14 miles.

3. If the force on an object is doubled, how does its acceleration change?

   A. It remains the same.
   B. It is halved.
   C. It is doubled.
   D. It is eliminated.

4. An object has a constant velocity of 50 m/s and travels for 10 s. What is the acceleration of the object?

   A. 0 m/s^2
   B. 5 m/s^2
   C. 60 m/s^2
   D. 500 m/s^2

GO ON TO THE NEXT PAGE

5. When calculating an object's acceleration, you must do which of the following?

   A. Divide the change in time by the velocity.
   B. Multiply the velocity by the time.
   C. Divide the change in velocity by the change in time.
   D. Find the difference between the time and velocity.

6. Which property of a substance does *not* change with a change in temperature?

   A. Volume
   B. Mass
   C. Phase
   D. Solubility

7. 100 N·m of work is done over 20 m. What force was applied to the object that was moved?

   A. 5 N
   B. 80 N
   C. 120 N
   D. 2,000 N

8. A 110-volt appliance draws 2.0 amperes. How many watts of power does it require?

   A. 55 watts
   B. 108 watts
   C. 112 watts
   D. 220 watts

9. A hummingbird's wings beat at 25 beats per second. What is the period of the wing beating in seconds?

   A. 0.04 s
   B. 0.25 s
   C. 0.4 s
   D. 4 s

GO ON TO THE NEXT PAGE

10. What is the kinetic energy of a 500-kg wagon moving at 10 m/s?

   A. 50 J
   B. 250 J
   C. 2.5×10^4 J
   D. 5.0×10^5 J

11. The specific heat capacity of tin is 0.217 J/(g°C). Which of these materials would require about twice as much heat as tin to increase the temperature of a sample by 1°C?

   A. Copper [0.3844 J/(g°C)]
   B. Iron [0.449 J/(g°C)]
   C. Gold [0.1291 J/(g°C)]
   D. Aluminum [0.904 J/g°C)]

12. A transverse wave transports energy from north to south. In what direction do the particles in the medium move?

   A. Only north to south
   B. Both eastward and westward
   C. Only east to west
   D. Both northward and southward

13. Which of the following describes a vector quantity?

   A. 13 miles
   B. 13 miles per hour
   C. 13 miles south
   D. 13 miles more

14. You drop a 50-g metal cube into a cylinder of water. How can you use displacement to find the density of the cube?

   A. Measure the volume of the displaced water and divide that into 50.
   B. Measure the volume of the displaced water and divide it by 50.
   C. Measure the mass of the displaced water and multiply it by 50.
   D. Measure the mass of the displaced water and divide it by 50.

GO ON TO THE NEXT PAGE

15. Two objects attract each other with a gravitational force of 12 units. If the distance between them is halved, what is the new force of attraction between the two objects?

A. 3 units

B. 6 units

C. 24 units

D. 48 units

16. Which of these can you conclude from Ohm's law?

A. Voltage and current are inversely proportional when resistance is constant.

B. The ratio of the potential difference between the ends of a conductor to current is a constant, R.

C. Voltage is the amount of charge that passes through a point per second.

D. Power (P) can be calculated by multiplying current (I) by voltage (V).

17. Coulomb's law has to do with _____.

A. electrostatic interaction

B. rigid body motion

C. heat conduction

D. universal gravitation

18. Jack stands in front of a plane mirror. If he is 2.5 feet away from the mirror, how far away from Jack is his image?

A. 2.5 feet

B. 3 feet

C. 4.5 feet

D. 5 feet

GO ON TO THE NEXT PAGE

19. Ocean waves build during a storm until there is a vertical distance from high point to low of 6 meters and a horizontal distance of 9 meters between adjacent crests. The waves hit the shore every 5 seconds. What is the speed of the waves?

    A. 1.2 m/s

    B. 1.8 m/s

    C. 2.0 m/s

    D. 2.4 m/s

20. If a 5.5-kg ball is moving at 4.5 m/s, what is its momentum?

    A. 10 kg·m/s

    B. 16.2 km/h

    C. 24.75 kg·m/s

    D. There is not enough information to calculate momentum.

21. Household alternating current typically has a frequency of 60 Hz. Which statement is true?

    A. The circuit is appropriate for lighting 60-watt bulbs.

    B. Circuits in the home may carry a current of 60 amperes.

    C. The expected voltage drop is 60 volts per meter.

    D. Electrons complete a cycle 60 times per second.

22. A 25-cm spring stretches to 28 cm when a force of 12 N is applied. What would its length be if that force were doubled?

    A. 31 cm

    B. 40 cm

    C. 50 cm

    D. 56 cm

23. A 2,100-kg car runs around a 5-km long circular track with a centripetal acceleration of 3 m/s^2. What is the net force acting upon the car?

    A. 450 N

    B. 700 N

    C. 1,500 N

    D. 6,300 N

GO ON TO THE NEXT PAGE

24. A circuit consists of three same-size resistors, wired in series to a 9-V power supply and producing 1 amp of current. What is the resistance of each resistor?

A. 9 ohms
B. 6 ohms
C. 3 ohms
D. 1 ohm

25. An object with a charge of 3 μC is placed 30 cm from another object with a charge of 2 μC. What is the magnitude of the resulting force between the objects?

A. 0.6 N
B. 0.18 N
C. 180 N
D. 9×10^{-12} N

**STOP. IF YOU HAVE TIME LEFT OVER,
CHECK YOUR WORK ON THIS SECTION ONLY.**

ANSWER KEY

Reading Comprehension

1. C	18. A	35. B
2. C	19. D	36. C
3. A	20. D	37. B
4. B	21. C	38. D
5. D	22. A	39. D
6. C	23. B	40. A
7. B	24. D	41. B
8. C	25. A	42. B
9. D	26. A	43. C
10. A	27. B	44. A
11. C	28. C	45. B
12. C	29. D	46. A
13. A	30. D	47. C
14. B	31. C	48. B
15. A	32. C	49. D
16. B	33. B	50. A
17. D	34. A	

Vocabulary and General Knowledge

1. D	18. A	35. C
2. C	19. B	36. D
3. A	20. B	37. A
4. A	21. A	38. C
5. B	22. A	39. D
6. C	23. D	40. B
7. D	24. D	41. A
8. B	25. B	42. B
9. C	26. B	43. C
10. A	27. C	44. D
11. C	28. A	45. A
12. B	29. B	46. B
13. D	30. D	47. B
14. C	31. C	48. C
15. B	32. D	49. D
16. C	33. A	50. A
17. D	34. B	

Grammar

1. B	18. C	35. D
2. D	19. C	36. D
3. A	20. D	37. A
4. D	21. A	39. C
5. C	22. B	39. C
6. C	23. D	40. C
7. A	24. B	41. C
8. D	25. B	42. A
9. A	26. A	43. B
10. D	27. C	44. D
11. C	28. A	45. D
12. B	29. C	46. C
13. A	30. C	47. A
14. D	31. D	48. B
15. D	32. B	49. B
16. B	33. A	50. B
17. B	34. A	

Basic Math Skills

1. A	18. D	35. A
2. C	19. A	36. C
3. B	20. C	37. 2
4. C	21. A	38. C
5. D	22. B	39. A
6. C	23. D	40. B
7. 3	24. 14	41. 12
8. B	25. B	42. C
9. C	26. D	43. D
10. B	27. A	44. A
11. A	28. B	45. D
12. B	29. D	46. A
13. D	30. B	47. D
14. B	31. C	48. C
15. C	32. A	49. 120
16. A	33. D	50. B
17. 31,200	34. B	

Biology

1. B	10. C	19. D
2. C	11. C	20. D
3. C	12. A	21. C
4. B	13. A	22. A
5. C	14. D	23. D
6. A	15. B	24. B
7. D	16. A	25. D
8. B	17. B	
9. A	18. C	

Chemistry

1. C	10. C	19. D
2. A	11. A	20. B
3. D	12. C	21. A
4. C	13. A	22. C
5. C	14. B	23. B
6. A	15. B	24. D
7. B	16. A	25. D
8. C	17. D	
9. B	18. D	

Anatomy and Physiology

1. A	10. D	19. B
2. D	11. C	20. C
3. A	12. D	21. D
4. A	13. B	22. B
5. A	14. C	23. A
6. C	15. D	24. D
7. D	16. A	25. C
8. B	17. B	
9. B	18. C	

Physics

1. B	10. C	19. B
2. D	11. B	20. C
3. C	12. B	21. D
4. A	13. C	22. A
5. C	14. A	23. D
6. B	15. D	24. C
7. A	16. B	25. A
8. D	17. A	
9. A	18. D	

EXPLANATORY ANSWERS

Reading Comprehension

1. (C) The main idea is the most important theme, one that carries throughout the passage. Although the other choices may connect to the topic, only choice C covers the overall passage.

2. (C) Although the relative size is mentioned (larger to smaller), specific size is never given. The other details appear in the passage.

3. (A) The basic purpose here is to provide information on a topic.

4. (B) The researchers did not look at reactions to violent videos (choice A). They did not compare boys in Australia to those in the United States (choice C), and there is no indication that they intend to study girls (choice D). Only choice B sticks to the material provided in the passage, as a summary must do.

5. (D) Light therapy is an "established form of medicine," meaning not only that it exists, but also that it is customary and reputable.

6. (C) Choices A, B, and D are details, but choice C expresses the main idea of the entire passage.

7. (B) A statement of fact can be proved or checked. If necessary, you could prove that untreated jaundice may cause brain damage. The other statements here express what someone thinks or believes.

8. (C) If a statement cannot be inferred by the reader, either there is not enough information to draw conclusions about it or the passage contradicts the inference. You can infer choice A from the fact that phototherapy has been around for more than a century. You can infer choice B from the final paragraph, and choice D from the fact that UV rays are filtered in light boxes to prevent such damage. Although you can infer that phototherapy is used to treat skin problems, there is no support for the conclusion that it is "most often" used for that purpose, making choice C correct.

9. (D) Skim the passage to identify the detail that does not appear.

10. (A) Substitute the choices in place of the vocabulary word. Only *central* (choice A) fits the context.

11. (C) Find the summary that best fits the overall substance of the passage. The passage never mentions studying the perpetrators of spankings (choice A) or spanking in various cultures (choice B). Choice D is a conclusion one might draw from the passage, but it is not a summary of the material in the passage.

12. (C) The author presents both sides but does not choose sides, as a persuasive essay might do (choice B).

13. (A) Choices B, C, and D have strong support in the passage. Choice A may or may not be true but is not supported by anything the author suggests.

14. (B) What is the passage mostly about? It is about napping and its effect on the brain.

15. (A) *Shifts* has a number of meanings, but in the context of "shifts in brain chemistry," the best choice is choice A, alterations, or changes.

16. (B) The author does not insert himself or his opinions into the text, making choices C and D unlikely, but he does directly address the reader in paragraph 1, which means that choice A is not quite right, either.

17. (D) All of the details are mentioned in the passage, with the exception of choice D.

18. (A) Choice B is contradicted by information in the last paragraph. The low-intensity exercise group experienced less fatigue but similar energy to the high-intensity exercise group, making choice C unlikely. There were three dozen participants in three groups, making choice D an unreasonable inference. The best choice is A—the passage states that this same team published a related study a few years ago.

19. (D) You could conclude this from the information given, but it would still be a matter of opinion rather than fact.

20. (D) If you don't read the word in context, you might choose any of the other choices. However, the author is clearly referring to the kind of track on which people jog or run.

21. (C) Choice A is a possible conclusion but not the main idea. Choice B refers to exercising hard, which is not what the passage suggests. Choice D is a detail. Choice C, the correct answer, reflects the overall theme of the passage.

22. (A) Ask yourself, "How does the author feel about drunkorexia? How does she make me feel about it?" The author's word choice evinces a feeling of dismay or concern.

23. (B) No one can abstain completely from food—no one can go without it.

24. (D) Choices A and B appear in paragraph 1, and choice C appears in paragraph 2. No mention is made of medical cures for this disorder.

25. (A) The answer would be choice B, to persuade, if the author were requesting an action or change in beliefs from the reader. Since the author is simply presenting facts and information, the better choice is A.

26. (A) Choices B, C, and D appear in a list in paragraph 2.

27. (B) To surf the Internet is to look at various websites.

28. (C) Choices A, B, and D receive clear support in the passage, but nowhere does the author imply that the majority of accidents are caused by sleepy drivers.

29. (D) *Irresponsible* is a value judgment; irresponsibility cannot be tested or proved. The other choices are testable.

30. (D) Choices A, B, and C are details from the passage, but only choice D covers the passage as a whole.

31. (C) Look for the statement that is unsupported by the information in the passage. That choice must be C—the passage states clearly that a vegan diet includes no animal products, and dairy products are animal products.

32. (C) Look back at the paragraph in question, and you will see the word defined in context.

33. (B) The author describes the positive aspects of vegetarianism as a means of improving health.

34. (A) Choices B, C, and D appear in paragraph 2, but protein is never mentioned.

35. (B) The passage does not support choices A or D, and choice C is just a small detail. The best choice is B.

36. (C) The CDC gives older adults an admonition to move slowly and carefully. In other words, it gives older adults a warning, or caution.

37. (B) All of the other choices have some support in the passage. However, the passage indicates that one-third of the people who fall sustain serious injury, of which some unnamed percentage is to the hip, making B the best choice.

38. (D) With the correct experimentation or testing, you could prove or disprove choices A, B, and C. Choice D, however, remains a judgment call, or opinion.

39. (D) The main idea is introduced in paragraph 2—although women's potential for bone brittleness has received attention, men have been overlooked until recently.

40. (A) When you book a bone density test, you schedule the test with your clinic or doctor.

41. (B) All of the choices but choice B are listed in paragraph 3.

42. (B) The question refers to the first sentence in the passage, so that is the sentence you must refer to in order to respond. The first sentence states, "Almost everyone knows, thanks to everything from newspaper articles to endless television commercials, that bone density is a major health concern for women." That does not mean that only women are at high risk (choice C); it simply means that the media give osteoporosis a lot of attention.

43. (C) Look for the idea that applies to the passage as a whole.

44. (A) Even if you do not recognize the word, you can use the context (especially the term *chronic fatigue*) to eliminate choices C and D entirely and focus on choice A as the best answer.

45. (B) The passage primarily gives information; it does not express an opinion or ask for the reader to act, as a persuasive essay would do (choice D).

46. (A) How does the author feel about the topic of SAD? The passage describes the negative aspects of SAD and its effects on patients, not in a lighthearted, irritated, or offended way, but in a relatively sympathetic way.

47. (C) Choice C is the only one that sticks to the basics of the passage without focusing too closely on one detail or moving beyond the scope of the essay.

48. (B) The author is mostly straightforward, but occasional phrases hint at some skepticism. These phrases include, "(C)annot always choose what hospital to go to the way we choose colleges," "Your acceptance of these scores will depend, in large part, on your belief in the abilities of doctors to stay up-to-date and assess their colleagues fairly," and, "We Americans love to evaluate everything, from restaurants to reality show contestants. Why not hospitals?"

49. (D) Orthopedics is not mentioned in the passage, although it is, in fact, one of the specialties considered. Choice A appears in paragraph 2, choice B in paragraph 4, and choice C in paragraph 1.

50. (A) You can infer this based on the sentence that starts the final paragraph: "The results this year are not unexpected." In other words, everyone would expect the Mayo Clinic to appear in the top five hospitals. There is no support for choices B and D, and choice C is the opposite of what is implied by the inclusion of "numbers of nurses" as a factor in the rankings.

Vocabulary and General Knowledge

1. (D) To waft is to propel lightly through the air.
2. (C) A feeling of contempt is a feeling of disdain, or scorn.
3. (A) *Ostracize* is from a Greek word meaning "banish" or "exile." If you ostracize someone, you exclude him or her from your social group.
4. (A) *Indigent* translates literally as "in need."
5. (B) A nit is the egg or young of a louse.
6. (C) If something is hypothetical, it is unproved but assumed to be true.
7. (D) To swathe is to wrap in a long strip of cloth, a blanket, or a bandage.

8. (B) A patient may be resistant to disease, or a microbe may be resistant to antibiotics. The effect is the same—they are unaffected.

9. (C) *Systematic* and *formulaic* both imply a sort of methodical arrangement.

10. (A) Although *synthetic* implies falseness (choice B), the better definition in the case of a drug is "man-made" (choice A).

11. (C) Often an antidote is given to counteract a poison.

12. (B) The root *sang* means "blood." Think *sangria*, which is the color of blood, or *sang-froid*, which translates directly to "cold-blooded" and is used to mean "self-possession."

13. (D) Someone who is puerile is childish. The word *puerperal* means "having to do with childbirth."

14. (C) Evisceration has to do with removal of the viscera, the internal organs—or removal of their contents.

15. (B) *Flux* has a variety of meanings, all related to flowing or outflow. In medical terms it often refers to a discharge from the bowels.

16. (C) Regulations are used to regulate, or control, conduct in a business or government.

17. (D) A product that is assembled is one that is constructed, or put together.

18. (A) A hose might emit water; a lamp might emit light. The word means "to discharge" or "to radiate."

19. (B) The parietal bones form part of the top and sides of the skull.

20. (B) The prefix *intra-* means "within" or "inside."

21. (A) The talus joins with the ends of the fibula and tibia to create the ankle joint.

22. (A) If it is derivative, it derives from something else.

23. (D) *Histrionics*, from a Latin word for "actor," implies overacting.

24. (D) To contravene is literally "to come against." If you contravene orders, you go against them, or disregard them.

25. (B) In four-legged creatures, the caudal part is nearest the tail. In humans, it is at the base of the body, toward the feet.

26. (B) The prefix *a-* means "not," so something that is aseptic is not septic, or not infected or diseased.

27. (C) A placebo is a harmless compound given as though it is medicine, usually as a control in an experiment testing new medication.

28. (A) From the same root as *same*, the word *simulated* means "gave the appearance of."

29. (B) The dosage would not restore the tenderness (choice D); it would make it feel better (choice B).

30. (D) *Doleful*, as *dolor*, derives from a root that means "to suffer." To be doleful is to be full of sorrow.

31. (C) The clavicle connects the scapula with the sternum.

32. (D) To be unruffled is to be "not ruffled," or undisturbed.

33. (A) Although *adverse* may mean "in an opposite direction" (choice B), when it relates to a reaction to medicine, it means "harmful," or "unfavorable."

34. (B) According to legend, Julius Caesar was born this way—delivered by cutting through his mother's abdominal and uterine walls.

35. (C) A contusion, unlike an abrasion (choice D), is an injury in which the skin is not broken.

36. (D) A chronic condition, from the root *chronos*, meaning "time," is one that continues or recurs. Examples include asthma or arthritis.

37. (A) *Alleviate* contains a root meaning "light." It means "to lighten" or "to relieve."

38. (C) The Latin is *bis in die*, meaning "twice a day."

39. (D) An inquest is essentially a coroner's investigation of a death, which typically includes an autopsy, or dissection of the corpse.

40. (B) *Corpus delicti* (choice A) means "the body of facts proving a crime." The corpus striatum (choice C) is the ganglia anterior to the thalamus. The corpus callosum (choice D) names the fibers that connect the cerebral hemisphere. The corpus luteum plays an important role in reproduction.

41. (A) Another word for this might be *clique*.

42. (B) *Verus*, as in *verify*, means "true."

43. (C) Businesses are in compliance when they comply with, or obey, the rules of the trade.

44. (D) The Centers for Disease Control and Prevention, based in Atlanta, is charged with monitoring health, overseeing prevention, performing research, and promoting healthy behavior nationwide.

45. (A) The PDR is the *Physicians' Desk Reference*, a compendium of prescription drugs, their dosages, interactions, functions, and chemical makeup.

46. (B) *Laceration* comes from a root that means "to tear." Any jagged wound can be considered a laceration.

47. (B) The root *hemo*, as in *hemoglobin*, means "blood." A hemostat compresses a blood vessel to reduce blood flow.

48. (C) To be enervated is to be nerveless, or weak. It may be used to describe someone who is exhausted or debilitated.

49. (D) To palpate something is to examine it by touching. A palpable lump can be touched, or felt.

50. (A) The affected area is the area that has an effect on it—the area that is involved. It does not necessarily imply that a disease is present (choice B).

Grammar

1. (B) The sentence is composed of two independent clauses. They could be written as two separate sentences, or they may be separated by a semicolon.
2. (D) The action takes place in the future—the time between now and when the semester ends. Therefore, the verb must be in the future tense.
3. (A) The foxes are not ingenuous, meaning "naive." They are ingenious, meaning "clever."
4. (D) Reading the choices aloud may help you determine which choice has a logical order of phrases and clauses. The least convoluted sentence is choice D.
5. (C) You can effect change, but you would affect a decision.
6. (C) The pronoun is the object of a preposition, so it must be an object pronoun. Object pronouns include *me, us, her, him, it,* and *them.*
7. (A) Jenny is a girl, so the feminine version of the object pronoun is required.
8. (D) A city may be a capital; a building may be a capitol.
9. (A) Try the choices in place of the blank. Only *despite* (choice A) fits the context.
10. (D) The words *these supplies* introduce a list. A colon should separate them from the list itself.
11. (C) Choice C is a compound sentence because it has two independent clauses joined by a semicolon.
12. (B) The infinitive phrase makes the most grammatical sense in context.
13. (A) To *loose* is to release; to *lose* is to misplace or use up.
14. (D) If you get rid of the intervening word, you can see that *have broken* is the correct construction.
15. (D) Reading the choices aloud may help you find the least tortuous one.
16. (B) The flock does not have feathers; the individuals in the flock have feathers. Since the flock is being treated as a group of individuals (as the verb *huddle* suggests), the pronoun should be plural.
17. (B) The pronoun required is a plural, first-person, subject pronoun.

18. (C) The adjective *delightful* describes the experience of having a late-night swim in the reservoir. It suggests that the experience is very enjoyable and pleasing.

19. (C) A comma should come between the introductory clause (*Although we had met earlier*) and the rest of the sentence.

20. (D) Thinking about laboring in the laboratory may help you remember how to spell this word.

21. (A) The sentence is composed of two independent clauses that could stand on their own as sentences. A semicolon must divide the clauses.

22. (B) The sentence calls for a word that indicates contrast, as *but* would—despite the fact that she is caring, she needs more training. *Nevertheless* is the correct word here.

23. (D) A menage is a household or group. To manage is to supervise.

24. (B) The pronoun must refer back to the subject, *centrifuge*, a genderless word that calls for a genderless pronoun.

25. (B) Was the family behind their house? No, the garden was. Choice B offers the best, most logical construction.

26. (A) I did not have torn pages; my book did. Placing the phrase closer to the word it modifies would improve the sentence.

27. (C) Choice A would be correct if the second verb in the sentence were in the present tense. *Operated* would be correct if it were presented as a choice. Only choice C works in the context of the sentence.

28. (A) To match the tense in the rest of the sentence, the verb phrase should be *Having completed*.

29. (C) The second half of the sentence talks about the future, so the first half should as well.

30. (C) This is a question that lacks end punctuation.

31. (D) The next few months are in the future, so the appropriate verbs will be in the future tense.

32. (B) Jeremiah could seem enthusiastic, an adjective, but he could not seem enthusiastically, an adverb. He could cheer enthusiastically, but *seem* is a linking verb that links Jeremiah to an adjective that describes him.

33. (A) Pronouns that are the objects of a preposition (*to*) must be object pronouns, and naming oneself last is a convention of standard English.

34. (A) The pronoun must replace *Kendra's*, so it must be a third-person, feminine, possessive pronoun. *Hers* (choice D) would only be correct if the pronoun were not modifying a noun (*books*).

35. (D) It may sound awkward, but choice D is correct. It features an object pronoun, which is the right choice when the pronoun is being used as an indirect object. Whom did Dr. Lucas show? He showed them.

36. (D) The following sentence is composed of two independent clauses: *Do not be afraid to ask questions in his class* and *he is very approachable and explains things well.* They should be separated by a semicolon.

37. (A) A dependent clause has a subject and a verb but cannot stand alone as a sentence. *After Marisa walked to the store* is a dependent clause because it does not express a complete thought.

38. (C) *Few* is a plural subject that requires a plural form of the verb—*deserve.*

39. (C) Read the whole sentence before you choose. Plugging each choice into the blank may help you select the verb that fits the tense and mood of the rest of the sentence.

40. (C) *Complements* is a verb, meaning enhances or goes perfectly with something.

41. (C) Who or what was lying on the sidewalk? Choices A and D make it seem as though Jon was on the sidewalk. Who or what was silver? Choice B makes it seem as though the woman was silver. Only choice C puts all modifiers near the words they modify, thus clarifying the meaning.

42. (A) The committee is working as a unit to produce a single report, so *its*, meaning "belonging to it," is an appropriate pronoun. If the committee worked as separate individuals to prepare a variety of reports, the pronoun might be *their* (choice B).

43. (B) Two independent clauses separated by *and* require a comma before the conjunction.

44. (D) The word means "not ceasing," which may help with its spelling.

45. (D) The coats belong to the patients. The coats are theirs.

46. (C) The pronoun is an indirect object, so it must be an object pronoun—*whomever.*

47. (A) What is now on blocks? The car with the broken axle is now on blocks. Choice A makes the description and action clearest.

48. (B) Of all the choices, only choice B, if moved to the beginning of the sentence, would make the action clear: "From my car window, I noticed a number of workers who were repairing the road alongside the mall."

49. (B) The word *still* is a clue here—even though the patients are resting comfortably, bed checks must be done. *However* best expresses this "in spite of X, Y" connection between ideas.

50. (B) Think about what happened to make Jessica mad. Her flight was cancelled. Then she drove home. Then she typed the letter. Choice B puts these actions in logical order.

Basic Math Skills

1. (A) Express the mixed numbers as improper fractions: $\frac{13}{5} \times \frac{9}{8}$. Then multiply numerators and denominators for a product of $\frac{117}{40}$. Finally, express this as a mixed number in lowest terms: $2\frac{37}{40}$.

2. (C) First find the difference in price: $75¢ - 25¢ = 50¢$. Then put the difference over the original price to find the percent change: $\frac{50¢}{25¢} = 2$, or 200%.

3. (B) To make a half batch, Amee will need to cut the amount of each ingredient in half. For the flour, that would be $2\frac{1}{2} \div 2$, which is $1\frac{1}{4}$.

4. (C) Takuo started with $5 and spent $1.35 + $1.75 in all. Subtract that total, $3.10, from $5 to get the amount left—$1.90.

5. (D) Percents are fractions of 100, so you must multiply numerator and denominator by 20 to find the percent.

6. (C) If 1 mile equals 1.6 kilometers, 12 miles equals 1.6×12, or 19.2 kilometers.

7. (3) There are 36 inches in a yard, so divide the total number of inches by 36: $108 \div 36 = 3$.

8. (B) First, find the total number of candies: $4 \times 36 = 144$. Then, divide the total by 16 students: $144 \div 16 = 9$.

9. (C) Multiplying two numbers with two digits to the right of the decimal point should result in a product with four digits to the right of the decimal point. However, in this case, the final digit, 0, is dropped off.

10. (B) One ton is approximately 907 kilograms. Set up a proportion: $\frac{1 \text{ ton}}{907 \text{ kg}} = \frac{x \text{ tons}}{2,267.5 \text{ kg}}; 2,267.5 \div 907 = 2.5$

11. (A) Add up her purchases: $12 + $19 + $8 + (6 \times $2) = $12 + $19 + $8 + $12 = $51. If she paid with three $20 bills, then subtract her total cost from $60: $60 - $51 = $9.

12. (B) Convert the decimal part to a fraction and reduce: $2\frac{68}{100} = 2\frac{17}{25}$. Now convert the mixed number to an improper fraction: $2\frac{17}{25} = \frac{(2 \times 25) + 17}{25} = \frac{50 + 17}{25} = \frac{67}{25}$.

13. (D) Substitute 7 for y in the equation: $\frac{x}{14} = 7 + 4$; $\frac{x}{14} = 11$. Now multiply both sides by 14: $\frac{x}{14} \times 14 = 11 \times 14$; $x = 154$.

14. **(B)** The actual population must be an equivalent ratio to 1:12. In the case of choice B, $(1 \times 85){:}(12 \times 85) = 85{:}1{,}020$.

15. **(C)** Express the mixed numbers as improper fractions, and multiply the first by the reciprocal of the second. $4\frac{5}{8} = \frac{37}{8}$. $1\frac{1}{2} = \frac{3}{2}$. $\frac{37}{8} \times \frac{2}{3} = \frac{74}{24}$. Now reduce to lowest terms and express the answer as a mixed number. $\frac{74}{24} = \frac{37}{12} = 3\frac{1}{12}$.

16. **(A)** There are about 3.79 liters in one gallon. Set up a proportion: $\dfrac{1\ \text{gal}}{3.79\ \text{L}} = \dfrac{x\ \text{gals}}{52\ \text{L}}$; $52 \div 3.79 = 13.7$.

17. **(31,200)** Multiply his hourly rate times 40 hours: $\$15 \times 40 = \$600$ per week. Multiply that times 52 weeks per year: $\$600 \times 52 = \$31{,}200$.

18. **(D)** Percent means "per 100," so divide the percent by 100 to find the decimal equivalent: $\dfrac{21.5}{100} = 0.215$.

19. **(A)** One milliliter = 0.001 liters, so 500 milliliters = 0.5 liters.

20. **(C)** You can find the answer by setting up a proportion. First convert the feet to inches: 4 feet = 48 inches. Then solve the proportion: $\dfrac{1}{10} = \dfrac{x}{48}$, so $x = 4.8$ inches. You do not even need to complete the proportion for 5 feet, or 60 inches.

21. **(A)** Estimation should eliminate choices C and D, and looking at place value should show you that $43.210 - 1.234$ will give you an answer whose last digit is 6, not 7. The correct answer is A.

22. **(B)** There are a few ways to do this, but the easiest way may be to simply add the two equations to make y drop out.

$$
\begin{array}{r}
x + y = 11 \\
+\ (3x - y = \ 9) \\
\hline
4x \qquad = 20
\end{array}
$$

Now divide both sides by 4 to find x: $\dfrac{4x}{4} = \dfrac{20}{4}$; $x = 5$.

23. **(D)** Express the mixed number as an improper fraction: $\frac{17}{3}$. Then find the lowest common denominator and restate the two fractions: $\frac{119}{21} + \frac{18}{21}$. Solve, and express as a mixed number in lowest terms: $\frac{137}{21} = 6\frac{11}{21}$.

24. **(14)** 1,000 grams is one kilogram, so 14,000 grams = 14 kilograms.

25. **(B)** Choice A would translate as 0920. The correct answer is choice B.

26. **(D)** Start by determining how many dozens are in 180: $180 \div 12 = 15$. The bakery must add 1 cupcake per dozen, or 15 in all.

27. **(A)** You may not need pencil and paper for this one. 110% is slightly more than 100%. Solve by thinking: $1.10 \times 40 = 44$.

28. **(B)** Think: $92 \div 11$ is around 8. $8 \times 11 = 88$. $92 - 88 = 4$, so the remainder is 4.

29. (D) If you know that there are 52 weeks in a year, this should be fairly simple. He runs 4 + 3 miles a week, so he runs 7 × 52 miles a year, or 364 miles.

30. (B) To find the total, multiply the price per drink by the number of drinks needed. The equation for that is $14 \times 1.5 = x$.

31. (C) You may not need to calculate this if you use common sense, but if you do need to calculate, simply divide 12 by 30. $12 \div 30 = 0.4$.

32. (A) Since 2.2 pounds = 1 kilogram, 11 pounds = $^{11}/_{2.2}$ kilograms, or 5 kilograms.

33. (D) Percent means "per 100," so multiply the decimal by 100 to find the percent: $0.502 \times 100 = 50.2$.

34. (B) If three cost $9.99, the unit price is $3.33. Dividing that into $50 gives you 15 with a bit left over. You might also consider that $9.99 is close to $10, and $50 = 5 \times $10, so he could buy approximately 5 times the three comic books, or 15 in all.

35. (A) 1,000 = M. 700 = DCC. 70 = LXX. 6 = VI.

36. (C) Call Europe x, Africa y, and Asia z. $x = 27$, so $y = 27 - 15$, or 12. Therefore, $z = 12 + 18$, or 30.

37. (2) It may be helpful to make a chart. Since the question doesn't ask about the amount of sugar, we can leave that out.

	Ratio	Multiplier	Actual
flour	4		
butter	2		1 cup

Use the information in the butter row to find the multiplier. Divide 1 cup by 2 to get the multiplier: $^1/_2$. Multiply the amount of flour by $\frac{1}{2}$ to find the actual amount. Flour: $4 \times \frac{1}{2} = \frac{4}{2} = 2$ cups.

38. (C) Try estimating. The numbers being multiplied are a little less than 1 and a little more than 2, so the answer will be around 2. You can find the answer without working out the computation.

39. (A) The formula is F = ($^9/_5$)C + 32. ($^9/_5$)15 + 32 = 59.

40. (B) In real life, the deck is 12 × 50 cm by 10 × 50 cm, or 600 cm by 500 cm. Since there are 100 centimeters in a meter, you should be able to tell right away that the answer will be 6 m by 5 m, or choice B.

41. (C) Rebecca's fence must have 144 pickets. She can paint 12 an hour, so she can do 144 in 144 ÷ 12, or 12 hours.

42. (C) Since you are essentially dividing 12 into 14, the answer must be close to 1. Only choice C makes sense.

43. (D) $^7/_4 = {}^{21}/_{12}$. $^{21}/_{12} - {}^1/_{12} = {}^{20}/_{12}$, which is the same as $1^8/_{12}$, or $1^2/_3$.

44. (A) One liter is about 1.06 quarts, so start by converting 460 ounces to quarts. There are 8 ounces in a cup and 4 cups in a quart, so a quart has 32 ounces. Now set up a proportion: $\frac{1\ qt}{32\ oz} = \frac{x\ qt}{460\ oz}$; $460 \div 32 = 14.375$ quarts. Now convert that to liters: $\frac{1\ L}{1.06\ qt} = \frac{x\ L}{14.375\ qt}$; $14.375 \div 1.06 = 13.56$ L.

45. (D) To add and subtract fractions, first find the lowest common denominator and convert each fraction to an equivalent fraction with that denominator. Here, the lowest common denominator is 48. $2\frac{44}{48} - \frac{9}{48} = 2\frac{35}{48}$. That fraction cannot be reduced further, so the answer is D.

46. (A) $85\% = \frac{85}{100}$. $\frac{85}{100} \div \frac{5}{5} = \frac{17}{20}$.

47. (D) Use the FOIL method of multiplying the first terms, then the outside terms, then the inside terms, then the last terms.
$$(4x+7)(x-3) = (4x)(x) + (4x)(-3) + (7)(x) + (7)(-3)$$
$$= 4x^2 - 12x + 7x - 21 = 4x^2 - 5x - 21$$

48. (C) Take 2% of $1,050. $0.02 \times \$1,050 = \$21$. Now add that to $1,050: $1,050 + $21 = $1,071.

49. (120) If 60% showed improvement, 40% did not. $0.40 \times 300 = 120$.

50. (B) There are about 3.28 feet in one meter. Set up a proportion: $\frac{1\ m}{3.28\ ft} = \frac{x\ m}{17\ ft}$; $17 \div 3.28 = 5.18$ meters.

Biology

1. (B) Vacuoles are saclike structures in eukaryotic cells that contain water and solutions of salt and food materials.

2. (C) Fermentation is an incomplete form of cellular respiration. When it occurs in yeast, pyruvic acid is converted into ethanol and carbon dioxide. When it occurs in muscle cells that are not receiving enough oxygen, pyruvic acid is converted into lactic acid.

3. (C) Telophase is the phase in which the spindle dissolves and new membranes and nucleoli form, leading to two new cells.

4. (B) In protein synthesis, coded information from DNA is translated into a finished protein. First, DNA unzips and RNA nucleotides bond with bases on each unzipped segment, forming messenger RNA. Then messenger RNA leaves the nucleus and attaches to a ribosome in the cytoplasm. Transfer RNA moves into position along the messenger RNA, and the amino acids attached to the transfer RNA molecules bond, forming the protein.

5. (C) If the trait is carried on the dominant allele, either an *AA* combination or an *Aa* combination result in the manifestation of the trait. On a Punnett square, that would represent 3 out of 4 choices.

6. (A) Osmosis is the process whereby molecules of water move from an area of greater concentration to an area of lesser concentration. Bacteria and fungi that land on salty foods lose water from their cells and die.

7. (D) A substance may move across a cell membrane from an area of low concentration to one of high concentration if it is pushed or pulled via the use of energy from ATP.

8. (B) Enzymes are proteins that function as catalysts in chemical reactions.

9. (A) Gymnosperms do not produce flowers or encase their seeds in fruit. Evergreens and conifers are gymnosperms.

10. (C) This is the definition of commensalism. An example might be cattle egrets and cattle. The cattle stir up insects, and the egrets consume them.

11. (C) In order, dogs belong to the kingdom Animalia, the phylum Chordata, the class Mammalia, the order Carnivora, the family Canidae, the genus *Canis*, and the species *lupus*.

12. (A) In saturated fats, all carbons are attached to two hydrogen atoms.

13. (A) The centriole is involved in animal cell reproduction. Vacuoles (choice C) are found in plant cells but not in animal cells.

14. (D) The asexual reproduction technique known as fragmentation is common in plants and less common in animals, but it does occur in sponges, coral, and some worms.

15. (B) Humans have 23 pairs of homologous chromosomes, for a total of 46.

16. (A) Messenger RNA carries the code to form a protein. Its first step once it receives that code is to leave the cytoplasm and attach to a ribosome, where its message is decoded by transfer RNA.

17. (B) Displayed on a Punnett square, the cross would yield one female carrier, one female hemophiliac, one male hemophiliac, and one normal male who neither carries nor manifests the disease. Only one of the four, a female X_hX, would be a carrier only.

18. (C) Cellular respiration breaks down glucose and oxygen into carbon dioxide and water, using ADP.

19. (D) The measurement is reliable, because repeating it yields the same result. However, because it does not equal Patient A's true weight, it is not valid.

20. (D) Digestive enzymes are manufactured by the stomach, small intestine, and pancreas. The pancreas makes enzymes that break down carbohydrates, proteins, and fats.

21. (C) Although it may be useful to compare men and women in a later study (choice D), the study in choice C does a good job of comparing yoga to another activity over a reasonable period of time.

22. (A) A nitrate is a nitrogen-containing material found in soil. Green plants take in nitrates through their roots and use them to make amino acids, the building blocks of proteins.

23. (D) Osmosis is the process by which water moves through a semi-permeable membrane from an area of high concentration to an area of lower concentration. In choice D, this occurs when water from the soil moves into the roots of a plant. Choice A is an example of diffusion.

24. (B) This is essentially the composition of a virus.

25. (D) Triglycerides, as their name suggests, are composed of three fatty acids attached to glycerol. Phospholipids contain two fatty acids, glycerol, and a phosphate group, so they lack one of the fatty acids found in triglycerides.

Chemistry

1. (C) Aluminum as an atom has 13 electrons. For an aluminum ion to have a +3 charge indicates that the atom lost 3 electrons and now has 10.

2. (A) The pH scale has a range of 1 to 14 with the number 7 indicating a neutral solution. An acidic sample will have a lower pH value, whereas a basic solution will have a higher pH value. Blood with a pH of 1.3 would be considered strongly acidic.

3. (D) Forty years represent two half-lives. After one half-life, 3 grams will remain. After two, 1.5 grams will remain.

4. (C) All of the compounds listed are covalently bonded because they contain all nonmetals. The equal sharing occurs when the electronegativity of the elements is the same.

5. (C) This combination of iron and sulfur forms iron (II) sulfide and is a synthesis reaction.

6. (A) Nonmetals are poor conductors (choice D), dull (choice B), and brittle (choice A) rather than malleable (choice C), at least in the solid state.

7. (B) A gas with low molar mass will diffuse more rapidly than one with greater molar mass.

8. (C) Molecular oxygen is O_2; ozone is O_3. It is thermodynamically unstable and highly reactive.

9. (B) Gases decrease in solubility as temperatures increase. Solids increase in solubility as temperatures increase.

10. (C) Hydrocarbons are formed of hydrogen and carbon. Complete combustion in oxygen forms CO_2 and H_2O.

11. (A) The zinc is balanced across the equation, but the chlorine and hydrogen are not. Choice A gives you two atoms of each on either side of the equation.

12. (C) On the periodic table, the atomic radii of atoms tend to decrease across a period from left to right and increase down a group, with the largest radii appearing in group I and at the bottoms of groups.

13. (A) An ionic bond is a chemical bond in which one atom loses an electron to become a positive ion, and another gains an electron to become a negative ion. Usually the bond is between a metal cation and a nonmetal anion. Sodium chloride is a typical example: $Na + Cl \rightarrow Na^+ + Cl^- \rightarrow NaCl$.

14. (B) A neutral atom has the same number of electrons as protons. Neon, with atomic number 10, has 10 protons and thus 10 electrons in its neutral state.

15. (B) The electron distribution of an atom is divided into shells, which in turn contain subshells composed of the orbitals in which the electrons reside. In electron configuration, the symbols 1s, 2s, 2p, and so on, are used to designate subshells, with superscripts indicating the number of electrons in each subshell. There is a maximum number of electrons per subshell. Carbon has atomic number 6, meaning that it has 6 protons, and in its balanced state, 6 electrons. Looking at the superscripts alone should tell you that only the superscripts in choice B add up to 6.

16. (A) The number of moles remains constant, but the volume increases tenfold, so the moles/volume (molarity) is $1/10$ the original.

17. (D) Acids turn litmus paper red.

18. (D) Hydrogen chloride, HCl, has a mass in grams equal to the atomic weight of one atom of hydrogen plus one atom of chlorine—about 1 + 35, or 36 g.

19. (D) Unlike alpha and beta radiation, gamma rays have no mass and no charge.

20. (B) Magnesium oxide is used in a variety of products, notably antacids.

21. (A) Since hydrogen has an oxidation state of +1, in this case the nitrogen requires a state of −3 to balance the +3 of the H_3 molecule.

22. (C) London dispersion forces are the only attractive forces between neutral atoms (as in a noble gas).

23. (B) There are 58.5 grams in 1 mole of NaCl. Setting up to calculate the molarity of the solution, you divide 1.0 mole by 0.500 liters: 1.0 moles ÷ 0.500 liters = 2.0 M.

24. (D) Sodium nitrite is $NaNO_2$ (choice C). Sodium nitrate is $NaNO_3$. It is used in fertilizer and as a preservative.

25. (D) Ionization energy is the minimum energy required to remove one electron from each atom in a mole of atoms in a gaseous state. On the periodic table, ionization potential tends to increase across a period, because the greater number of protons (not neutrons) attract orbiting electrons more strongly, thus requiring more energy to remove those electrons from orbit.

Anatomy and Physiology

1. (A) Something that is anterior is toward the front of the body. The nose is the most anterior feature on the list of choices.

2. (D) Thyroxine (T4) aids in the regulation of metabolism.

3. (A) A goiter may put pressure on the trachea and esophagus, causing difficulty in breathing or swallowing.

4. (A) Peristalsis is mainly involuntary, taking part in the smooth muscles that line the intestines and other parts of the digestive tract.

5. (A) This is a common cause of underweight in adolescents. Choices B and C would be more likely to lead to overweight.

6. (C) The parietal lobe integrates sensory input and creates a spatial grid from which we perceive the world.

7. (D) The urinary system eliminates water, urea, and other waste products from the body in the form of urine.

8. (B) The adrenals sit atop the kidneys and produce a variety of hormones, from cortisol and testosterone to epinephrine (adrenaline) and norepinephrine.

9. (B) In men, the urethra is part of both the reproductive and the urinary systems.

10. (D) The axial skeletal system is the system of bones in the head and torso, encompassing the skull, spinal column, sternum, and ribs. The radius (choice D) is a bone in the arm.

11. (C) The gallbladder stores the fat-digesting bile produced by the liver.

12. **(D)** In nonspecific immunity, the response is immediate and antigen-independent, meaning that the invading organism need not be identified by the body. In specific immunity, the response takes some time and is antigen-dependent, as the production of specific antibodies would be.

13. **(B)** The body's electrolytes must be maintained at very precise concentrations. Excess water dilutes the body's electrolytes, whereas water restriction concentrates them. The kidneys regulate and help maintain the balance of water and electrolytes in the body.

14. **(C)** Choice A describes the pulmonary vein, and choice B describes the pulmonary artery. Most of the arteries of the body perform the function described in choice D, but the coronary artery's main function is to feed blood to the heart muscle to allow it to pump.

15. **(D)** Scurvy was once the disease of sailors because months at sea without fruits and vegetables led to vitamin C deficiency. Without vitamin C, the human body cannot synthesize collagen, leading to spongy tissue and bleeding sores.

16. **(A)** Messages from the nervous system tell the muscles to contract, which in turn moves the bones.

17. **(B)** FSH (choice A) and LH (choice C) regulate reproduction. ADH (choice D) promotes water retention. TRH (choice B) is produced in the hypothalamus and releases thyroid-stimulating hormone.

18. **(C)** The ribs are in front of the lungs in the human body, making them closer to the front of the body, or anterior.

19. **(B)** The range is about 7.35 to 7.45, making blood fairly neutral. Excess carbon dioxide can lead to acidosis, a pH below 7.35.

20. **(C)** A transverse section is a cross section; it separates the body horizontally into upper and lower sections.

21. **(D)** Lactase breaks down lactose into simpler sugars.

22. **(B)** The hypothalamus regulates the body's internal balance, or homeostasis. It also controls the pituitary gland and links the endocrine system to the nervous system.

23. **(A)** Fluid balance is connected to electrolyte balance. The key electrolytes in the human body include sodium, potassium, calcium, chloride, and bicarbonate.

24. **(D)** The skull sits atop the spinal cord, making it superior in position.

25. **(C)** The nervous system controls the voluntary movements of the skeletal system.

Physics

1. (B) Cork has holes throughout that reduce the volume of matter present (the cork is replaced by air), making it less dense than many other materials.

2. (D) Marilyn made a round trip of 8 miles to return to her starting point. Then she drove 1 mile plus 5 miles for a total of 6 miles to the wedding. Her displacement is 6 miles—the distance from her home to the wedding—but she drove a total distance of 14 miles.

3. (C) As long as the mass of the object remains the same, the relationship between force and acceleration is direct. Doubling the force will double the acceleration.

4. (A) An object that has a constant velocity does not experience any acceleration. Change in velocity is needed to calculate acceleration.

5. (C) Acceleration is defined as the change in velocity over time. In other words, $a = \Delta v / \Delta t$.

6. (B) Energy changes cannot affect mass. Increase and decrease in temperature can change volume (choice A), phase (choice C), and solubility (choice D). For example, heating water changes both its volume and its phase from liquid to gas. Sugar is more soluble in boiling water than in cold water.

7. (A) $W = Fd$, or $F = W/d$. The work, 100 N·m, divided by 20 meters, gives a force of 5 N.

8. (D) Power equals voltage times current. The voltage is 110, and the current is 2.0, making the power 220 watts.

9. (A) The period is the time it takes for an event to repeat itself, measured in seconds. If the wings beat at 25 beats per second, the period of each wing beat is $\frac{1}{25}$ of a second, or 0.04 s.

10. (C) Kinetic energy can be found using this formula: $KE = \frac{1}{2} m(v^2)$, where m = mass and v = speed. In this problem, that would be $\frac{1}{2}(500 \times 100)$, or 2.5×10^4 Joules.

11. (B) Because the specific heat capacity of iron is close to twice that of tin, iron would require about twice as much heat to increase 1°C in temperature.

12. (B) In transverse waves, particle action is perpendicular to the motion of the wave.

13. (C) A vector quantity has both direction and magnitude.

14. (A) Density = mass/volume. Measuring the volume of the displaced water gives you the volume of the cube, and dividing that volume into the mass, 50, gives you the cube's density.

15. (D) Decreasing distance by a factor of 2 increases force by a factor of 2^2. In this problem, $F = 48$.

16. (B) Ohm's law says that electric current is directly proportional to voltage and inversely proportional to resistance: $I = V/R$. The resistance is constant, independent of the current.

17. (A) According to Coulomb's law, like charges repel and opposite charges attract with a force proportional to the product of the charges and inversely proportional to the square of the distance between them.

18. (D) With a plane mirror, the distance from an object to the mirror is identical to the distance from the mirror to the image.

19. (B) The period is 5 seconds. From that you can determine the frequency; it is the reciprocal of the period, or $\frac{1}{5}$. The wavelength is 9 meters. Knowing that and the frequency, you can determine the speed using the equation $v = f\lambda$. $\frac{1}{5}(9) = \frac{9}{5}$, or 1.8 m/s.

20. (C) Multiply velocity by mass to find momentum. 4.5 m/s × 5.5 kg = 24.75 kg·m/s.

21. (D) Named for Heinrich Hertz, the hertz (Hz) is a unit of frequency defined as the number of cycles per second of a periodic phenomenon.

22. (A) Use the equation $k = Fx$, where k is the spring constant, F is the force, and x is the elongation. The spring elongated by 3 cm when stretched by a force of 12 N, so the constant is $\frac{12}{3} = 4$ N/cm. Applying that constant to the new equation with double the force gives you $x = \frac{24}{4}$, or 6 cm. Finally, add that number of centimeters to the original length, 25 cm, to get a total of 31 cm.

23. (D) Use the equation $F_{net} = ma$. The answer is $2,100 \times 3$, or 6,300 N.

24. (C) Resistance equals voltage divided by current, so the resistance must equal 9 ohms, divided over three same-size resistors, for 3 ohms apiece.

25. (A) Use Coulomb's law to find the force. The equation to use is this:

$$F_{elect} = \frac{k \times Q_1 \times Q_2}{d^2}$$

Remember that 1 coulomb = 10^6 microcoulombs. Q_1 in this case equals 3×10^{-6} C, Q_2 equals 2×10^{-6} C, and d, distance, equals 30 cm, or 0.3 m. Now, you must recall Coulomb's constant, $k = (9.0 \times 10^9$ N·m²/C²). Once more, it's all about computation:

$$\frac{9.0 \times 10^9 \, \text{N·m}^2 \times (3 \times 10^{-6} \, \text{C}) \times (2 \times 10^{-6} \, \text{C})}{\text{C}^2 \cdot (0.3 \, \text{m})^2} = \frac{54 \times 10^{-3}}{0.09} = 0.6 \, \text{N}$$

CHAPTER 6

A2 Practice Test 4

READING COMPREHENSION

50 items | Suggested time: 55 minutes

Universal Flu Vaccine May Be a Reality

People in search of protection against the flu must obtain a vaccine annually, and the vaccine itself changes year to year depending on the strain of flu most prevalent. These annual flu vaccines target a particular protein, but the head of that protein mutates quickly. One part of the protein, the stalk, however, seems to remain consistent from one flu strain to the next, so researchers are now focusing on that stalk as the best way forward toward a universal vaccine.

Ideally, a universal flu vaccine would last longer than a year and would not need to be altered or redeveloped regularly. There is no other virus that requires annual vaccination; the influenza virus is currently unique in that regard. Its ability to mutate has led to constant scrambling in laboratories to design new vaccines that can provide the correct immunity. Since the flu kills nearly 36,000 people annually in the United States alone, a universal vaccine would be an enormous step forward.

Trials began in 2019 on human patients, but it will take some time and a good deal of tweaking to create the vaccine hoped for by researchers and doctors. Many researchers feel that they are racing against the clock, trying to develop a universal vaccine before yet another new pandemic flu virus appears somewhere in the world.

GO ON TO THE NEXT PAGE

1. What is the main idea of the passage?

    A. Annual flu vaccines are not as efficacious as they could be.
    B. The influenza virus continues to mutate, flummoxing scientists.
    C. The threat of a pandemic leads researchers to race for a cure.
    D. Progress is being made in creating a vaccine for all flu strains.

2. Which of the following is *not* listed as a detail in the passage?

    A. Flu vaccines target a particular protein.
    B. Flu vaccines currently change year to year.
    C. Flu vaccines protect children and older adults.
    D. Flu vaccines are typically given annually.

3. What is the author's primary purpose in writing this essay?

    A. To inform
    B. To persuade
    C. To entertain
    D. To reflect

4. Choose the best summary of the passage.

    A. The flu vaccine has been required annually because the virus is constantly changing.
    B. Targeting the stalk of a protein in the flu virus offers promise for the development of a universal vaccine.
    C. In 2019, researchers developed a universal vaccine to protect against influenza.
    D. The possibility of a pandemic is the number one reason to develop a universal vaccine quickly.

GO ON TO THE NEXT PAGE

New Gout Treatment

Gout is a form of arthritis that typically comes on suddenly, causing intense joint pain, especially in the feet, ankles, wrists, or fingers. It is caused by the accumulation of urate crystals in the joint. Whereas normally, uric acid dissolves in the bloodstream and passes out of the body in the urine, at times, uric acid builds up, forming crystals. A diet rich in the foods that increase levels of uric acid—meat, seafood, fructose— may be a risk factor for gout. It now appears that nurse-led treatments that focus on lifestyle may provide significant aid for gout patients.

Medical treatment for gout has usually involved pain relievers and corticosteroids. In addition, doctors may prescribe uric acid inhibitors for patients who have recurrent gout attacks.

A recent British study indicates that nurse-led care that includes holistic education, lifestyle advice, and some form of urate-lowering therapy is not only cheaper but also more successful than the usual, physician-led treatment. Nurses were trained thoroughly in causes and management of gout and were encouraged to include patients in decisions involving their own treatment. After two years, outcomes largely favored the nurse-led patients.

5. What does the term *inhibitors* mean, as used in the second paragraph?

   A. Protectors
   B. Deterrents
   C. Stressors
   D. Transporters

6. Which is the best title for this passage?

   A. "Medical Treatment for Gout"
   B. "Uric Acid Affects the Joints"
   C. "Risk Factors for One Type of Arthritis"
   D. "Nurse-Led Care Aids Gout Patients"

7. Which of the following statements is an opinion?

   A. Nurse-led care can be cheaper than traditional care.
   B. A diet rich in meat may increase uric acid.
   C. Gout is both unpleasant and debilitating.
   D. Uric acid usually dissolves in the bloodstream.

GO ON TO THE NEXT PAGE

8. Which statement would *not* be inferred by the reader?

    A. Vegetarians may be less prone to gout.

    B. Gout may affect the joints of the toes.

    C. Nurse training is a key part of nurse-led care.

    D. Doctors never involve patients in their own care.

Get the Lead Out

In California, three paint manufacturers recently settled a 19-year lawsuit for $305 million. Their crime (to which they did not admit) was marketing lead paint while knowing its toxicity. It was a surprising ending for many who believed that because the companies sold the paint prior to the government ban on its use, they could not be held liable for its harmful effects years afterward.

The money will be used by municipalities to mitigate lead hazards in older homes, inspecting, evaluating, and removing paint where warranted. The money will go fast; there are thousands of such houses, and each could cost over $1,000 to remediate.

Even small amounts of lead in the body can result in serious health problems, but the symptoms are often difficult to associate with lead. In young children, there may be brain damage leading to developmental delays, or there may be seizures, fatigue, or irritability. Adults may show signs of high blood pressure, muscle pain, or memory loss. Pregnant women exposed to lead over time are prone to miscarriages and stillbirths.

Although lead paint has been banned in the United States since 1978, and US manufacturers stopped using lead-soldered cans in 1991, older buildings still have lead pipes, and lead may appear in bullets or batteries as well as in some pottery and toys made overseas. A major lead disaster occurred in 2015, when tests indicated dangerous lead levels in residents' water in Flint, Michigan. In that case, lead leached from the water pipes when the state failed to treat the water with an anticorrosive agent. It took months for the city to declare a state of emergency, during which time thousands of children and adults had been poisoned.

GO ON TO THE NEXT PAGE

9. Which of the following is *not* listed as a detail in the passage?

  A. Appetite loss and stomach pain are signs of lead poisoning.
  B. The lawsuit against the paint manufacturers was settled.
  C. Dangerous lead levels were found in Flint drinking water.
  D. Lead appears in some materials manufactured overseas.

10. What is the meaning of the word *leached* as used in the last paragraph?

  A. Sucked
  B. Compressed
  C. Seeped
  D. Materialized

11. Choose the best summary of the passage.

  A. Although lead has been banned from most uses in the United States, its effects continue to cause health problems that need mitigation.
  B. Because of government failure to react in a timely fashion, people in Flint, Michigan, were hit hard with the effects of lead poisoning.
  C. Children and adults react differently to lead in their systems, but both may have serious symptoms that require immediate attention.
  D. Lead from paint that was applied prior to the government ban continues to be hazardous to the present day.

12. What is the author's primary purpose in writing this essay?

  A. To entertain
  B. To analyze
  C. To reflect
  D. To inform

13. Which statement would *not* be inferred by the reader?

  A. Paint applied in the 1960s may contain lead.
  B. Not all countries have stringent antilead laws.
  C. Lead may be inhaled or absorbed through the skin.
  D. Lead-poisoned children may have difficulty in school.

GO ON TO THE NEXT PAGE

Resources for Seniors

States offer a variety of home and community-based services, with the goal of enabling seniors to remain in their homes rather than transitioning to assisted-living or nursing homes. Caregiver and respite services are also available in most states.

Senior Companion or Friendly Visitor Programs are designed to provide social interaction for seniors. Volunteers, usually older retirees, visit the senior for conversation or simple recreational activities. In addition to preventing the isolation that often poses a mental and physical health risk to seniors, companions may alert families and doctors to new and potentially troubling health conditions.

Local offices for aging are usually able to provide short- or long-term assistance with household chores. They offer transportation services to medical appointments, pharmacies, or grocery stores.

For low-income seniors or seniors on fixed incomes, home repair assistance and heating or cooling assistance is available. Seniors who require wheelchairs may request modifications such as ramps and grab bars to make their homes more accessible.

By the year 2030, one in five Americans will be retirement age, and seniors will outnumber children for the first time in history. The state resources we provide for our older relatives will become increasingly important as the population ages.

14. What is the main idea of the passage?

    A. The nation is growing older, leading to new problems.
    B. States provide many types of assistance for seniors.
    C. Most seniors need help to stay in their homes.
    D. Low-income seniors are eligible for many resources.

15. What is the meaning of the word *respite* as used in the first paragraph?

    A. Relief
    B. Treatment
    C. Guardian
    D. Specialist

GO ON TO THE NEXT PAGE

16. Identify the overall tone of the essay.

    A. Instructive

    B. Forceful

    C. Sentimental

    D. Urgent

17. Which of the following is *not* listed as a detail in the passage?

    A. Soon, 20 percent of Americans will be of retirement age.

    B. Seniors on fixed incomes may qualify for heating assistance.

    C. Offices for Aging frequently offer elder transportation aid.

    D. Only about 5 percent of seniors are in assisted living or nursing care.

Nails Give Clues to Health

Most nail abnormalities are innocuous, but some may be clues to underlying health problems. Everyone should be alert to changes in the color, shape, or texture of his or her nails. Nails may provide an early warning sign to serious illness.

White nails may indicate liver problems, especially when they are accompanied by yellowish skin on the fingers. Yellow nails, on the other hand, usually just mean you have a treatable fungal infection. Pale nails can be a sign of anemia, whereas blue nails usually mean a lack of oxygen due to a lung or heart problem.

If your usually smooth nails become pitted, this could be a sign of rheumatoid or psoriatic arthritis. If they are indented and soft, you may have a serious iron deficiency. If normally healthy nails suddenly crack and split, you may need to get your thyroid checked. Dark lines under the nail may indicate the deadly skin cancer, melanoma.

Any unusual changes in your nails should lead you to make an appointment with your general practitioner or with a dermatologist. Your nails may be trying to tell you something about what's going on in the rest of your body.

GO ON TO THE NEXT PAGE

18. A reader might infer from this passage that _____.

    A. taking care of one's nails can improve one's overall health
    B. self-care may include being aware of changes to nails
    C. doctors regularly repair damage and problems with nails
    D. melanoma attacks the nail bed before attacking other skin

19. Which of the following statements is an opinion?

    A. Blue nails may indicate a lack of oxygen.
    B. An iron deficiency can soften nails.
    C. Pitted nails are a sign of real trouble.
    D. Dermatologists can check your nails.

20. What is the meaning of the word *innocuous* as used in the first paragraph?

    A. Undiscovered
    B. Harmless
    C. Imperceptible
    D. Purposeless

21. What is the main idea of the passage?

    A. Keeping nails strong is one way to ensure good health.
    B. Cancer or arthritis may alter fingernails and toenails.
    C. Changes in nails' color or texture may indicate illness.
    D. Healthy nails are smooth and strong without discoloration.

The Essential Omega-3

Omega-3 fatty acids include alpha-linolenic acid (ALA), docosahexaenoic acid (DHA), and eicosapentaenoic acid (EPA). Your body needs omega-3s; they appear in the membranes that surround every cell in your body. Some people take omega-3 supplements such as cod liver oil, but with a little dietary care, you should be able to obtain adequate omega-3s from your daily nutrition.

GO ON TO THE NEXT PAGE

ALA is available in plant-based oils, especially flaxseed and canola oils. Some leafy greens, wheat germ, and walnuts also contain ALA. DHA and EPA occur naturally in fatty fish such as tuna, mackerel, sardines, bluefish, and salmon. Vegetarians may obtain some DHA and EPA from algal sources.

The positive effects on health of a diet rich in omega-3s are clear, although further research is needed to know exactly how omega-3s help. They seem to reduce inflammation, lower blood pressure, and reduce the buildup of plaque in the arteries, making them critical in maintaining heart health. Researchers have found that people with a high omega-3 intake seem to have fewer colon and breast cancers. Because of the fatty acids' effect on inflammation, some doctors find omega-3 supplements useful for asthma and arthritis patients.

Less clear are the effects on mental health, although there are health professionals who believe strongly that high levels of omega-3s can reduce depression, improve memory, and moderate symptoms of attention deficit hyperactive disorder. Until more research takes place, it is unwise to rely on omega-3s to cure mental health issues. However, ensuring that your diet contains ample amounts of these critical fatty acids is still a good idea.

22. Identify the overall tone of the essay.

    A. Humorous
    B. Scornful
    C. Confessional
    D. Pragmatic

23. What is the meaning of the word *moderate* as used in the last paragraph?

    A. Diminish
    B. Facilitate
    C. Enhance
    D. Conclude

GO ON TO THE NEXT PAGE

24. The passage lists all of these benefits of omega-3s EXCEPT
_____.

    A. reduced blood pressure
    B. less risk of diabetes
    C. improved memory
    D. alleviated depression

25. What is one of the author's primary purposes in writing this essay?

    A. To persuade
    B. To entertain
    C. To analyze
    D. To reflect

A Brief History of Microsurgery

Microsurgery as we know it today was developed in Sweden in the 1920s for use on animals. The first microsurgery used a monocular microscope, but soon a Swedish doctor developed a surgical binocular microscope, which became widely used in delicate ear operations.

It was not until the 1960s that microscopy was first used to augment neurovascular surgery. Surgeons found that with the help of the microscope, they could repair the tiniest of blood vessels and even reconstruct vessels in partially amputated limbs.

In that same decade, a German surgeon developed the diploscope, two independent binocular microscopes, so that a surgeon may use a high magnification while his or her surgical assistant follows along at a lower magnification, thus observing more of the area of operation in case of problems. This improvement in microscopy led to advances in plastic surgery, an area of medicine that regularly requires work on the tiniest of blood vessels and nerves.

GO ON TO THE NEXT PAGE

Technological advances have made it possible for surgeons to perform microsurgery on cerebral aneurysms, to use it as a means for reversing vasectomies, and to improve breast reconstruction after cancer surgery. New tools such as telerobotic arms connected to microsurgical forceps, or video microscopy, in which the operative field is displayed in high definition on a TV monitor, continue to make the most complex surgeries everyday events.

26. The passage mentions all of these uses for microscopy EXCEPT
_____.

    A. ear surgery
    B. amputations
    C. vasectomies
    D. reconstructions

27. What is the meaning of the word *delicate* as used in the first paragraph?

    A. Subtle
    B. Fragile
    C. Refined
    D. Intricate

28. Which statement would *not* be inferred by the reader?

    A. Most surgical advances were first performed on animals.
    B. Binocular microscopy is preferable to monocular microscopy.
    C. Europeans were involved in the development of microscopy.
    D. More than one doctor at once may assist in microsurgery.

29. Which of the following statements is an opinion?

    A. Surgeons can reconstruct vessels in amputated limbs.
    B. A diploscope lets doctors use two different magnifications.
    C. Microscopy continues to improve with new technology.
    D. Telerobotic arms may be attached to surgical forceps.

GO ON TO THE NEXT PAGE

30. What is the main idea of the passage?

   A. Microscopy uses microscopes to allow surgeons to have clear views of a wider area of operation.

   B. The repair of tiny blood vessels is a critical part of many surgeries related to the nervous system.

   C. A variety of technological advances have been developed since the 1920s to make surgery easier on patients and doctors.

   D. Microscopy, which continues to evolve and improve, allows surgeons to perform complex and delicate surgeries.

Tick Tock

According to the Centers for Disease Control and Prevention (CDC), tickborne diseases doubled in the United States between the years 2004 and 2016. Because Lyme disease is difficult to diagnose, with disparate symptoms that mimic other diseases, it is greatly underreported, and the prevalence of Lyme is thought to be even higher than the CDC suggests.

Lyme disease is caused by the bacterium *Borrelia burgdorferi*, which is spread through a relationship with three animals. That relationship starts with the white-footed mouse (or in California, the Western gray squirrel), which is prone to infection by the bacterium. Ticks in their larval form feed on the blood of the mouse. If the mouse is infected, the tick becomes infected as well, and after passing through a dormant phase, the tick nymph, usually the size of a poppy seed, looks for another blood meal. This might come from another mouse, or it might come from a human or a dog or cat. The nymphs then molt, becoming active adults, whose food of choice is the whitetail deer. They mate on the deer, drop off, and lay their eggs, starting the cycle over again.

Humans may be bitten by an infected nymph or by a full-grown adult tick. The tick needs to attach for 36 hours or so to infect a human with Lyme disease. Unfortunately, the tick bite is easy to ignore; it does not itch like a mosquito bite or sting like a deerfly bite. Many people go without treatment for months until a test explains their seemingly unrelated symptoms, which may include joint pain, a rash, fatigue, swollen glands, chills or fever, headache, or even paralysis. Time is of the essence if you know you have been bitten by a tick. See a doctor, get tested, and get treated.

GO ON TO THE NEXT PAGE

31. Which of the following is a conclusion that a reader can draw from this passage?

    A. Humans are the only mammals for whom infection by *Borrelia burgdorferi* causes symptoms.

    B. The life cycle of an uninfected tick may omit the dormancy preceding the nymph stage.

    C. Unless a tick feeds on an infected mouse or squirrel, its bite will not spread Lyme disease.

    D. The combination of fever, headache, and joint pain is clear evidence of Lyme disease.

32. What is the meaning of the word *disparate* as used in the first paragraph?

    A. Unusual

    B. Diverse

    C. Trivial

    D. Damaging

33. Identify the overall tone of the essay.

    A. Cautionary

    B. Defensive

    C. Enthusiastic

    D. Indignant

34. Which of the following is *not* listed as a detail in the passage?

    A. Ticks must attach for many hours to infect a human.

    B. Tick nymphs may feed on mice or other mammals.

    C. Humans may not feel a tick bite as it occurs.

    D. Humans can avoid ticks by staying in open spaces.

GO ON TO THE NEXT PAGE

Dance Your Way to Fitness

In 1998, Colombian choreographer and aerobics instructor Beto Pérez introduced the world to a new exercise craze. Apparently, it was a bit of serendipity that led him to invent Zumba. He left his usual music for class at home and had to improvise around a series of hip-hop cassettes he happened to have. The resulting dance moves were a hit with the class, and in 2001, Pérez, who had moved to Miami, released some videos featuring his new Rumbacize, or Zumba, routines. The rest is history; Zumba remains wildly popular, and classes may be found all over the world.

Zumba features four Caribbean and South American rhythms: merengue, from the Dominican Republic; salsa, from Cuba; reggaeton, from Puerto Rico; and cumbia, from Colombia. Instructors often include other styles such as flamenco, mambo, samba, and tango. The object is to get people moving for an hour of aerobic dance.

A study at the University of Wisconsin–La Crosse determined that Zumba is a highly effective, full-body workout that allows heart rates to alternate as with more typical interval workouts, thus burning more calories than many exercise programs, including kickboxing and power yoga. The dance movements aid with flexibility and core strength. Importantly, the classes provide good workouts both for very fit and for less-fit participants. Even better, because the movements are fun and the music is lively, participants tend to come back.

35. Which might be a good title for this passage?

    A. "South American Exercise Craze Is Popular Further North"
    B. "Dance-Inspired Zumba Provides a Full-Body Workout"
    C. "Forgetful Aerobics Instructor Discovers a New Routine"
    D. "Zumba Beats Kickboxing as the Best All-Around Exercise"

36. What is the meaning of the word *serendipity* as it is used in the first paragraph?

    A. Chance
    B. Persistence
    C. Foreboding
    D. Expertise

GO ON TO THE NEXT PAGE

37. Which statement would *not* be inferred by the reader?

    A. People return to routines when they enjoy them.

    B. Power yoga does not burn many calories.

    C. Zumba can help you become more flexible.

    D. Zumba grew in popularity due to videos.

38. Which of the following statements is an opinion?

    A. Zumba provides aerobic exercise.

    B. Cumbia is not a Caribbean rhythm.

    C. Dancing is an easy way to get fit.

    D. Zumba classes are found worldwide.

Heat Exhaustion

One of the human effects of the climate crisis is that as temperatures climb, more and more people are in danger of heat exhaustion. A recent spate of temperatures in triple digits occurred in states where such temperatures are rare. Municipalities provided cooling centers, which doubtless saved some lives.

Knowing the signs of heat exhaustion can help you protect yourself on the hottest of days. Left untreated, heat exhaustion may lead to heat-stroke, which can be fatal.

If you are forced to be outside and active in a place where high temperatures combine with high humidity, monitor your body for unusual reactions. People with heat exhaustion may sweat heavily yet have skin that feels clammy or cold. They may have a sudden sharp headache or muscle cramps. They may experience dizziness when standing up, which can lead to nausea.

If you notice that your heart is racing and you feel faint, stop your activity at once. Find a cool place to rest, and hydrate immediately with water or an electrolyte-fortified sports drink. If you suddenly stop sweating entirely, become confused, or cannot drink, you need immediate medical attention.

Be aware that certain medical conditions—obesity, or any condition that requires you to take beta blockers, tranquilizers, or antipsychotics—may exacerbate your reaction to excessive heat. If your weight or medications make you susceptible to heat exhaustion, avoid all physical activity when the heat index is over 90 degrees.

GO ON TO THE NEXT PAGE

39. What is the main idea of the passage?

    A. Cease all activity when the weather is especially hot.

    B. High temperatures and high humidity cause heatstroke.

    C. Certain medical conditions contribute to heat exhaustion.

    D. Knowing the signs of heat exhaustion can help prevent harm.

40. The term *exacerbate*, as used in the last paragraph, can best be defined as _____.

    A. to soothe

    B. to intensify

    C. to adapt

    D. to disclose

41. In this passage, which of these is *not* mentioned as a possible sign of heat exhaustion?

    A. Dizziness

    B. Nausea

    C. Headache

    D. Drowsiness

42. Which conclusion can the reader draw after reading this passage?

    A. The climate crisis has increased deaths from heatstroke.

    B. Heat exhaustion rarely occurs in dry environments.

    C. The cessation of sweat is not necessarily a positive sign.

    D. Temperatures below 90 degrees are usually not dangerous.

Dr. Sophia Bethena Jones

In a student union at the University of Michigan is a conference room named the Sophia B. Jones Room. The woman for whom it is named came from a family of impressive activists and revolutionaries and went on to have a remarkable career in medicine and education.

Sophia was born in 1857 in Chatham, Ontario, Canada. Her father was one of the first black graduates of Oberlin College in Ohio and was a strong abolitionist. Sophia had an older sister, Anna, and a younger sister, Fredericka. Both became teachers, and Anna was a suffragist who later helped create the National Association of Colored Women's Clubs.

GO ON TO THE NEXT PAGE

Sophia took a different path; she started at the University of Toronto, but dissatisfied with the medical education afforded to women there, she moved to Michigan and graduated in 1885 as the university's first black female doctor of medicine. She was quickly hired by the historically black women's school of higher learning, Spelman College, to create a nursing program, thus becoming Spelman's first black faculty member.

Following her work at Spelman, Sophia moved on to Wilberforce University in Ohio, a school that was the first to be owned and run by African-Americans, and one at which W. E. B. Du Bois had been an esteemed professor. She continued to believe and teach that education was the path to public health. She worked in hospitals in Philadelphia, St. Louis, and Kansas City until her retirement, at which time she and her sister Anna moved to California.

A society named for Sophia continues to provide medical students and alumni at Spelman with scholarships and financial support. In this way, Spelman maintains Sophia's inspiring goals of educating health workers and improving public health.

43. What is the main idea of the passage?

    A. Sophia Jones was recognized not only for her medical prowess but also for her teaching.
    B. Few black Canadians of her time achieved what Sophia Jones managed to do.
    C. Sophia Jones and her family made valuable contributions to American politics.
    D. Unlike her sisters and father, Sophia Jones worked in the field of medical training.

44. The term *afforded to*, as used in the third paragraph, can best be defined as _____.

    A. traversed by
    B. presented to
    C. removed from
    D. paid for by

GO ON TO THE NEXT PAGE

45. What is the author's primary purpose in writing this essay?

A. To persuade
B. To reflect
C. To entertain
D. To inform

46. Identify the overall tone of the essay.

A. Modest
B. Concerned
C. Admiring
D. Impartial

47. Choose the best summary of the passage.

A. As the first black woman graduate of her university's medical program, Sophia was honored to be acknowledged years later.
B. Coming from a family of distinction, Sophia Jones excelled, becoming a doctor, professor, and instructor of nurses.
C. Moving from Canada when its system failed her, Sophia Jones found a new life and professional fulfillment in the American Midwest.
D. Working within a system that rarely rewarded women and people of color, Sophia Jones defied expectations and became a renowned doctor.

The NASA Twins Study

Mark Kelly and his identical twin, Scott, were professional astronauts. They served as space shuttle pilots, with each logging multiple flights.

In 2015, Scott began a year's service aboard the International Space Station. NASA cleverly recognized this as an opportunity to do a longitudinal study on the effects of space flight and weightlessness on the human body. By comparing Scott in space to Mark on the ground, researchers could draw some important and valuable conclusions that could be used to plan for extended space travel in the future.

Ten teams of researchers developed a plan to test both men preflight, inflight, and postflight over 25 months. For the most part, the results showed the resilience of the human body even when under such unusual stress as a year in space.

GO ON TO THE NEXT PAGE

Among some of the findings were these: Scott's cognitive performance was similar to Mark's on the ground. Scott's body mass decreased substantially, probably due to his diet of prepackaged food and his increased exercise, but it stabilized and returned to normal postflight. His gut bacteria were significantly different from Mark's inflight, but they, too, returned to normal afterward.

A potentially troubling finding had to do with inflammation and arterial wall thickening, which appeared in Scott during and postflight but did not appear in Mark. Astronauts have often suffered from vision problems, and a study of fluid shifts determined that a certain protein was elevated in Scott's system during flight. Some slight DNA damage, possibly due to radiation exposure, also appeared in Scott but not in Mark.

Perhaps the most fascinating finding had to do with telomeres, the caps on chromosomes that shorten with age. Unexpectedly, Scott's telomeres lengthened over his year in space, decreased after landing, and then shortened even more or vanished in the months that followed. Because telomere shortening and loss is connected to age-related diseases, this is an aspect of space travel that researchers want to understand better.

48. What is the overall tone of the essay?

    A. Approving
    B. Hypercritical
    C. Incredulous
    D. Flippant

49. Which of the following is *not* listed as a detail in the passage?

    A. Who conducted the study
    B. When the inflight study took place
    C. Why the inflight study was conducted
    D. Where the postflight study took place

50. A reader might infer from this passage that NASA _____.

    A. plans new twin studies as it aims for Mars
    B. allows other agencies to study its astronauts
    C. will use these data in planning future trips
    D. cares more about physiology than psychology

**STOP. IF YOU HAVE TIME LEFT OVER,
CHECK YOUR WORK ON THIS SECTION ONLY.**

VOCABULARY AND GENERAL KNOWLEDGE

50 items | Suggested time: 45 minutes

1. Select the meaning of the underlined word in the sentence.

   If the companies <u>amalgamate</u>, some employees may lose their jobs.

   A. Disband
   B. Move
   C. Merge
   D. Regroup

2. What is another word for *compendium*?

   A. Collection
   B. Aptitude
   C. Conclusion
   D. Humor

3. What is the meaning of *impugn*?

   A. To instill with
   B. To instruct about
   C. To dispute the truth of
   D. To lament or complain about

4. Select the meaning of the underlined word in the sentence.

   Those who are <u>maladroit</u> should not become surgeons.

   A. Clumsy
   B. Romantic
   C. Untrained
   D. Self-conscious

5. If a patient is especially obdurate, she is _____.

   A. very large
   B. quite stubborn
   C. easily upset
   D. ready to go home

GO ON TO THE NEXT PAGE

6. *Replete* is best defined as being _____.

    A. hardy

    B. quiet

    C. full

    D. sad

7. Select the meaning of the underlined word in the sentence.

    Patients in this wing often have a <u>tenuous</u> hold on reality.

    A. Judicious

    B. Deleted

    C. Frantic

    D. Fragile

8. An alarm that is strident is _____.

    A. shrill

    B. muted

    C. constant

    D. resonant

9. A remedy may cure certain ailments. Another word for this might be _____.

    A. inoculation

    B. indicator

    C. nostrum

    D. serum

10. A vertiginous patient is _____.

    A. on a liquid diet

    B. lying flat

    C. burned

    D. dizzy

11. What is another word for *latent*?

    A. Flagrant

    B. Dormant

    C. Deceased

    D. Postponed

GO ON TO THE NEXT PAGE

12. Select the meaning of the underlined word in the sentence.

Each shiver made his muscles <u>undulate</u> beneath his skin.

A. Ripple
B. Shake
C. Flatten
D. Unknot

13. Select the meaning of the underlined word in the sentence.

The <u>tumult</u> in the emergency room seemed to last a long time.

A. Siren
B. Distress
C. Suffering
D. Commotion

14. Which word describes a screen or filter?

A. Permeable
B. Incendiary
C. Exuding
D. Resilient

15. What is another word for *putrefy*?

A. Discharge
B. Harden
C. Panic
D. Rot

16. What is the meaning of *superfluous*?

A. Maximum
B. Excessive
C. Insipid
D. Soggy

GO ON TO THE NEXT PAGE

17. What is the best description of the phrase *suggests that* in this sentence?

> A study suggests that vaping may reduce cigarette smoking but also lead to higher relapse.

A. Makes a suggestion about
B. Gives evidence about
C. Hints at the idea that
D. Promotes a plan to

18. What is the best description for the abbreviation *EEG*?

A. A test of brain activity
B. A medical service
C. A heartbeat monitor
D. A specialist in dentistry

19. The shorter bone in the forearm is the _____.

A. humerus
B. radius
C. scapula
D. fibula

20. Select the meaning of the underlined word in the sentence.

> The typical patellar <u>reflex</u> takes only 50 milliseconds between the initial tap and the leg extension.

A. Replication
B. Convulsion
C. Reaction
D. Stretching

21. The breastbone may be called the _____.

A. stelic
B. steres
C. sterol
D. sternum

GO ON TO THE NEXT PAGE

22. Select the meaning of the underlined word in the sentence.

The students approached the cadaver with some <u>trepidation</u>.

A. Wonder
B. Confusion
C. Eagerness
D. Apprehension

23. What is the meaning of *venal*?

A. Vibrant
B. Savage
C. Greedy
D. Fortunate

24. Select the meaning of the underlined word in the sentence.

The researcher's <u>spurious</u> argument confused even the experts.

A. Bogus
B. Obscure
C. Baffling
D. Outrageous

25. *Superior* refers to which part of the human body?

A. Front
B. Bottom
C. Top
D. Back

26. What is the best description for the term *flaccid*?

A. Light-colored
B. Drooping or loose
C. Uncontaminated
D. Unusually aggressive

GO ON TO THE NEXT PAGE

27. Select the meaning of the underlined word in the sentence.

    The patient's <u>corpulence</u> made him difficult to handle.

    A. Belligerence
    B. Gassiness
    C. Wariness
    D. Stoutness

28. What does *bifurcate* mean?

    A. Fold twice
    B. Flower biannually
    C. Divide in two forks
    D. Pierce two openings

29. Select the meaning of the underlined word in the sentence.

    Always <u>dilute</u> that medicine before dosing a patient.

    A. Add water to
    B. Reduce by half
    C. Warm up
    D. Decontaminate

30. What is the best description for the term *cathartic*?

    A. Infested
    B. Therapeutic
    C. Fatiguing
    D. Supplementing

31. Your "funny bone" is actually your _____.

    A. humerus
    B. ulnar nerve
    C. carpal bone
    D. biceps brachii

GO ON TO THE NEXT PAGE

32. What is another word for *acrid*?

A. Bitter
B. Smoky
C. Nimble
D. Severe

33. Select the meaning of the underlined word in the sentence.

One by one, the applicants were <u>winnowed</u> out of the group.

A. Escorted
B. Separated
C. Elevated
D. Summoned

34. If you are at the zenith of your career, you are _____.

A. just getting started
B. preparing for retirement
C. at the pinnacle of success
D. having trouble with your superiors

35. Select the meaning of the underlined word in the sentence.

The robotic arm may <u>yaw</u> too much and need adjusting.

A. To gape open
B. To move up and down
C. To close tightly
D. To move side to side

36. A symptom that is transitory is _____.

A. short-lived
B. damaging
C. fluctuating
D. degenerating

GO ON TO THE NEXT PAGE

37. To take umbrage at something is to _____.

    A. reprimand it
    B. stand beneath it
    C. speak well of it
    D. be offended by it

38. The abbreviation *HPV* on a medical form refers to a particular _____.

    A. blood condition
    B. viral infection
    C. heart rate
    D. therapy

39. Select the meaning of the underlined word in the sentence.

    The nurses and teenage aides developed a quick <u>rapport</u>.

    A. Performance
    B. Narrative
    C. Manner
    D. Bond

40. The electrolytes in human bodies include sodium, potassium, calcium, and _____, among others.

    A. magnesium
    B. manganese
    C. magnetite
    D. manganite

41. Select the meaning of the underlined word in the sentence.

    The patient held out a <u>tremulous</u> hand and grasped the paperwork.

    A. Wrinkled and wizened
    B. Pale and lifeless
    C. Clenched and arthritic
    D. Quivering and weak

GO ON TO THE NEXT PAGE

42. What is tepid bathwater?

    A. Water that is salty
    B. Water that is lukewarm
    C. Water that is icy
    D. Water that is half-full

43. What is the best description for the word *operated* in this sentence?

    > Rural communities are increasingly taking ownership of their hospitals, which may be operated by administrative medical groups.

    A. Performing surgery
    B. In effect
    C. Managed and run
    D. Brought about

44. A stye is an infection of the _____.

    A. eyelid
    B. eardrum
    C. nostril
    D. scalp

45. The abbreviation *LBW* on an infant's chart refers to the baby's

    _____.

    A. genetic makeup
    B. feeding schedule
    C. Babinski response
    D. weight at birth

46. Select the meaning of the underlined word in the sentence.

    > The professor <u>sanctioned</u> our field trip to the chemistry lab.

    A. Organized
    B. Deterred
    C. Authorized
    D. Neglected

GO ON TO THE NEXT PAGE

47. If tubes distend, they _____.

    A. flex

    B. stretch

    C. solidify

    D. collapse

48. To aspirate fluid, you might use a _____.

    A. syringe

    B. beaker

    C. test tube

    D. flange

49. When people masticate, what do they use?

    A. Fingers

    B. Eyes and ears

    C. Gums and teeth

    D. Heels and toes

50. Select the meaning of the underlined word in the sentence.

    The elderly patient has been fighting a <u>persistent</u> cold.

    A. Typical

    B. Harmless

    C. Without cure

    D. Lasting a long time

**STOP. IF YOU HAVE TIME LEFT OVER,
CHECK YOUR WORK ON THIS SECTION ONLY.**

GRAMMAR

50 items | Suggested time: 45 minutes

1. Which sentence is written correctly?

    A. After completing her nightly duties Anya left for home.
    B. After completing her nightly duties; Anya left for home.
    C. After completing her nightly duties, Anya left for home.
    D. After completing, her nightly duties, Anya left for home.

2. Select the phrase that will make this sentence grammatically correct.

    Once they pass the exam, the students _____.

    A. being certified
    B. have been certified
    C. will be certified
    D. are certifying

3. Which word is not spelled correctly in the context of the sentence?

    Unfortunately, her absences were becoming a regular ocurrence.

    A. Unfortunately
    B. absences
    C. regular
    D. ocurrence

4. Which sentence is grammatically correct?

    A. As Katie went to return the library book, she noticed an envelope stuck to the cover.
    B. Katie, going to return the library book, did notice an envelope stuck to the cover.
    C. Having noticed an envelope stuck to the cover, Katie gone to return the library book.
    D. Noticing an envelope stuck to the cover of the library book, Katie going to return the book.

GO ON TO THE NEXT PAGE

5. Which word is used incorrectly in the following sentence?

> Professor Turnbull will appraise us of the correct procedure for submitting our work.

A. appraise
B. correct
C. procedure
D. submitting

6. Select the correct word for the blank in the following sentence.

> The intern and _____ are folding the bandages.

A. us
B. he
C. them
D. her

7. What word is best to substitute for the underlined words in the following sentence?

> Several nursing students stayed behind after class, but the instructor advised <u>the students</u> to ask questions during office hours.

A. them
B. him
C. they
D. those

8. Which word is used incorrectly in the following sentence?

> Which criteria was used to draw a conclusion about their findings?

A. Which
B. was
C. draw
D. their

GO ON TO THE NEXT PAGE

9. Which of the following words fits best in the sentence below?

_____ she is the youngest member of her class, Octavia is taller than her classmates.

A. Despite
B. Since
C. Although
D. Provided

10. What punctuation is needed in this sentence to make it correct?

"Can you help me carry these items" Ji-yoo asked her colleague.

A. Period
B. Question mark
C. Comma
D. Semicolon

11. Which of the following is spelled correctly?

A. Exercise
B. Excercise
C. Exersize
D. Excersize

12. Select the word or phrase that makes this sentence grammatically correct.

The children started _____ away their trash without being asked.

A. throw
B. to throw
C. threw
D. threwing

GO ON TO THE NEXT PAGE

13. Select the word in the sentence that is *not* used correctly.

    The staunch hikers took a torturous downhill path that wound through thick vegetation.

    A. staunch
    B. vegetation
    C. wound
    D. torturous

14. Select the word or phrase that makes this sentence grammatically correct.

    Before _____ this medicine, consume a modest meal.

    A. having taken
    B. taking
    C. took
    D. will take

15. Which sentence is grammatically correct?

    A. Thoroughly, Mateo read the instructions before he began.
    B. Before he began thoroughly, Mateo read the instructions.
    C. Mateo read the instructions thoroughly before he began.
    D. The instructions were thoroughly read by Mateo before he began.

16. Select the word that makes this sentence grammatically correct.

    The board of education _____ to hold a special meeting.

    A. plan
    B. plans
    C. planning
    D. do plan

GO ON TO THE NEXT PAGE

17. What word is best to substitute for the underlined words in the following sentence?

> The children loved having <u>the children's</u> photographs taken.

A. its
B. his
C. they
D. their

18. Which word is not spelled correctly?

> The goverment official was grateful to receive that award.

A. goverment
B. official
C. grateful
D. receive

19. What punctuation is needed in this sentence to make it correct?

> I finished the project early however, I really should edit my work.

A. Apostrophe
B. Colon
C. Comma
D. Semicolon

20. Identify the type of sentence.

> Did Adam return the library book he borrowed last week?

A. Interrogative
B. Imperative
C. Declarative
D. Exclamatory

GO ON TO THE NEXT PAGE

21. Which sentence is written correctly?

    A. Because we have been friends for over ten years we often finish each other's sentences.
    B. Because we have been friends, for over ten years, we often finish, each other's sentences.
    C. Because we have been friends, for over ten years, we often finish each other's sentences.
    D. Because we have been friends for over ten years, we often finish each other's sentences.

22. Select the word that makes this sentence grammatically correct.

    We had been working _____ nine hours.

    A. since
    B. near
    C. for
    D. in

23. What part of speech is the word *on* in the sentence below?

    Early on Tuesday morning, Raegan took her first steps.

    A. Preposition
    B. Conjunction
    C. Pronoun
    D. Adverb

24. Select the word that makes this sentence grammatically correct.

    People often believe _____ to be morally superior to their friends.

    A. oneself
    B. themself
    C. theirselves
    D. themselves

GO ON TO THE NEXT PAGE

25. Which sentence is the clearest?

    A. As the wind picked up, we saw trash cans rolling down the street.
    B. Rolling down the street, we saw trash cans as the wind picked up.
    C. We saw trash cans as the wind picked up rolling down the street.
    D. Down the street we saw trash cans rolling as the wind picked up.

26. Select the word or phrase that is misplaced in the sentence.

    There was a long fence behind the farmhouse made of crisscrossed logs.

    A. There
    B. a long fence
    C. the farmhouse
    D. made of crisscrossed logs

27. Select the word or phrase that makes this sentence grammatically correct.

    Sadie and her mother were excited to _____ the award.

    A. be received
    B. receiving
    C. receive
    D. have been received

28. Select the phrase in the sentence that is *not* used correctly.

    Until his trip to Puerto Rico, Javier had never seeing his ancestral home.

    A. Until his trip
    B. had never
    C. never seeing
    D. his ancestral home

GO ON TO THE NEXT PAGE

29. Select the word that makes this sentence grammatically correct.

I added _____ pepper to the casserole.

A. too
B. more
C. those
D. many

30. What punctuation is needed in this sentence to make it correct?

Remember the old saying Out of sight, out of mind.

A. Exclamation point
B. Apostrophe
C. Colon
D. Semicolon

31. Select the phrase that will make this sentence grammatically correct.

As the concert ended, my friends _____.

A. ask for a ride home
B. asked for a ride home
C. have asked for a ride home
D. are asking for a ride home

32. Which word is used incorrectly in the following sentence?

Follow the instructions you received in you're packet.

A. Follow
B. instructions
C. packet
D. you're

33. Select the sentence that is grammatically correct.

A. My roommate and me studied together in the library.
B. My roommate and I studied together in the library.
C. I and my roommate studied together in the library.
D. Me and my roommate studied together in the library.

GO ON TO THE NEXT PAGE

34. What word is best to substitute for the underlined words in the following sentence?

The nursing staff appreciate occasional thank-you cards.

A. They
B. It
C. Them
D. Us

35. Which sentence is grammatically correct?

A. I helped me to the delicious fruit salad.
B. I helped ourselves to the delicious fruit salad.
C. I helped myself to the delicious fruit salad.
D. Myself helped me to the delicious fruit salad.

36. What punctuation is needed in this sentence to make it correct?

I will check the supply closet and you can look in the laundry.

A. Period
B. Comma
C. Colon
D. Semicolon

37. A compound complex sentence must have _____.

A. at least two independent clauses and at least one dependent clause
B. at least one independent clause and at least one dependent clause
C. at least one independent clause and at least two dependent clauses
D. at least two independent clauses and at least two dependent clauses

38. Which word is used incorrectly in the following sentence?

Fredericka always orders pancakes, but Louis prefer waffles.

A. always
B. orders
C. but
D. prefer

GO ON TO THE NEXT PAGE

39. Which of the following words or phrases fits best in the sentence below?

Derek insists on working out daily _____ his time is limited.

A. despite
B. due to
C. even if
D. whereas

40. What part of speech is the word *counsel* in the sentence below?

You will need counsel if you are accused of a serious crime.

A. Noun
B. Verb
C. Adjective
D. Adverb

41. Which sentence is the clearest?

A. Reading between the lines, his meaning was interpreted by us.
B. His meaning, having read between the lines, we interpreted.
C. Reading between the lines, we interpreted his meaning.
D. We interpreted his meaning, having read between the lines.

42. Select the word that makes this sentence grammatically correct.

Our subcommittee _____ on the fourth Wednesday of each month.

A. meet
B. meets
C. meeting
D. are meeting

43. What punctuation is needed in this sentence to make it correct?

Take this fast acting cough medicine after your next meal.

A. Period
B. Comma
C. Colon
D. Hyphen

GO ON TO THE NEXT PAGE

44. Which of the following is spelled correctly?

   A. State of the art
   B. State-of the art
   C. State-of the-art
   D. State-of-the-art

45. What word is best to substitute for the underlined words in the following sentence?

   Mr. Karnicki invited <u>all of his relatives</u> to visit him in the hospital.

   A. his
   B. theirs
   C. them
   D. their

46. Which word is used incorrectly in the following sentence?

   The design was incredible complex, with multicolored, repeating patterns.

   A. incredible
   B. complex
   C. multicolored
   D. repeating

47. Which sentence is the clearest?

   A. Raising his bow once again, we heard the violinist's passion.
   B. Raising his bow once again, the violinist expressed his passion.
   C. The violinist expressed his passion once again raising his bow.
   D. The violinist once again expressed his passion, raising his bow.

GO ON TO THE NEXT PAGE

48. Select the phrase or clause that is misplaced in the sentence.

> The children and their parents handed water to the runners in tiny cups.

A. and their parents
B. handed water
C. the runners
D. in tiny cups

49. Select the word or phrase that will make the sentence grammatically correct.

> The village is not very far _____ the railway station.

A. to
B. from
C. by
D. next

50. Which sentence is grammatically correct?

A. Having read the directions twice, we were still having trouble put the chair together.
B. We were still having trouble putting the chair together despite our have read the directions twice.
C. Despite having read the directions twice, we still had trouble putting the chair together.
D. Despite we have read the directions twice, still having trouble putting the chair together.

STOP. IF YOU HAVE TIME LEFT OVER, CHECK YOUR WORK ON THIS SECTION ONLY.

BASIC MATH SKILLS

50 items | Suggested time: 45 minutes

1. Multiply and simplify: $2\frac{1}{4} \times \frac{1}{9} =$

   A. ¼
   B. ⅔
   C. $\frac{7}{36}$
   D. $3\frac{1}{36}$

2. 6 is 15% of what number?

   A. 0.9
   B. 40
   C. 80
   D. 90

3. If Jolene averages 5 miles for every 30 minutes of biking, how far will she bike in 2 hours?

   A. 10 miles
   B. 15 miles
   C. 20 miles
   D. 30 miles

4. Three pints is approximately how many liters?

   A. 1.42 liters
   B. 1.89 liters
   C. 2.83 liters
   D. 3.18 liters

5. Express 35% as a fraction in lowest terms.

   A. $\frac{35}{100}$
   B. ¾
   C. $\frac{3}{10}$
   D. $\frac{7}{20}$

GO ON TO THE NEXT PAGE

6. About how many kilograms are there in 20 pounds?

    A. 44 kilograms

    B. 16 kilograms

    C. 9 kilograms

    D. 3 kilograms

7. If $x = 7y - 6$, what is the value of x when $y = -2$?

    A. −20

    B. −13

    C. −1

    D. 8

8. Mayor Ali is running for re-election and has asked each of her 2,304 best donors to contribute $1,500 each to her campaign. If each donor sends that amount, how much money will the campaign raise? (Enter numeric values only.)

————————————

9. Approximately how many miles are in 8 kilometers?

    A. 4.6 miles

    B. 5.0 miles

    C. 10.0 miles

    D. 12.8 miles

10. A potter finished a series of coffee mugs. She glazed 3 blue mugs, 4 gray mugs, 6 yellow mugs, and 3 violet mugs. What is the ratio of gray mugs to the total number of mugs?

    A. 2:3

    B. 3:8

    C. 1:4

    D. 3:16

11. Express 0.846 as a fraction.

    A. $^{423}/_{500}$

    B. $^{21}/_{25}$

    C. $^{4}/_{5}$

    D. $^{17}/_{200}$

GO ON TO THE NEXT PAGE

12. When Jay was born, he weighed 8 lbs 7 oz. How many ounces is that?

    A. 15 oz

    B. 56 oz

    C. 128 oz

    D. 135 oz

13. Translate this phrase into an equation: A number is seven more than half of a given number.

    A. $x = \dfrac{n}{2} + 7$

    B. $x = \dfrac{n}{2} - 7$

    C. $x = \dfrac{(n+7)}{2}$

    D. $x = n + 7$

14. Solve for x. $2 : 5 :: 64 : x$

    A. 32

    B. 70

    C. 128

    D. 160

15. Divide and simplify: $2\frac{1}{9} \div \frac{1}{3} =$

    A. $1\frac{1}{3}$

    B. $6\frac{1}{27}$

    C. $6\frac{1}{3}$

    D. 28

16. Isabella wins $25 in a raffle at the fair. She spends $7 on an apple pie and $2 on lemonade. How much of her winnings does she take home?

    A. $9

    B. $16

    C. $18

    D. $23

17. Sarah currently works 40 hours a week for $13 an hour. If her wages go up to $15 per hour, how much more will she make each week? (Enter numeric value only. _____

GO ON TO THE NEXT PAGE

18. Chun Mei earns a 5% commission on each appliance she sells. If she sells a washer for $749 and a dryer for $689, what will her commission be?

    A. $37.45

    B. $71.90

    C. $149.80

    D. $287.60

19. How many centimeters are there in 5.5 meters? (Enter numeric value only.) _____

20. A plan for a barn is drawn on a 1:30 scale. If the width of a barn door on the plan measures 3 inches, what is the actual width of the finished door?

    A. 90 feet

    B. 10 feet

    C. 9 feet

    D. 7.5 feet

21. Add: $3.12 + 31.2 + 312 =$

    A. 936

    B. 374.4

    C. 346.32

    D. 318.24

22. The number 51 is 60% of what number? (Enter numeric value only.) _____

23. Add and simplify: $3\frac{1}{3} + 8\frac{1}{4} =$

    A. $11\frac{2}{3}$

    B. $11\frac{7}{12}$

    C. $11\frac{1}{16}$

    D. $12\frac{1}{3}$

GO ON TO THE NEXT PAGE

24. At the deli, Sam bought a sandwich for $7.89 and chips for $1.49. If he gave the cashier $20, how much change did he receive?

    A. $0.62

    B. $5.02

    C. $9.38

    D. $10.62

25. Convert this military time to regular time: 1010 hours.

    A. 10:10 A.M.

    B. 10:10 P.M.

    C. 1:01 A.M.

    D. 1:01 P.M.

26. Which equation expresses the relationship between x and y?

x	y
2	6
3	9
4	12
5	15

    A. $x = 3y$

    B. $x = y + 4$

    C. $x = \dfrac{1}{3}y$

    D. $x = y - 4$

27. Approximately how many kilograms are there in 11 pounds?

    A. 4.6 kilograms

    B. 5.0 kilograms

    C. 5.5 kilograms

    D. 24.2 kilograms

28. Divide: $2{,}032 \div 25 =$

    A. 91 r3

    B. 81 r28

    C. 81 r7

    D. 9 r3

GO ON TO THE NEXT PAGE

29. Gwen's favorite summer drink is 2 parts fruit juice to 3 parts seltzer. If she is making drinks for friends and starts with a gallon of fruit juice, how many quarts of seltzer will she need?

  A. 3 quarts
  B. 4.5 quarts
  C. 5 quarts
  D. 6 quarts

30. Approximately how many millimeters are there in 1 foot?

  A. 304.8 millimeters
  B. 30.48 millimeters
  C. 3.048 millimeters
  D. 0.305 millimeters

31. Express $14\frac{1}{4}$ as a decimal.

  A. 3.25
  B. 3.45
  C. 3.5
  D. 3.75

32. How many liters are in 120 milliliters?

  A. 1.2 liters
  B. 12 liters
  C. 1,200 liters
  D. 0.12 liters

33. Express the ratio of 12:15 as a percentage.

  A. 58.8%
  B. 62%
  C. 75.25%
  D. 80%

GO ON TO THE NEXT PAGE

34. A package containing 3 bars of soap costs $6.90. How much do you save per bar if you purchase a value pack of 8 bars for $17.20?

    A. 15¢

    B. 40¢

    C. 75¢

    D. $1.20

35. What number in Arabic numerals is Roman numeral CIX? (Enter numeric value only.) _____

36. At the fair, Serena sold 6 fewer balloons than Tommy, who sold 2 more balloons than Uri sold. If Uri sold 28 balloons, how many did Serena sell?

    A. 20

    B. 22

    C. 24

    D. 32

37. 0.845 is equal to _____ percent. (Enter numerical value only.)

38. Multiply: $2.8 \times 8.2 =$

    A. 16.16

    B. 22.16

    C. 22.96

    D. 23.6

39. If the outside temperature is 59 degrees on the Fahrenheit scale, what is the approximate temperature on the Celsius scale?

    A. −9°C

    B. 15°C

    C. 23°C

    D. 87°C

GO ON TO THE NEXT PAGE

40. A scientific illustrator uses a scale of 3:1 for his drawings of insects. If the length of a cicada in his drawing is 12.6 centimeters, how long is the actual cicada in real life?

   A. 37.8 centimeters
   B. 6.3 centimeters
   C. 4.6 centimeters
   D. 4.2 centimeters

41. At Bethesda Junior High, there are two grade levels: seventh and eighth. If there are 342 students at the school and 188 of them are seventh graders, what is the ratio of seventh to eighth graders?

   A. 94:77
   B. 77:94
   C. 94:171
   D. 77:171

42. Divide: $25.3 \div 4 =$

   A. 5.75
   B. 5.875
   C. 6.25
   D. 6.325

43. Subtract and simplify: $\frac{3}{8} - \frac{1}{6} =$

   A. $\frac{1}{2}$
   B. $\frac{3}{16}$
   C. $\frac{5}{24}$
   D. $\frac{7}{48}$

44. There are about 3 medium apples in a pound. If 3 pounds of Honeycrisp apples are selling for $6.99, what is the approximate cost per apple?

   A. $0.61
   B. $0.78
   C. $0.81
   D. $2.33

GO ON TO THE NEXT PAGE

45. Subtract and simplify: $8\frac{1}{4} - 1\frac{1}{2}$.

    A. $4\frac{1}{4}$

    B. $6\frac{3}{4}$

    C. $6\frac{7}{8}$

    D. $7\frac{1}{4}$

46. Express 36% as a decimal.

    A. 0.036

    B. 0.36

    C. 3.6

    D. 36

47. 3 is 15% of what number? (Enter numeric value only.) _____

48. Olivia makes $51,200 in her teaching job. This year, her salary will increase by 4%. What will her salary be then?

    A. $52,348

    B. $52,736

    C. $53,040

    D. $53,248

49. Joel's $1,200 monthly rent is currently $\frac{1}{3}$ of his take-home monthly income. His rent is about to increase by $150 per month. How much more a month would Joel need to make to keep his rent as $\frac{1}{3}$ of his take-home pay? (Enter numeric value only.) _____

50. Approximately how many gallons are there in 1.2 kiloliters?

    A. 317 gallons

    B. 379 gallons

    C. 455 gallons

    D. 3,166 gallons

STOP. IF YOU HAVE TIME LEFT OVER, CHECK YOUR WORK ON THIS SECTION ONLY.

BIOLOGY

| 25 items | Suggested time: 21 minutes |

1. Which cellular structure is largely protective in function?

   A. Mitochondrion
   B. Vacuole
   C. Cell membrane
   D. Ribosome

2. Which form of fermentation is used to produce beer?

   A. Lactic acid fermentation
   B. Acetic acid fermentation
   C. Propionic acid fermentation
   D. Ethyl alcohol fermentation

3. Which event takes place during telophase?

   A. The nuclear envelope disappears.
   B. Organelles double in number.
   C. Chromosomes separate.
   D. Two nuclei are formed.

4. Which is *not* part of a nucleic acid?

   A. Sulfate
   B. Phosphate
   C. Carbon
   D. Nitrogen

5. Queen Victoria and her daughters Alice and Beatrice carried the recessive, X-linked hemophilia gene, and her son, Prince Leopold, died of the disease at age 30. Of their descendants, whom would you expect to show symptoms of hemophilia?

   A. Princess Beatrice's daughter, Princess Victoria Eugenie
   B. Princess Alice's daughter, Princess Irene
   C. Prince Leopold's daughter, Princess Alice
   D. Princess Beatrice's grandson, Prince Alfonso

| **GO ON TO THE NEXT PAGE** |

6. Why do gardeners sometimes use salt to get rid of slugs?

  A. The salt moves from the exterior into the slug's body.
  B. The salt causes water in the slug to move outward.
  C. The salt and slug slime merge to form a new compound.
  D. The salt's corrosiveness breaks down the slug's cell walls.

7. Which of the following are found both in open and closed circulatory systems?

  A. Arteries
  B. Red blood cells
  C. Capillaries
  D. Immune cells

8. Most enzymes are made up of _____.

  A. proteins
  B. lipids
  C. starches
  D. simple sugars

9. Which plant part produces pollen?

  A. Anther
  B. Style
  C. Stigma
  D. Pistil

10. As cattle graze, cattle egrets consume the insects they stir up. This is an example of _____.

  A. Mutualism
  B. Parasitism
  C. Commensalism
  D. Competition

11. Humans, or *Homo sapiens*, are part of the family _____.

  A. Animalia
  B. Hominidae
  C. Mammalia
  D. Chordata

GO ON TO THE NEXT PAGE

12. Which of these is *not* an example of a lipid?

   A. Butter

   B. Wax

   C. Canola oil

   D. Honey

13. Which cells in the human body lack nuclei?

   A. Nerve cells

   B. Red blood cells

   C. Liver cells

   D. Connective tissue cells

14. Which organism reproduces via spore formation?

   A. Shelf fungus

   B. Lemon tree

   C. Smallmouth bass

   D. Staphylococcus

15. A cell containing 12 chromosomes divides into daughter cells in mitosis. How many chromosomes are in each daughter cell?

   A. 3

   B. 6

   C. 12

   D. 24

16. RNA is made from DNA through a process called _____.

   A. transcription

   B. synthesis

   C. translation

   D. replication

GO ON TO THE NEXT PAGE

17. Duchenne muscular dystrophy is a recessive sex-linked trait carried on the X chromosome. In an example of an unaffected father and a female carrier who have two daughters and two sons, which is the predicted outcome?

    A. Both daughters will carry the disease.
    B. Both sons will carry the disease.
    C. One daughter may have the disease.
    D. One son may have the disease.

18. Which one is *not* a reactant in photosynthesis?

    A. Water
    B. Light energy
    C. Glucose
    D. Carbon dioxide

19. If a test has poor internal consistency, which statement is true?

    A. The test produces different results at different times.
    B. The items do not correlate or measure similar things.
    C. The test produces different results depending on the researcher.
    D. The items never vary even when the test environment changes.

20. Which of the following does *not* affect the basal metabolic rate (BMR)?

    A. Muscle mass
    B. Hormones
    C. Blood type
    D. Age

GO ON TO THE NEXT PAGE

21. How should a researcher test the hypothesis that a particular species of bird vocalizes most in the hours around dawn?

   A. Observe a flock of the birds in captivity and record them at two-hour intervals from predawn until sunset for a month.
   B. Observe a flock of the birds in the wild and record them at one-hour intervals from predawn until sunset in several seasons.
   C. Observe a flock of the birds in the wild and record them in predawn and postdawn hours every day for six months.
   D. Observe a flock of the birds in the wild, record them at one-hour intervals for a month, and compare that recording to recordings of other species.

22. In nature, water vapor becomes liquid water through the process of _____.

   A. condensation
   B. sublimation
   C. precipitation
   D. absorption

23. What is another name for the light-independent reaction in plants?

   A. Photosynthesis
   B. Calvin cycle
   C. Germination
   D. Phosphorus cycle

24. *Bacillus subtilis* may be described as _____.

   A. spiral
   B. globular
   C. rod-shaped
   D. grape-like clusters

25. Which type of sugar is a disaccharide?

   A. Sucrose
   B. Fructose
   C. Glucose
   D. Galactose

**STOP. IF YOU HAVE TIME LEFT OVER,
CHECK YOUR WORK ON THIS SECTION ONLY.**

CHEMISTRY

25 items | Suggested time: 21 minutes

1. Which of these names a hydride ion?

   A. OH^-
   B. H^+
   C. H^-
   D. HCl

2. Which substance forms hydroxide ions when placed in water?

   A. Lemon juice
   B. Battery acid
   C. Vinegar
   D. Lye

3. Cobalt-60 has a half-life of 5 years. If you start with 20 g of cobalt-60, how much is left after 10 years?

   A. 15 g
   B. 10 g
   C. 5 g
   D. 2.5 g

4. Which one does *not* name a polar molecule?

   A. NH_3
   B. H_2S
   C. SO_2
   D. CO_2

5. What happens in a single displacement reaction?

   A. A compound breaks down into two substances.
   B. An active element replaces a less active element.
   C. A precipitate solid forms from two mixed solutions.
   D. The oxidation states of atoms in the chemicals change.

GO ON TO THE NEXT PAGE

6. Arsenic and silicon are examples of _____.

    A. metals

    B. metalloids

    C. nonmetals

    D. heavy metals

7. Why does the diffusion rate increase as a substance is heated?

    A. The kinetic energy of particles increases.

    B. The space between particles increases.

    C. The density of particles decreases.

    D. The size of particles increases.

8. What is always different from one allotrope to another?

    A. Arrangement of atoms

    B. Gram atomic mass

    C. Physical state

    D. Stability

9. Which is true of a saturated solution?

    A. It has more solute than can dissolve in the solvent.

    B. It has less solute that can dissolve in the solvent.

    C. It has the maximum concentration of the solute dissolved in the solvent.

    D. It contains a precipitate that lowers the concentration of the solute in the solvent.

10. Which one is *not* a hydrocarbon?

    A. Methane (CH_4)

    B. Pyridine (C_5H_5N)

    C. Ethane (C_2H_6)

    D. Propane (C_3H_8)

11. Balance this equation: $Fe + Cl_2 \rightarrow FeCl_3$

    A. $2Fe + 2Cl_2 \rightarrow 2FeCl_3$

    B. $2Fe + 3Cl_2 \rightarrow 2FeCl_3$

    C. $3Fe + 2Cl_2 \rightarrow 3FeCl_3$

    D. $3Fe + 3Cl_2 \rightarrow 6FeCl_3$

GO ON TO THE NEXT PAGE

12. On the periodic table, families of elements with similar properties appear in the same _____.

    A. row
    B. principal energy level
    C. period
    D. column

13. What is the net charge of an ionic compound?

    A. 0
    B. −1
    C. +1
    D. Variable

14. How many neutrons are in an atom of helium-4?

    A. 2
    B. 3
    C. 4
    D. 6

15. What is the correct electron configuration for nitrogen?

    A. $1s^2 2s^2$
    B. $1s^2 2s^2 2p^2$
    C. $1s^2 2s^2 2p^3$
    D. $1s^2 2s^2 2p^4$

16. Which best defines the molarity of an aqueous sugar solution?

    A. Grams of sugar per milliliter of solution
    B. Moles of sugar per milliliter of solution
    C. Grams of sugar per liter of solution
    D. Moles of sugar per liter of solution

17. Which of these represents a strong acid?

    A. CH_3COOH
    B. H_2SO_4
    C. NH_3
    D. KOH

GO ON TO THE NEXT PAGE

18. To the nearest whole number, what is the mass of one mole of hydrogen iodide?

    A. 2 g/mol
    B. 58 g/mol
    C. 87 g/mol
    D. 128 g/mol

19. What is the charge of a beta particle?

    A. −1
    B. +1
    C. +2
    D. No charge

20. What is the correct formula for calcium carbonate?

    A. $CaSO_4$
    B. $CaCO_3$
    C. $Ca(OH)_2$
    D. CH_3OH

21. What is the oxidation state of the potassium ion in the compound KCl?

    A. +1
    B. −1
    C. +2
    D. −2

22. Which of these types of intermolecular force is weakest?

    A. Dipole–dipole interaction
    B. London dispersion force
    C. Hydrogen bonding
    D. Ionic bonding

GO ON TO THE NEXT PAGE

23. How many moles of potassium bromide are in 25 mL of a
1.4 M KBr solution?

  A. 0.035 mol

  B. 0.056 mol

  C. 0.18 mol

  D. 1.6 mol

24. What is the correct formula for iron III oxide?

  A. I_2O

  B. FeS

  C. Fe_2O_3

  D. O_2Fe_3

25. Which element has an atomic mass greater than that of sodium?

  A. Boron

  B. Oxygen

  C. Fluorine

  D. Silicon

**STOP. IF YOU HAVE TIME LEFT OVER,
CHECK YOUR WORK ON THIS SECTION ONLY.**

ANATOMY AND PHYSIOLOGY

25 items | Suggested time: 21 minutes

1. Which is a posterior feature of the human leg?

   A. Patella
   B. Quadriceps sartorius
   C. Triceps brachii
   D. Achilles tendon

2. What is probably torn in a rotator cuff tear?

   A. Tendon and possibly ligament
   B. Muscle and possibly tendon
   C. Ligament and possibly muscle
   D. Tendon only

3. Which bones does the rotator cuff help stabilize?

   A. Radius and humerus
   B. Scapula and clavicle
   C. Humerus and scapula
   D. Ulna and radius

4. Primary peristalsis occurs in the _____.

   A. esophagus
   B. stomach
   C. nervous system
   D. small intestine

5. Which of these can provide significant protein to a person on a vegan diet?

   A. Eggs
   B. Fish
   C. Tofu
   D. Leafy greens

GO ON TO THE NEXT PAGE

6. Which lobe of the brain controls speech?

   A. Frontal lobe
   B. Temporal lobe
   C. Parietal lobe
   D. Occipital lobe

7. How does the circulatory system work with the digestive system?

   A. The circulatory system removes undigested solids from the body.
   B. The circulatory system filters and collects digested materials.
   C. The circulatory system moves absorbed nutrients through the body.
   D. The circulatory system releases enzymes that control digestion.

8. When are gallstones most problematic?

   A. When they block a duct
   B. When they contain cholesterol
   C. When they contain bilirubin
   D. When they begin to dissolve

9. Where might a gallstone be most likely to create pain?

   A. In the upper right quadrant of the abdomen
   B. In the lower right quadrant of the abdomen
   C. In the umbilical region
   D. Along the pelvic girdle

10. How many bones are in the human foot?

   A. 6
   B. 16
   C. 26
   D. 36

11. The retinas are part of the _____.

   A. skeletal system
   B. nervous system
   C. lymphatic system
   D. circulatory system

GO ON TO THE NEXT PAGE

12. Which are *not* part of the body's secondary defense system?

   A. Microphages
   B. Leukocytes
   C. T cells
   D. Cilia

13. Which organ system is primarily responsible for maintaining temperature control?

   A. The skeletal system
   B. The digestive system
   C. The nervous system
   D. The integumentary system

14. Which is the first step in pulmonary circulation?

   A. Blood moves toward the heart through the pulmonary veins.
   B. The pulmonary artery carries blood from the heart to the lungs.
   C. Carbon dioxide is exchanged for oxygen.
   D. Oxygenated blood moves through the aorta.

15. Which is another name for thiamine?

   A. Vitamin B_1
   B. Vitamin B_3
   C. Vitamin B_{12}
   D. Vitamin D

16. How does the skeletal system work with the nervous system?

   A. The bones send signals about body position to the brain.
   B. Pain nerves inside bones alert the brain to injuries.
   C. The vertebrae of the spine protect the spinal cord.
   D. Bone marrow produces and stores nerve cells.

17. Which hormone is produced by the pineal gland?

   A. Corticosteroid
   B. Oxytocin
   C. Prolactin
   D. Melatonin

GO ON TO THE NEXT PAGE

18. The anterior chamber of the eye lies between the _____.

    A. iris and lens
    B. lens and retina
    C. cornea and iris
    D. retina and optic nerve

19. Which of the following is the average normal body temperature in degrees Celsius?

    A. 30°C
    B. 32°C
    C. 35°C
    D. 37°C

20. The coronal plane of the body may also be called the _____ plane.

    A. sagittal
    B. frontal
    C. median
    D. axial

21. What does trypsin break down in the body?

    A. Fat
    B. Starch
    C. Proteins
    D. Nucleic acids

22. The sebaceous glands are part of the _____.

    A. endocrine system
    B. digestive system
    C. respiratory system
    D. integumentary system

23. Which mineral is considered an antioxidant?

    A. Selenium
    B. Calcium
    C. Sulfur
    D. Iron

GO ON TO THE NEXT PAGE

24. The shoulder is _____ to the elbow.

    A. posterior

    B. proximal

    C. distal

    D. medial

25. Which organ system is largely responsible for controlling stress?

    A. The endocrine system

    B. The digestive system

    C. The lymphatic system

    D. The respiratory system

**STOP. IF YOU HAVE TIME LEFT OVER,
CHECK YOUR WORK ON THIS SECTION ONLY.**

PHYSICS

| 25 items | Suggested time: 50 minutes |

1. A rock has a volume of 6 cm^3 and a mass of 24 g. What is its density?

   A. 4 g/cm^3
   B. 4 cm^3/g
   C. 144 g/cm^3
   D. 144 cm^3/g

2. Jon walks all the way around a rectangular park that is 1 km × 2 km. Which statement is true about Jon's walk?

   A. The displacement of his walk is 3 kilometers, and the distance traveled is 0 kilometers.
   B. The displacement of his walk is 0 kilometers, and the distance traveled is 16 miles.
   C. The displacement of his walk is 6 kilometers, and the distance traveled is 0 kilometers.
   D. The displacement of his walk is 0 kilometers, and the distance traveled is 6 kilometers.

3. Which point on a roller coaster represents the car's greatest potential energy?

   A. The start of the ride
   B. The highest peak
   C. The lowest trough
   D. The end of the ride

4. A caterpillar starts moving at a rate of 14 in/hr. After 15 minutes, it is moving at a rate of 20 in/hr. What is the caterpillar's rate of acceleration?

   A. 6 in/hr^2
   B. 12 in/hr^2
   C. 24 in/hr^2
   D. 280 in/hr^2

GO ON TO THE NEXT PAGE

5. A pitcher throws a 45-g baseball at a velocity of 42 meters per second. What is the ball's momentum?

   A. 189 kg·m/s
   B. 1.89 kg·m/s
   C. 1.07 kg·m/s
   D. 0.93 kg·m/s

6. Which of these substances is most compressible?

   A. Gold
   B. Water
   C. Mercury
   D. Methane

7. Amanda uses 100 N of force to push a lawnmower around her lawn. If she mows 20 rows measuring 30 meters per row, how much work does she do?

   A. 3,000 N·m
   B. 6,000 N·m
   C. 60,000 N·m
   D. The answer cannot be determined from the information given.

8. A 780-watt refrigerator is powered by a 120-volt power source. What is the current being drawn?

   A. 660 amperes
   B. 150 amperes
   C. 6.5 amperes
   D. 0.15 amperes

9. As the frequency of a sound wave increases, what else is true?

   A. Its wavelength decreases.
   B. Its wavelength increases.
   C. Its amplitude decreases.
   D. Its amplitude increases.

GO ON TO THE NEXT PAGE

10. A car is traveling on the highway. In town, its speed drops from 60 mph to 30 mph. What happens to its kinetic energy?

    A. Its energy is halved.
    B. Its energy is doubled.
    C. Its energy is quadrupled.
    D. Its energy is divided by 4.

11. The specific heat capacity of water is about 4.2 J/g°C. How much energy would you need to heat 1 kilogram of water 10°?

    A. 420 J
    B. 4,200 J
    C. 42,000 J
    D. 420,000 J

12. If a wave has a frequency of 60 hertz, which of the following is true?

    A. It completes one cycle per minute.
    B. It measures 60 m from crest to crest.
    C. It completes 60 cycles per second.
    D. It measures 60 m from crest to trough.

13. Which mathematical quantity is scalar?

    A. Distance
    B. Velocity
    C. Acceleration
    D. Displacement

14. A block of an alloyed metal has a density of 2.5 g/cm³. Which object below has the same density?

    A. A block with a mass of 6.5 grams and a volume of 16.25 cm³
    B. A block with a mass of 80 grams and a volume of 32 cm³
    C. A block with a mass of 48 grams and a volume of 22 cm³
    D. A block with a mass of 100 grams and a volume of 250 cm³

GO ON TO THE NEXT PAGE

15. The Law of Universal Gravitation states that the gravitational force between two objects is directly proportional to _____.

   A. the gravitational constant
   B. the distance between them
   C. the product of their masses
   D. the square of the distance between them

16. In a parallel circuit, the _____ through each component is the same.

   A. current
   B. wattage
   C. resistance
   D. voltage

17. In Einstein's mass-energy equation, what is represented by c?

   A. Distance in centimeters
   B. The speed of light
   C. Degrees Celsius
   D. Centrifugal force

18. A concave mirror with a focal length of 2 cm forms a real image of an object at an image distance of 6 cm. What is the object's distance from the mirror?

   A. 3 cm
   B. 6 cm
   C. 12 cm
   D. 30 cm

19. The speed of sound in dry air at 20°C is 343 m/s. If the wavelength of a sound wave is 5 m, what is its frequency?

   A. 171.5 Hz
   B. 79 Hz
   C. 68.6 Hz
   D. 63.6 Hz

GO ON TO THE NEXT PAGE

20. An object with a mass of 45 kg has momentum equal to 180 kg·m/s. What is the object's velocity?

A. 4 m/s

B. 8.1 km/s

C. 17.4 km/h

D. 135 m/s

21. In the mechanical power equation $P = E/t$, power is measured in

_____.

A. ohms

B. Joules

C. volts

D. watts

22. A spring has a spring constant of 20 N/m. How much force is needed to compress the spring from 40 cm to 30 cm?

A. 200 N

B. 80 N

C. 5 N

D. 2 N

23. A fair ride takes riders in a circular loop. At the top of the loop, they have a velocity of 6 m/s and centripetal acceleration of 6 m/s². What is the diameter of the loop?

A. 6 m

B. 12 m

C. 18 m

D. 36 m

24. A 120-volt heat lamp draws 1.25 amps of current. What is the lamp's resistance?

A. 96 ohms

B. 104 ohms

C. 150 ohms

D. 245 ohms

GO ON TO THE NEXT PAGE

25. An object with a charge of 4 μC is placed 50 cm from another object with a charge twice as great. What is the magnitude of the resulting repulsive force?

A. 0.1152 N

B. 1.152 N

C. 10^{-3} N

D. 2.5×10^{-3} N

STOP. IF YOU HAVE TIME LEFT OVER, CHECK YOUR WORK ON THIS SECTION ONLY.

ANSWER KEY

Reading Comprehension

1. D	18. B	35. B
2. C	19. C	36. A
3. A	20. B	37. B
4. B	21. C	38. C
5. B	22. D	39. D
6. D	23. A	40. B
7. C	24. B	41. D
8. D	25. A	42. C
9. A	26. C	43. A
10. C	27. D	44. B
11. A	28. A	45. D
12. D	29. C	46. C
13. C	30. D	47. B
14. B	31. C	48. A
15. A	32. B	49. D
16. A	33. A	50. C
17. D	34. D	

Vocabulary and General Knowledge

1. C	18. A	35. D
2. A	19. B	36. A
3. C	20. C	37. D
4. A	21. D	38. B
5. B	22. D	39. D
6. C	23. C	40. A
7. D	24. A	41. D
8. A	25. C	42. B
9. C	26. B	43. C
10. D	27. D	44. A
11. B	28. C	45. D
12. A	29. A	46. C
13. D	30. B	47. B
14. A	31. B	48. A
15. D	32. A	49. C
16. B	33. B	50. D
17. B	34. C	

Grammar

1. C	19. D	37. A
2. C	20. A	38. D
3. D	21. D	39. C
4. A	22. C	40. A
5. A	23. A	41. C
6. B	24. D	42. B
7. A	25. A	43. D
8. B	26. D	44. D
9. C	27. C	45. C
10. B	28. C	46. A
11. A	29. B	47. B
12. B	30. C	48. D
13. D	31. B	49. B
14. B	32. D	50. C
15. C	33. B	
16. B	34. A	
17. D	35. C	
18. A	36. B	

Basic Math Skills

1. A	18. B	35. 109
2. B	19. 550	36. C
3. C	20. D	37. 84.5
4. A	21. C	38. C
5. D	22. 85	39. B
6. C	23. B	40. D
7. A	24. D	41. A
8. 3,456,000	25. A	42. D
9. B	26. C	43. C
10. C	27. B	44. B
11. A	28. C	45. B
12. D	29. D	46. B
13. A	30. A	47. 20
14. D	31. C	48. D
15. C	32. D	49. 450
16. B	33. D	50. A
17. 80	34. A	

Biology

1. C
2. D
3. D
4. A
5. D
6. B
7. D
8. A
9. A
10. C
11. B
12. D
13. B
14. A
15. C
16. A
17. D
18. C
19. B
20. C
21. B
22. A
23. B
24. C
25. A

Chemistry

1. C
2. D
3. C
4. D
5. B
6. C
7. A
8. A
9. C
10. B
11. B
12. D
13. A
14. A
15. C
16. D
17. B
18. D
19. A
20. B
21. A
22. B
23. A
24. C
25. D

Anatomy and Physiology

1. D
2. B
3. C
4. A
5. C
6. B
7. C
8. A
9. A
10. C
11. B
12. D
13. D
14. B
15. A
16. D
17. D
18. C
19. D
20. B
21. C
22. D
23. A
24. B
25. A

Physics

1. A
2. D
3. B
4. C
5. B
6. D
7. C
8. C
9. A
10. D
11. C
12. C
13. A
14. B
15. C
16. D
17. B
18. A
19. C
20. A
21. D
22. D
23. B
24. A
25. B

EXPLANATORY ANSWERS

Reading Comprehension

1. (D) If you were asked what this passage was about, you would probably respond, "It's about how a new universal vaccine is being developed." Only choice D matches that overall topic.

2. (C) Detail C is never mentioned in the passage, whereas details A, B, and D are discussed in paragraph 1. Just because detail C is true does not mean it is part of this particular essay.

3. (A) The author is not trying to convince you of anything, as a persuasive essay might do (B). The basic purpose here is to provide information on a topic.

4. (B) Summaries A and D may be true, but they do not cover the key points in the passage, as any summary must. The title of the passage is a clue to the main idea, and summary B briefly restates the point of the whole passage.

5. (B) The prescribed drugs do not protect uric acid from forming (A); they deter, or prevent, it.

6. (D) A question that asks you to suggest a title is really asking you to identify the main idea of a passage. Do not be fooled by the fairly vague title that already exists. Instead, think about what the entire passage tells you—that gout is a painful form of arthritis whose treatment usually involves pain relievers, corticosteroids, and inhibitors, but most importantly that nurse-led care is proving quite beneficial to gout patients. The title that best captures that critical point is choice D.

7. (C) A statement of opinion is what someone thinks or believes. You cannot test the premise in an opinion to see whether it is true or false. In this case, statements A, B, and D can be proved scientifically, but statement C is subjective and descriptive.

8. (D) If a statement cannot be inferred by the reader, either there is not enough information to draw conclusions about it, or the passage contradicts the inference. In this case, you do not learn enough about doctors and patients to infer that doctors never involve patients in their own care—it may be that nurses do that more frequently, but *never* is not implied here. On the other hand, statement A might be inferred from the fact that a diet rich in meat may lead to gout. Statement B might be inferred from the fact that gout affects feet, ankles, wrists, and fingers. Statement C might be inferred from the fact that the nurses in the study were trained thoroughly.

9. (A) Skim the passage to identify the detail that does not appear. Choice B is mentioned in paragraph 1, choices C and D are mentioned in paragraph 4, but choice A is never mentioned.

10. (C) Read the word in context. Lead "leached" from the pipes, meaning that it trickled out slowly, or seeped.

11. (A) Choice D is close, but it only deals with lead paint, whereas the paragraph mentions lead in other forms. Choices B and C are much too limited in scope.

12. (D) This passage is primarily informative, providing facts and data about the topic.

13. (C) Choice A may be inferred because laws restricting lead did not appear until the 1970s. Choice B may be inferred because toys and pottery from overseas may contain lead. Choice D may be inferred because lead poisoning may cause developmental delays. Choice C is never suggested.

14. (B) The passage is mostly about state and local offerings for seniors.

15. (A) Respite services give relief for caregivers.

16. (A) Although the final sentence suggests a sort of urgency, the majority of the paragraph is neutral and instructive.

17. (D) Detail A is found in paragraph 5, detail B is found in paragraph 4, and detail C is found in paragraph 3. The author does not mention the number of seniors in assisted living or nursing care, making choice D correct.

18. (B) The passage has nothing to do with taking care of or repairing nails (choices A and C), and there is no indication that melanoma attacks the nail bed before it is seen elsewhere (choice D). The point of the article is to make readers aware of how changes in nails may indicate health issues, making choice B correct.

19. (C) The words *real trouble* are subjective and tell what someone thinks or believes. The other statements can be checked or proved.

20. (B) Look at the context, which contrasts innocuous abnormalities with "clues to underlying health problems." The only word that makes sense in context is choice B.

21. (C) Choice C is the only one that applies to every paragraph in the passage. Again, the passage is not about healthy nails (choices A and D).

22. (D) The author's attitude toward omega-3s is positive, but it is also practical, or *pragmatic*. Only choice D fits.

23. (A) The word *moderate* has many meanings, but here it refers to tempering or lessening symptoms, making choice A the best answer.

24. (B) This question asks you to locate the detail that is missing from the passage. Skim the paragraphs and you will see that choice A appears in paragraph 3, while choices C and D are mentioned in paragraph 4. Choice B is never mentioned.

25. (A) Although this passage is partly informative, that is not a choice here. The author does present the opinion that "ensuring that your diet contains ample amounts of these critical fatty acids is still a good idea," making this a persuasive essay.

26. (C) Detail A appears in the first paragraph, and detail D is mentioned several times throughout the passage. Detail B is in the last paragraph. Only the reversal of vasectomies is described, meaning that choice C is correct.

27. (D) *Delicate* has a variety of shades of meaning. Here it is used to describe complex and difficult ear surgeries.

28. (A) Although choice A may well be true, there is not enough information about the topic to draw this conclusion from the passage alone. The other choices are all supported by details in the passage.

29. (C) *Improvement* is a matter of opinion. The other choices are testable facts.

30. (D) Look for the choice that covers the passage as a whole. Choice A is close, but choice D is better, because it mentions improvements as well as the effects of those improvements.

31. (C) The passage does not include enough information to assume conclusions A, B, or D. However, it is clear that to become a carrier of the disease, the tick must first attach to a mouse or squirrel with the disease, making choice C correct.

32. (B) The symptoms are varied, or diverse.

33. (A) Think about the author's overall attitude about Lyme disease. The author makes clear that the disease is difficult to diagnose and easy to ignore at first, but that early diagnosis is important— "time is of the essence." The tone is cautionary.

34. (D) Details A and C appear in paragraph 3, and detail B is in paragraph 2. Detail D is never mentioned.

35. (B) What is the passage mostly about? It is about Zumba and its benefits as an exercise. Choices A, C, and D are not untrue, but they are also not as clearly the main idea of the passage.

36. (A) The aerobics instructor left his music somewhere and had to invent something on the spot. In other words, Zumba was developed by chance rather than by design.

37. (B) The last sentence in the passage implies choice A, and choice C is mentioned in that final paragraph as well. Once Pérez released some videos in Miami, his routines became "wildly popular," making choice D inferable as well. Since kickboxing and power yoga are compared to Zumba, you can infer that both of them burn calories, even a lot of calories—just not quite as many as Zumba does. This makes choice B correct.

38. (C) Some people may find dancing "easy," but some will not. It is not a testable description. The other choices may be proved or disproved.

39. (D) The passage as a whole has to do with knowing the signs of heat exhaustion.

40. (B) Consider each choice in context. Medical conditions may intensify the effects of heat.

41. (D) Skim the passage to find each choice. The effects of heat exhaustion appear in paragraphs 3 and 4. Drowsiness is never mentioned.

42. (C) There is not enough information in the passage to infer choices A or B, although high humidity is certainly a factor in heat exhaustion. The heat index may be over 90 degrees while the temperature is under that number, making choice D incorrect. Clearly, cessation of sweat (choice C) can be a very bad sign, as described in paragraph 4.

43. (A) The passage as a whole is really about Sophia Jones and her medical successes, not just her family (choice C and D) and not her life as a Canadian (choice B)

44. (B) Try the choices in place of *afforded to* in context. Choice B is the only one that makes sense.

45. (D) The passage is biographical, which is typically informational in purpose.

46. (C) It is fair to infer that the author admires the subject of the passage; the phrase "inspiring goals" and the emphasis on Sophia's legacy make that clear.

47. (B) Choice B is the only one that covers all of the key details of the passage—Sophia's family and her own distinguished career. Choice A goes beyond the scope of the passage, choice C never mentions her work, and choice D contains opinions that the passage does not share.

48. (A) The author is not critical of the study (choice B), doubtful about it (choice C), or dismissive of it (choice D). Use of words such as *important* and *valuable* indicate the author's approval.

49. (D) Ten teams of researchers conducted the study (choice A). The inflight study started in 2015 (choice B). The scientists intended to draw conclusions about long space flights (choice C). Choice D is never mentioned.

50. (C) This conclusion is clear from the information in paragraph 2. None of the other choices is supported by the text.

Vocabulary and General Knowledge

1. (C) Any of the choices works in context, but the meaning of *amalgamate* is "to combine into one."

2. (A) The root *com-* means "together." A compendium is a collection of things or information.

3. (C) If you impugn someone's motives, you doubt their sincerity.

4. (A) *Maladroit* means "badly adroit," or clumsy.

5. (B) The *dur* in *obdurate* means "hard," as in *durable*. An obdurate person is hard-headed.

6. (C) You may be replete after a large meal.

7. (D) *Tenuous* is from a root that means "thin." A tenuous hold on reality is a very thin or fragile hold on reality.

8. (A) A strident sound is loud and harsh, or shrill.

9. (C) *Nostrum* is sometimes used to refer to fake remedies, or cure-alls.

10. (D) If you have vertigo, you are dizzy.

11. (B) A latent disease has symptoms that are not yet apparent. A latent bud or virus is simply dormant, or inactive.

12. (A) An undulating motion is a surging up-and-down movement. The word comes from the Latin word for *wave*.

13. (D) Any of the choices might work in context, but *tumult* means "confusion and disorder," such as that caused by a lot of people milling about.

14. (A) Something that is permeable allows liquid or gas to flow through it.

15. (D) Putrefaction is the process of decay.

16. (B) *Super* means "over," and *fluous* means "flow," so something that is superfluous is overflowing, or excessive.

17. (B) When we say that a written work "suggests" something, we usually mean that it provides evidence from which we can conclude something.

18. (A) *EEG* stands for "electroencephalography." The process of EEG measures the electrical activity in the brain.

19. (B) The radius is the shorter and thicker of the two forearm bones; it is paired with the ulna. The other choices are in the upper arm (choice A), shoulder (choice C), and leg (choice D).

20. (C) A reflex is an unconscious action in response to a stimulus.
21. (D) *Sternum* is from the Greek word for "chest."
22. (D) *Trepidation* is from a Latin word meaning "alarmed."
23. (C) *Venal* is from the same root as *vendor*. It is used especially to describe people susceptible to bribery—those who can be "bought."
24. (A) If your argument is spurious, it is invalid because it is bogus or fake.
25. (C) Apart from anatomy, we know *superior* as "higher in rank." In anatomy, it is similarly "higher in position."
26. (B) The word *flaccid* is from the same root as *flabby*.
27. (D) From *corpus*, meaning "body," corpulence is obesity.
28. (C) A tree or river may bifurcate, and so might a blood vessel.
29. (A) If you dilute a liquid, you make it weaker or thinner by adding water or another solvent to it.
30. (B) *Cathartic* is from a root meaning "cleansing." Something that is cathartic may provide relief by releasing strong emotions or by purging the body.
31. (B) When you hit your so-called "funny bone," you cause numbness and pain along the ulnar nerve.
32. (A) An acrid smell or taste is bitter and unpleasant.
33. (B) You winnow grain by tossing it into the air to separate out the chaff. You winnow people by separating out the unfit to leave the best.
34. (C) At the zenith of your career, you are at your most powerful and successful point.
35. (D) A yawing motion is a movement around a vertical axis, as when a ship loses control and yaws to starboard.
36. (A) A transitory symptom is temporary; it passes or transits quickly.
37. (D) To take umbrage is to be offended or indignant, usually about someone's remarks or behavior.
38. (B) *HPV* stands for "human papillomavirus," the most common sexually transmitted disease.
39. (D) Rapport is an affinity for another person—a harmonious relationship.
40. (A) Electrolytes are minerals that are or can be ionized.
41. (D) *Tremulous* is from the same root as *tremble*.
42. (B) Tepid water is neither cold nor hot.
43. (C) *Operated* has several meanings, but only choice C makes sense here.
44. (A) An infection of the gland at the base of an eyelash can cause the inflamed swelling known as a *stye*.

45. (D) *LBW* means "low birth weight."
46. (C) *Sanctioned* is the rare word that has two meanings that are nearly antonyms. It may mean "imposed a penalty on" or "gave permission for."
47. (B) To distend is to swell or expand.
48. (A) To aspirate is a medical procedure to draw fluid out via suction; it may be done with a syringe or with suction tubes.
49. (C) Masticating is chewing.
50. (D) Something that continues over a long period of time may be said to be *persistent*.

Grammar

1. (C) This question tests your knowledge of basic punctuation. A comma must appear between the phrase *After completing her nightly duties* and the independent clause *Anya left for home*. No other commas are needed.
2. (C) The students have not yet passed the exam, so the future-tense verb is required.
3. (D) *Occurrence* has two *c*s and two *r*s.
4. (A) Reading the choices aloud may help you determine which choice has a logical order of phrases and clauses. What happened first? Katie went to return the book. What happened then? She noticed the envelope. Only choice A shows that logical order of events.
5. (A) The correct word in this sentence would be *apprise*, meaning "explain," rather than *appraise*, meaning "evaluate."
6. (B) No matter who is folding bandages with the intern, the pronoun required must be a subject pronoun. Only *he* fulfills this requirement. Do not be confused by the plural verb form; it matches the compound subject.
7. (A) The pronoun must be a plural, third-person, object pronoun. When in doubt, test the choices in place of the underlined phrase.
8. (B) *Criteria* is a plural noun, so the verb that agrees with it must be *were*, not *was*.
9. (C) Read the whole sentence before choosing the answer. Octavia is taller than her classmates, yet she is the youngest in her class. The word you choose must reflect that unexpected contrast. Choice A is ungrammatical, so only choice C works.
10. (B) Ji-yoo is asking a question, so a question mark should appear before the closing quotation marks.
11. (A) This is a frequently misspelled word.
12. (B) Substituting each choice in place of the blank should prove to you that the only answer that sounds correct is the infinitive phrase.

13. (D) *Tortuous* means "twisting." The word here, *torturous*, means "causing pain."

14. (B) *You take* would be another possibility, but *taking* (choice B) is correct.

15. (C) Another way to state this would be "Before he began, Mateo read the directions thoroughly." The word *thoroughly* modifies *read*, not *began* (choice B). Choice A is unidiomatic, and choice D is passive.

16. (B) The board is acting as a unit, not planning as individuals. For that reason, the verb should be singular.

17. (D) The pronoun should be plural, third-person, and possessive.

18. (A) *Government* contains the word *govern*.

19. (D) The sentence contains two independent clauses. A semicolon should separate them after the word *early*.

20. (A) Since the sentence ends in a question mark, it is an interrogative sentence.

21. (D) Only the introductory clause requires a comma to separate it from the independent clause it precedes.

22. (C) Choices A and B are unidiomatic, and choice D makes no sense.

23. (A) The word *on* is a preposition that begins the prepositional phrase *on Tuesday morning*.

24. (D) Choices B and C are ungrammatical, and choice A does not match its antecedent, *people*.

25. (A) The cans are rolling, not the people (choice B) or the wind (choice C). Choice D makes it seem as though the action is taking place down the street, whereas choice A clarifies that the cans are rolling down the street.

26. (D) *Made of crisscrossed logs* describes the fence, not the farmhouse. Placing that phrase in the middle of the sentence would make it grammatical: "There was a long fence made of crisscrossed logs behind the farmhouse."

27. (C) The correct verb completes the infinitive phrase.

28. (C) The correct sentence would be "Until his trip to Puerto Rico, Javier had never seen his ancestral home."

29. (B) The only grammatical choice is B.

30. (C) This construction makes sense if you use a colon before the saying.

31. (B) In this type of question, you must make sure that the tense of verbs remains consistent. Because *ended* is past tense, the correct answer contains another past-tense verb, *asked*.

32. (D) The pronoun should be the possessive form, *your*.

33. (B) The pronoun must be a subject pronoun, and it should follow the other subject in the compound subject of the sentence.

34. (A) The correct pronoun is plural and third-person, because it replaces a plural noun in the subject.

35. (C) The reflexive pronoun *myself* is never used as a subject (choice D). It is the only reflexive pronoun that matches the subject *I*.

36. (B) A comma should follow *closet* to separate the two independent clauses that are joined with the word *and*.

37. (A) A compound complex sentence must have at least two independent clauses and at least one dependent clause.

38. (D) The verb *prefer* does not agree with the singular noun *Louis*. The word should be *prefers*.

39. (C) Try reading the sentence aloud with each choice replacing the blank. Only choice C makes sense and is grammatical.

40. (A) *Counsel* is a noun meaning lawyer.

41. (C) Read the choices aloud if you have any doubts. Only choice C is both concise and logical.

42. (B) The subcommittee meets as a unit, making the singular form of the verb correct here.

43. (D) *Fast-acting* is a hyphenated adjective.

44. (D) Hyphens should separate each word of this hyphenated adjective.

45. (C) Test the pronouns in the sentence, and you will see that only the object pronoun makes sense.

46. (A) The adverb *incredibly* should modify the adjective *complex*.

47. (B) Choice A misplaces the modifier, making it seem as though we are raising the violinist's bow. Choices C and D are convoluted and confusing.

48. (D) In questions like this one, try to find the phrase that, if moved around, would improve the sentence. In this case, *in tiny cups* describes the water, not the runners. The phrase should come immediately after *water*.

49. (B) *Far from* is idiomatically correct here.

50. (C) Read the choices aloud if you are in doubt. The only one that contains phrases in logical order and correct verb forms is choice C.

Basic Math Skills

1. (A) To multiply mixed numbers and fractions, first express mixed numbers as fractions. In this case, 2¼ may be expressed as 9/4. Next, multiply numerators and denominators. $9 \times 1 = 9$. $4 \times 9 = 36$. The answer is 9/36, or ¼.

2. (B) Think: $0.15x = 6$. Solve: $x = 6 \div 0.15$. The answer is 40.

3. (C) Think: How far does Jolene bike in 1 hour? If she bikes 10 miles in 1 hour, she bikes 20 miles in 2 hours.

4. (A) One liter is about 1.06 quarts, so start by converting 3 pints to quarts. There are 2 pints in a quart, so 3 pints = 1.5 quarts. Now set up a proportion:
$$\frac{1 \text{ L}}{1.06 \text{ qt}} = \frac{x \text{ L}}{1.5 \text{ qt}}; \ 1.5 \div 1.06 = 1.42 \text{ liters}.$$

5. (D) 35% is the same as $^{35}/_{100}$. Reduce that to lowest terms by dividing the numerator and denominator by 5: $^{7}/_{20}$.

6. (C) If 1 kilogram equals 2.2 pounds, 20 pounds equals $20 \div 2.2$, or about 9.09 kilograms.

7. (A) Substitute -2 for y and solve for x:
$x = 7(-2) - 6 = -14 - 6 = -20$.

8. (3,465,000) Multiply the number of donors by the amount per donor: $2,304 \times \$1,500 = \$3,456,000$.

9. (B) There are about 1.6 kilometers in a mile, so set up a proportion: $\frac{1 \text{ mi}}{1.6 \text{ km}} = \frac{x \text{ mi}}{8 \text{ km}}; 8 \div 1.6 = 5 \text{ miles}$.

10. (C) Add up the number of each color mug to find the total: $3 + 4 + 6 + 3 = 16$. There are 4 gray mugs, so the ratio of gray to total is 4:16, which can be reduced to 1:4.

11. (A) Since there are three decimal places, put the decimal over 1,000 and then reduce: $\frac{846}{1,000} = \frac{423}{500}$.

12. (D) There are 16 ounces in one pound, so 8 pounds = $8 \times 16 = 128$ oz. Add the extra 7 oz. to that: $128 + 7 = 135$ oz.

13. (A) Let n represent the "given number." Half of that number can be written as $\frac{n}{2}$. Seven more than that is $\frac{n}{2} + 7$.

14. (D) Think of the ratio this way: 2 is to 5 as 64 is to x. You may solve this by setting up an equation and cross-multiplying. $\frac{2}{5} = \frac{64}{x}$. $5 \times 64 = 2x$. $320 = 2x$. $x = 160$.

15. (C) Begin by expressing the mixed number as an improper fraction: $2\frac{1}{9} = {^{19}/_9}$. To divide by a fraction, multiply by its reciprocal. Therefore, $^{19}/_9 \div ^{1}/_3 = {^{19}/_9} \times {^{3}/_1}$, or $^{57}/_9$. Divide the numerator and denominator by 3 to express the improper fraction in lowest terms: $^{19}/_3$. Now express $^{19}/_3$ as a mixed number: $6\frac{1}{3}$.

16. (B) Add up what she spent: $\$7 + \$2 = \$9$. Subtract that from her winnings: $\$25 - \$9 = \$16$.

17. (80) She has a $2 per hour raise, so multiply that by 40 hours to find the increase in weekly pay: $\$2 \times 40 = 80$.

18. (B) Solve by adding the prices: $\$749 + \$689 = \$1,438$. Multiply that by 5%: $\$1,438 \times 0.05 = \$71.90$.

19. (550) One meter = 100 centimeters, so 5.5 meters = 550 centimeters.

20. (D) Find the answer by setting up a proportion and then converting the answer to feet: $\dfrac{1}{30} = \dfrac{3}{x}$. Cross-multiplication leads to $x = 3(30)$, or $x = 90$ inches. Converting that to feet gets you an answer of $^{90}\!/_{12}$, or 7.5 feet.

21. (C) You should not need to compute if you estimate first. Your answer will be greater than 312 by around $31 + 3$. The only possible answer is C.

22. (85) Think of this as an equation, and use the decimal equivalent of 60%: $0.6x = 51$. Then divide to find the answer: $51 \div 0.6 = x$. $x = 85$.

23. (B) Express $3\frac{1}{3}$ as $^{10}\!/_3$ and $8\frac{1}{4}$ as $^{33}\!/_4$. Next, find the common denominator—12. $^{10}\!/_3 = {}^{40}\!/_{12}$, and $^{33}\!/_4 = {}^{99}\!/_{12}$. Add the numerators: $40 + 99 = 139$. $^{139}\!/_{12} = 11^{7}\!/_{12}$.

24. (D) Add to find the amount Sam spent: $\$7.89 + \$1.49 = \$9.38$. Subtract from the total to find his change: $\$20.00 - \$9.38 = \$10.62$.

25. (A) 10:10 A.M. is correct. Choice B would be 2210 in military time.

26. (C) In the table, each value for x has been multiplied by 3 to get the y value. If $y = 3x$, then $x = \frac{1}{3}y$.

27. (B) There are about 2.2 pounds in a kilogram, so set up a proportion: $\dfrac{1 \text{ kg}}{2.2 \text{ lb}} = \dfrac{x \text{ kg}}{11 \text{ lb}}$; $11 \div 2.2 = 5$ kilograms.

28. (C) The calculation would look like this:

$$
\begin{array}{r}
81 \text{ r}7 \\
25\overline{)2032} \\
\underline{200} \\
32 \\
\underline{25} \\
7
\end{array}
$$

29. (D) The ratio is 2:3 juice to seltzer. Gwen is using a gallon of fruit juice, or 4 quarts of juice. $\dfrac{2}{3} = \dfrac{4}{x}$, so $x = 6$.

30. (A) There are about 2.54 cm in an inch. There are 12 inches in a foot, so there are $2.54 \times 12 = 30.48$ cm in a foot. A millimeter is a tenth of a centimeter, so multiply that by 10 to get the number of millimeters in a foot: $30.48 \times 10 = 304.8$ mm.

31. (C) Decimals must have denominators of 10, 100, and so on. You can make $^{14}\!/_4$ into a fraction with a numerator of 100 by multiplying both numerator and denominator by 25: $^{14}\!/_4 \times {}^{25}\!/_{25} = {}^{350}\!/_{100}$. $^{350}\!/_{100} = 3.5$.

32. (D) Because 1 milliliter = 0.001 liters, 120 milliliters = 0.12 liters.

33. (D) A percentage is equivalent to a fraction with a denominator of 100. Think: $\frac{12}{15} = \frac{x}{100}$. Cross-multiply to get the answer: $1,200 = 15x$, so $x = 80$.

34. (A) If 3 bars normally cost $6.90, the unit price is $2.30 per bar. In a value pack of 8 for $17.20, the unit price is $17.20 ÷ 8, or $2.15 per bar. The amount saved per bar is 15¢.

35. (109) C = 100, and IX = 9.

36. (C) Start with Uri's number, 28. Tommy sold 28 + 2 = 30 balloons. Serena sold 30 − 6 = 24 balloons.

37. (84.5) Percent means "per 100," so multiply the decimal by 100 to convert it to a percent: $0.845 \times 100 = 84.5$ percent.

38. (C) Rounding the factors should prove to you that choice A is impossible; the answer will be closer to 3 × 8. Since there is one digit to the right of the decimal point in each factor, there should be two digits to the right of the decimal point in the product.

39. (B) The formula is $(F − 32) \times \frac{5}{9} = C$. So $(59 − 32) \times \frac{5}{9} = 15$.

40. (D) The scale is 3:1. If the length of the real cicada is 12.6 centimeters, the real cicada is one-third that length, or 4.2 centimeters.

41. (A) First, find the number of eighth graders. There are 342 students total and 188 of those are seventh graders. That means there are $342 − 188 = 154$ eighth graders. The ratio of seventh to eighth graders is 188:154, which can be reduced to 94:77.

42. (D) If it helps, move the decimal points to the right and divide 253 by 40. The answer will be the same.

43. (C) First find the least common denominator. Then subtract the numerators. $\frac{9}{24} − \frac{4}{24} = \frac{5}{24}$.

44. (B) If there are 3 apples in 1 pound, there are 9 in 3 pounds. Divide 9 into $6.99 to find the answer, and round to the nearest penny.

45. (B) You may think $1\frac{1}{2} = 1\frac{2}{4}$ and subtract that way, or you may change the mixed fractions to improper fractions: $\frac{33}{4} − \frac{3}{2} = \frac{33}{4} − \frac{6}{4} = \frac{27}{4} = 6\frac{3}{4}$.

46. (B) Percent means "per 100," so divide the percent by 100 to convert it to a decimal: $36 ÷ 100 = 0.36$.

47. (20) 15% is the same as 0.15, which may be an easier way to think about this. If $0.15x = 3$, $x = 3 ÷ 0.15$, or 20.

48. (D) If she gets a 4% raise, she will receive $51,200 + (0.04 × $51,200). $51,200 + $2,048 = $53,248.

49. (450) If $1,200 is $\frac{1}{3}$ of Joel's take-home income, he must make $3,600/month. If his rent will soon be $1,350, that number is $\frac{1}{3}$ of $4,050. Joel needs to make $4,050 − $3,600, or $450 more per month. However, you need not do all of this calculation if you just think: He needs $150 more per month for rent, which is $\frac{1}{3}$ of $450.

50. (A) One gallon is about 3.79 liters. Convert liters to kiloliters first. A kiloliter is 1,000 liters, so 3.79 liters = 3.79 ÷ 1,000 = 0.00379 kiloliters. Now set up a proportion to convert kiloliters to gallons: $\dfrac{1 \text{ gal}}{0.00379 \text{ kL}} = \dfrac{x \text{ gal}}{1.2 \text{ kL}}$; $1.2 ÷ 0.00379 \approx 317$ gallons.

Biology

1. (C) The membrane that surrounds the cell functions much as human skin does—it forms a protective layer against the outside world.

2. (D) In beer production, yeast metabolizes sugar from grain, producing alcohol and carbon dioxide.

3. (D) Telophase is the final phase of mitosis, in which the daughter cells are formed from the separated chromosomes. The nuclear envelope reforms, and two nucleoli appear. In the cytokinesis that follows, the new cells separate from each other.

4. (A) A nucleic acid is composed of a five-carbon sugar, a phosphate group, and a nitrogenous base.

5. (D) If the recessive gene is carried on an X chromosome, it is more likely to manifest in a male, who is XY, than in a female, who is XX.

6. (B) This practical, if unkind, form of osmosis creates a saltwater solution outside of the slug, causing water from the slug's cells to move outward to dilute and balance the solution. Excess salt can cause slugs to lose too much water, killing them.

7. (D) Arthropods such as insects or crustaceans have open circulatory systems, in which hemolymph flows freely rather than being locked into vessels (choices A and C). Hemolymph does not transport oxygen, so it contains no red blood cells (choice B). Within the hemolymph are hemocytes, which are immune cells, making choice D correct.

8. (A) The vast majority of enzymes are proteins, although it appears that RNA may also serve as a catalyst. All enzymes bind with substrates to produce products; for example, maltase catalyzes the hydrolysis of maltose to produce glucose.

9. (A) The anther is part of the stamen. It produces pollen, which later lands on the stigma, descends down the style, and enters the ovary.

10. (C) In the symbiotic relationship known as commensalism, one species benefits from another without harming the other species.

11. (B) Humans are in the kingdom Animalia, phylum Chordata, class Mammalia, order Primates, family Hominidae, genus *Homo*, and species *sapiens*.

12. (D) Waxes, oils, and fats are lipids, but honey is primarily carbohydrate (glucose and fructose), although it does contain a small percentage of lipids.

13. (B) Red blood cells lack many of the features of ordinary cells, because their only function is to fill themselves with hemoglobin in order to transport oxygen. Unlike most cells, they cannot replicate or synthesize protein.

14. (A) Fungi, algae, moss, and ferns may release spores, which allow them to reproduce asexually. If the spores land in a place hospitable to germination, they will grow into a clone of the parent plant.

15. (C) Following mitosis, each daughter cell will contain the exact number of chromosomes that appeared in the parent cell. Following meiosis II, on the other hand, each of four daughter cells will have half that number of chromosomes (choice B).

16. (A) Transcription is the process by which genetic information is copied into new molecules of RNA. Translation (choice C) is the process by which the sequence of messenger RNA is translated to a sequence of amino acids during protein synthesis. Replication (choice D) refers to the separation of DNA strands to serve as a template for the synthesis of new strands.

17. (D) Picture a Punnett square. The mother, $X_d X$, would be a carrier only. The father, XY, would be unaffected. One daughter, $X_d X$, would be a carrier like her mother. One, XX, would be unaffected. One son, XY, would be unaffected, but a second son, $X_d Y$, would manifest the disease.

18. (C) The reactants in photosynthesis are water, light energy, CO_2, and chlorophyll. The products are glucose, O_2, and water.

19. (B) If the internal consistency is poor, items do not correlate well with each other. If the internal consistency is good, the items all measure similar things.

20. (C) There is no evidence to suggest that blood type has any effect on BMR.

21. (B) Birds in captivity are unlikely to give you results that can be replicated in the wild (choice A). To be sure that the birds vocalize most around dawn, you need to test them at all hours, not just at the hours around dawn (choice C). Because your hypothesis only involves the one species, there is no need to compare it with other species (choice D). The best choice is B, which considers both multiple hours and multiple times of year, just in case the vocalization is seasonal.

22. (A) Condensation occurs in the atmosphere as warm air rises and cools, losing its capacity to hold water vapor. The excess vapor condenses to form droplets, and when the water droplets in clouds combine, they may become heavy enough to begin the process of precipitation.

23. (B) Photosynthesis (choice A) encompasses both light-dependent and light-independent reactions in plants. The Calvin cycle (choice B) is light-independent, although it uses the products of light-dependent reactions. During the Calvin cycle, the plant uses ATP and NADPH to convert CO_2 and water into organic compounds that the plant can use.

24. (C) Most bacteria are spiral (spirillum or spirochete), spherical (coccus), or rod-shaped (vibrio or bacillus).

25. (A) Sucrose, lactose, and maltose are all disaccharides, formed of two monosaccharides. Sucrose is made up of glucose and fructose. The other choices listed here are monosaccharides, or simple sugars.

Chemistry

1. (C) A hydride ion is the anion of hydrogen, or H^-. A hydride may be a compound in which hydrogen bonds with more electropositive elements.

2. (D) A base forms hydroxide ions when placed in water. Of the choices given, only lye (choice D) is a base. If you add lye, NaOH, to water, it dissociates into Na^+ and OH^-, the latter of which is a hydroxide ion.

3. (C) Half of the cobalt-60 remains after 5 years, and half of that remains after 10. So you would have 10 g after 5 years and 5 g after 10.

4. (D) Polar molecules have an uneven distribution of electrons. Generally, molecules with a linear structure are nonpolar, with an even distribution of electrons pulling equally on both sides of a central atom. CO_2 is an example of that linear structure—two oxygen atoms pull carbon equally. SO_2 (choice C), on the other hand, is polar—there is a difference in electronegativity between sulfur and oxygen that causes the molecule to bend.

5. (B) In a single displacement reaction, one or more elements replace another element or elements. Usually this happens when the replacement is more reactive than the element being replaced, creating a more stable compound.

6. (C) Like silicon, arsenic has properties of both metals and solid nonmetals, making it a metalloid. Arsenic looks like a metal but is a poor conductor of electricity. Silicon is a great semiconductor, but unlike metals, it improves in conductivity with an increase in temperature.

7. (A) As particles heat, they start to move around rapidly, making diffusion easier and quicker.

8. (A) Some elements exist in two or more different forms in the same physical state. Allotropes differ from each other in physical form because their atoms are bonded differently. They may or may not differ in mass (choice B) or stability (choice D).

9. (C) This is the definition of a saturated solution.

10. (B) A hydrocarbon contains only hydrogen and carbon. Hydrocarbons are important ingredients of petroleum and natural gas.

11. (B) The original equation has 1 iron atom on both sides, but 2 chlorines on one side and 3 on the other. Using the lowest possible factor of 2 and 3, you can change each of those to 6:

$$\text{\_\_}Fe + 3Cl_2 \rightarrow 2FeCl_3$$

Now there are six atoms of chlorine on each side, but you need a coefficient on the left side to balance the iron atoms:

$$2Fe + 3Cl_2 \rightarrow 2FeCl_3$$

12. (D) Typically, columns designate elements that have similar properties, which often means that they share the same number of valence electrons. For example, noble gases form the family that runs down the rightmost column of the periodic table.

13. (A) Ionic compounds are balanced and neutral, meaning that their net charge is zero.

14. (A) Calculate the number of neutrons in an element by subtracting the number of protons from the mass number. Helium has 2 protons, as designated by its atomic number. Because we are looking at helium-4, there are 2 protons and 2 neutrons present in the nucleus.

15. (C) In electron configuration, the symbols 1s, 2s, 2p, and so on are used to designate subshells, with superscripts indicating the number of electrons in each subshell. There is a maximum number of electrons per subshell. Nitrogen has atomic number 7, meaning that it has 7 protons, and in its balanced state, 7 electrons. Looking at the superscripts alone should tell you that only choice C offers a solution with 7 electrons—3 in the first subshell, 2 in the next, and 2 in the last.

16. (D) Molarity of a solution is expressed as moles of solute per liter of solution.

17. (B) A strong acid ionizes in water, losing a proton, H^+. Of the choices here, only sulfuric acid (H_2SO_4) is a strong acid. Choice A, acetic acid, and choice B, ammonia, are weak acids. Choice C, potassium hydroxide, is a strong base.

18. (D) A mole of atoms consists of Avogadro's number of atoms and has a mass in grams numerically equal to the atomic weight of the element. So, one mole of HI has a mass in grams equal to the atomic weight of one atom of hydrogen plus one atom of iodine— about $1 + 127$, or 128 g/mol.

19. (A) Alpha rays have a positive charge, but beta particles have a negative charge.

20. (B) Calcium (Ca) will be the first part of the formula, making choice D incorrect. A carbonate is the ion CO_3.

21. (A) Oxidation numbers for atoms in a neutral molecule must add up to zero. Chlorine, bromine, and iodine have an oxidation number of -1 unless they are combined with oxygen or fluorine. If the chlorine in KCl is -1, the potassium (K) must be $+1$.

22. (B) Generally, the rule is
    London dispersion $<$ dipole-dipole $<$ H-bonding $<$ ion-ion

23. (A) Convert the milliliters to liters first. Multiply the molarity (1.4) by the volume (0.025 L) to find the number of moles.

24. (C) Iron is Fe, and an oxide is a compound containing oxygen and another element. The elements appear in the order in which they are named.

25. (D) Sodium has an atomic number of 11 on the periodic table, so the atomic mass of any element from atomic number 12 up will be greater than sodium's mass. Of the choices given, boron (choice A) is 5, oxygen (choice B) is 8, and fluorine (choice C) is 9. Silicon (choice D) is 14, and its mass of around 28 AMU is greater than that of sodium, which is around 23 AMU.

Anatomy and Physiology

1. (D) The posterior section of the leg is the rear section. The patella (choice A) is anterior, as is the quadriceps sartorius (choice B). The triceps brachii (choice C) is a posterior muscle in the arm.

2. (B) The rotator cuff is a set of muscles and tendons that stabilize the shoulder joint and aid in the lifting and rotation of the arms.

3. (C) The rotator cuff muscles arise in the scapula and insert into the humerus.

4. (A) As chewed food enters the esophagus, primary peristalsis forces it downward to the stomach.

5. (C) A vegan would not eat eggs (choice A) or fish (choice B) but could derive protein from soy products such as tofu. Leafy greens (choice D) provide very little protein.

6. (B) The temporal lobe is responsible for speech, comprehension, and memory.

7. (C) Although the circulatory system transports enzymes (choice D), it does not release them. It does work to distribute nutrients throughout the body, making C the correct choice.

8. (A) Gallstones form from cholesterol and bilirubin. They cause symptoms when they lodge in a duct and block it.

9. (A) The most likely site of gallstone pain is near where the gallbladder empties into the bile duct, in the upper right above the stomach. Pain may radiate as far as the right shoulder.

10. (C) The foot contains 26 bones and 33 joints. The bones include seven types of tarsals, five metatarsals, and the phalanges that make up the toes.

11. (B) The retinas and optic nerves are considered part of the central nervous system. There are five distinct types of neurons in each retina.

12. (D) Our primary immune defense system is composed of skin and mucous membranes, with ciliated cells (choice D) a key part. Phagocytes of all kinds make up the secondary defense system; the other choices are part of that system.

13. (D) Although it gets help from the circulatory system and endocrine system, and occasionally from the muscular and respiratory systems as well, it is the body's skin that bears the primary responsibility for controlling body temperature.

14. (B) Pulmonary circulation is that process that begins with the removal of deoxygenated blood from the heart to the lungs. It then returns oxygenated blood to the heart through the pulmonary veins (choice A).

15. (A) Thiamine helps convert food into energy. It is available in meat, eggs, legumes, nuts, and whole grains. A severe thiamine deficiency may result in beriberi.

16. (C) One of the key duties of the skeleton is to protect the softer parts of the body, and the spinal cord would be in danger without the vertebrae to provide a bulwark.

17. (D) Melatonin helps regulate sleep patterns, with more released by the pineal gland at night than in the daytime.

18. (C) The anterior chamber of the eye is the fluid-filled part closest to the surface, the space between the iris and the cornea.

19. (D) Normal body temperature has a range of about 1.1 degrees Celsius, but the average is 37 degrees (98.6°F).

20. (B) The coronal, or frontal, plane divides the body into front and back sections, beginning at the corona, or crown of the head.

21. (C) Trypsin is produced in the pancreas and works in the small intestine to break down proteins into peptides.

22. (D) The sebaceous glands are oil-producing glands located most often in the hair follicles. They release sebum, a waxy substance that lubricates and helps waterproof the skin and hair.

23. (A) Antioxidants protect cells from damage caused by free radicals. Vitamins A, C, and E have antioxidant properties. So, too, do certain minerals, including selenium, which is found in a variety of protein-rich foods.

24. (B) The shoulder is closer to the center of the body than the elbow is, making it proximal to the elbow.

25. (A) Stress responses start in the nervous system, but the stress response comes from the endocrine system, which releases cortisol from the adrenal glands. Cortisol, in turn, sends messages to the body that clear the mind, energize muscles, and increase heart and breathing rates.

Physics

1. (A) Density = mass/volume, in this case grams per centimeter cubed.

2. (D) He walked all the way around, ending up where he began, for a displacement value of 0. The circumference of the rectangular park was 1 km + 2 km + 1 km + 2 km = 6 km.

3. (B) Potential energy has to do with an object's position, among other factors. When the car is perched at the top of the track, about to roll downward, it is at its peak potential energy.

4. (C) Subtract the initial velocity from the final velocity to find the change in velocity: 20 in/hr − 14 in/hr = 6 in/hr. The change in time is 15 minutes, or 0.25 hr. Divide the change in velocity by the change in time to find the rate of acceleration: 6 in/hr ÷ 0.25 hr = 24 in/hr^2.

5. (B) Momentum is calculated by multiplying mass by velocity, $p = mv$. The mass of the ball is 45 g, or 0.045 kg. The velocity is 42 m/s. So the momentum is 0.045 × 42, or 1.89 kg·m/s.

6. (D) Gases are more compressible than either solids or liquids.

7. (C) Work is equal to force times distance. Amanda mowed 600 meters using 100 N of force, so she did 60,000 N·m worth of work

8. (C) Watts divided by volts equals amperes. The current being drawn is 780 watts ÷ 120 volts = 6.5 amps.

9. (A) You can easily see this if you draw a diagram. As the frequency of waves increases, you have more waves per second, so the wavelength of each wave decreases.

10. (D) Kinetic energy is proportional to velocity squared. If speed doubles, kinetic energy quadruples (choice C). If speed is cut in half, kinetic energy is divided by 4.

11. (C) Heat capacity equals energy divided by change in temperature. In this case, 4.2 J/g°C = $E \div 10$, so $E = 42$ J for 1 gram of water, but for 1 kilogram of water, $E = 42,000$ J.

12. (C) One hertz is equal to one cycle per second.

13. (A) A vector quantity has both magnitude and direction. A scalar quantity has only magnitude.

14. (B) Divide mass by volume to find density. Only choice B offers a quotient of 2.5 g/cm^3.

15. (C) Newton's law states that gravitational force between objects is directly proportional to the product of their masses. It is inversely proportional to the square of the distance between them (choice D).

16. (D) A parallel circuit has two or more paths through which current may flow. The voltage is the same across each component. The current (choice A) may vary, but the sum of the current between or among components equals the total current that flows from the source. The resistance (choice C) is variable.

17. (B) In the equation $E = mc^2$, E is units of energy, m is units of mass, and c is the speed of light.

18. (A) You are looking first at the relationship between the object distance (d_o), the image distance (d_i), and the focal length (f). Use the formula $1/f = 1/d_o + 1/d_i$, where $f = 2$ cm and $d_i = 6$ cm. In this case, $\frac{1}{2} = 1/d_o + \frac{1}{6}$, or $\frac{3}{6} = 1/d_o + \frac{1}{6}$. So $d_o = 3$ cm.

19. (C) Calculate frequency by dividing the speed of sound by the wavelength: $343 \div 5 = 68.6$ Hz.

20. (A) Momentum is the product of velocity and mass, so you can calculate velocity by dividing momentum by mass. Here, $180 \div 45 = 4$ m/s.

21. (D) The SI unit for power is the watt.

22. (D) The equation to use is $K = f/x$, where K is the spring constant, f is force, and x is distance. Here, you are given spring constant and the compression distance, 10 cm, or 0.1 m. So you can calculate that 20 N/m = f/0.1 m, meaning that $f = 2$ N.

23. (B) Centripetal acceleration equals velocity squared divided by the radius of the loop: $a = v^2/R$. In this case, $a = 6$, and $v^2 = 36$, so $6 = 36/R$, and $R = 6$ m. However, you are asked to find the diameter, which is $2R$, or 12 m.

24. (A) According to Ohm's Law, resistance (R) equals voltage (ΔV) divided by current (I), or $R = \Delta V/I$. In this case, you know voltage and amps of current, so $R = 120 \div 1.25$, or 96 ohms.

25. (B) Use Coulomb's Law to find the force. The equation to use is this:

$$F_{elect} = \frac{k \times Q_1 \times Q_2}{d^2}$$

Remember that 1 Coulomb = 10^6 microCoulombs. $Q_1 = 4 \times 10^{-6}$ C, and $Q_2 = 8 \times 10^{-6}$ C, and d, distance, = 50 cm, or 0.5 m. Now, you must recall Coulomb's constant, $k = (9.0 \times 10^9 \text{ N·m}^2/\text{C}^2)$. From this point, it's all about computation:

$$\frac{90 \times \frac{10^9 \text{N} \cdot \cancel{\text{m}}^2}{\cancel{\text{C}}^2} \times (4 \times 10^{-6} \cancel{C}) \times (8 \times 10^{-6} \cancel{C})}{(0.5 \cancel{\text{m}})^2} = \frac{288 \times 10^{-3}}{0.25} = 1.152 \text{ N}$$

NOTES

NOTES

NOTES

NOTES